Defining Sport

Studies in Philosophy of Sport

Series Editor: Shawn E. Klein, Arizona State University

The Studies in Philosophy of Sport series encourages scholars from all disciplines to inquire into the nature, importance, and qualities of sport and related activities. This series aims to encourage new voices and methods for the philosophic study of sport while also inspiring established scholars to consider new questions and approaches in this field.

This series encourages scholars new to the philosophy of sport to bring their expertise to this growing field. These new voices bring innovative methods and different questions to the standard issues in the philosophy of sport. Well-trodden topics in the literature will be reexamined with fresh takes and new questions and issues will be explored to advance the field beyond traditional positions.

Titles in the Series

Defining Sport: Conceptions and Borderlines, edited by Shawn E. Klein

Defining Sport

Conceptions and Borderlines

Edited by Shawn E. Klein

LEXINGTON BOOKS
Lanham • Boulder • New York • London

Published by Lexington Books
An imprint of The Rowman & Littlefield Publishing Group, Inc.
4501 Forbes Boulevard, Suite 200, Lanham, Maryland 20706
www.rowman.com

Unit A, Whitacre Mews, 26–34 Stannary Street, London SE11 4AB

British Library Cataloguing in Publication Information Available
The hardback edition of this book was previously catalogued by the Library of Congress as follows:

Library of Congress Cataloging-In-Publication Data Available

Includes bibliographic references and index.
ISBN 9781498511575 (cloth : alk. paper)
ISBN 9781498511599 (pbk. : alk. paper)
ISBN 9781498511582 (electronic)

Printed in the United States of America

To Kristen Klein
For giving me the inspiration and courage to start the SportsEthicist.com.

Contents

Acknowledgments

First, I thank my friend and colleague Michael Perry. Mike and I worked together at Rockford University and organized several conferences on sport. The early impetus for this book derived from some of that work and the conversations around it. Mike was my first guest on my Sports Ethics Podcast and our topic was: "What Is Sport?" In 2014, Mike and I organized the Third Annual Sports Studies Symposium at Rockford University, and our topic that year was "Defining Sport" (two of the talks at that symposium, Brian Glenney's and Kevin Schieman's, eventually made their way into this volume).

Second, I thank my friend and colleague Stephen Hicks and the Center for Ethics and Entrepreneurship that he founded and directs. The Center helped support the Sports Studies Symposiums and my work at Rockford University. In particular, Stephen encouraged me to develop the Sports Ethics class that I taught for many years at Rockford (and now at Arizona State University). Without Stephen and the Center, I might not have had the opportunity to teach and research the Philosophy of Sport and Sports Ethics.

I extend sincere gratitude to the reviewers of the chapters in his book: Jack Bowen, Colleen English, Aaron Harper, Victoria Jackson, and Emily Ryall. Their feedback and suggestions helped make the book better.

I thank Jana Hodges-Kluck and Lexington Books for giving me the opportunity to work on this book and to support the book series, *Studies in the Philosophy of Sport*, which will encourage scholars from all disciplines to inquire into the nature, importance, and qualities of sport and related activities.

Finally, I thank my wife Kristen. Her unwavering support, guidance, and love have been invaluable to me. She is also the one who first told me to get off my *tuches* and start the SportsEthicist.com blog—which played no small part in this book coming to be. The hours that Kristen, our son Sammy, and I spend together (usually playing *Minecraft*) are my happiest.

Introduction

Shawn E. Klein

Sport is everywhere, and for many, everything. Whether one is a participant, a casual spectator, a die-hard fan, or even a critic, sport plays a significant role in the lives of most people throughout the world. It is the topic of daily conversation and frequently the lead story on news. Sport unites (and sometimes divides) cities and nations—even families. It transcends ethnic, national, gender, age, religious, and belief boundaries. It is probably as old as human civilization itself. In these ways it is no exaggeration to say that the study of sport is the study of humanity.

But what is sport? How do we define this thing that we all seem to know about and talk about? And if we able to talk about it as much as we do, why should we even bother defining it?

JUST LOOK IT UP

Many of my students, when asked this, tell me to just look it up in the dictionary. Increasingly, they pull out their iPhone and look up "sport" online. The definition they find, if they come across a good dictionary, is usually perfectly fine. It tells us how the term is most frequently used, when it first came in to use, and what its etymological origins are.

One problem with this approach is that it ignores *why* this is the definition. In failing to take into account the process of defining the concept and merely looking at the final product, we miss the opportunity to gain a better understanding of the concept itself and how it relates to other concepts. For example, one dictionary defines sport as "[a]n activity involving physical exertion and skill that is governed by a set of rules or customs and often undertaken competitively."[1] This is, in many ways, a good definition;

it includes many of the key elements discussed in this volume. If, however, we don't probe this more or don't understand the process of forming this definition, we miss out such things as why physical skills or rules are part of the definition. For this, we need to think about the activities from which sport is being distinguished. For example, the physical skills element distinguishes sport from nonphysical skill–based games or activities, such as chess. This definition uses "activity" as the genus, but maybe there is a narrower genus we could use. But, then, we run the risk of being too narrow (this is part of the issue at stake, and discussed in several of our chapters, of whether all sports are types of games). These issues are essential to understanding sport, but they are only discovered and dealt with through the definitional inquiry.

Another issue with dictionary definitions is that they tend to focus on the term and its usage. But, when philosophers ask for the definition, we are not concerned merely with the term "sport." The term, or word, is the linguistic marker for the concept and it is the concept with which we are concerned. The term is not the same thing as the concept. The marker can take many forms: dog, perre, cane, mbwa, inu, kehlev, and so on,[2] but these terms all stand for the concept of the domesticated, barking mammal with superior olfactory faculties. It is what the concept picks out (and the how and the why these things are able to be treated as part of one concept) that we are concerned with, not the particular term used.

When we confuse the term for the concept, we look too much at word usage. Usages change and shift; terms gain or lose connotations. The concept, though, if it is formed properly, rarely changes. The term used might change or we might, with new knowledge, reclassify something into a new or different concept; but the core concept doesn't change. For example, as we learned more about whales, we reclassified them as mammals instead of fish. Or poor Pluto gets demoted to a planetoid. The conception of what a mammal is or what a planet is didn't change. Someone in the United States might use the term "soccer," in England, "football"; yet both are employing the same concept and referring to the same activity. Usage is important to understand and can help us to discover important things about concepts, but they are not sufficient for identifying the concept and its definition.

This volume is not about the variations of usage of the term "sport." It is about the concept; the range of activities in the world that we unite into one idea: sport. The task is to find the rules, for lack of a better word, that tell us what can be united into this idea and what cannot. It is through this project of defining sport that we can come to understand these activities better, how they are similar or different, and how they related to other human endeavors.

BORDERLINE CASES

Someone suggests a definition of sport: sport is X. Almost immediately someone else points to a kind of X that doesn't seem to be a sport; or, they find some sport that is a non-X but seems to be excluded. The most interesting of these are the borderline cases. These are the cases that look in some ways like they fit the definition, but in other ways like they do not. These challenge us to think a little harder about not just the definition, but more importantly, the activities themselves. They are opportunities to know more about our world and the myriad activities to which we dedicate ourselves. Like Nozick's mountain villager who thinks he is a good basketball player until Jerry West shows up,[3] we might think we know what sport is until we start thinking about competitive eating or cheese-rolling.[4] It is only by first thinking about how to draw the boundaries that we discover the borderline cases. Then we are able to rethink how we draw those conceptual boundaries and how better to understand the borderline cases and the paradigmatic cases. Along the way, we gain a deeper appreciation and apprehension of the activities and their participants.

THE ORGANIZATION OF THE VOLUME

This definitional inquiry and the deeper appreciation and apprehension of sport that follows is the goal of this volume. Part I examines several of the standard and influential approaches to defining sport. Part II uses these approaches to examine various challenging borderline cases. Rather than use these borderline cases as counterexamples to merely knock down proposed definitions only to move on to the next proposal, these chapters explore the interplay of the borderline cases with the definition to provide a more thorough and clearer understanding of the definition and the given cases. This understanding will then hopefully help to resolve the theoretical concern posed by the borderline cases in the first place.

The first three chapters in part I examine the most influential definitional approaches in the philosophy of sport. While Bernard Suits was by no means the first to attempt to define sport, his approach remains one of the most important. This is not to suggest that most sport philosophers are Grasshopperians.[5] But most approaches to defining sport or games in sport philosophy have to contend with Suits—either by agreeing broadly with his view or presenting their view in contradistinction to Suits. We can see this in Chad Carlson's look at the history of the definitional inquiry in the philosophy of sport. In his "A Three-Pointer: Revisiting Three Crucial Issues in the

'Tricky Triad' of Play, Games, and Sport," Carlson details the influence and sustained impact of Suits' approach to defining sport and games. Through his analysis of the "Tricky Triad," the complex interplay of the concepts of sport, game, and play first introduced by Suits,[6] Carlson draws our attention to the essential role of intentionality in the attempt to understand the nature of sport. That is, we can't just describe the visible aspects of the activities of sport, we have to look as well to the attitude of the players and the experience of engaging in these activities. Carlson uses this added element to examine the apparently paradoxical nature of professional athletes. Since professionals are being paid to play a sport, many have claimed they can't actually be playing but are instead working. Carlson argues for a more nuanced way of understanding the relationship of play and work.

Suits' view is that games, and by extension sport, are entirely defined by their formal structures: there are certain features of an activity (rules, institutions, etc.) that provide the necessary and sufficient conditions for something to be a sport or not. However, this formalism is viewed by many as being too reductive and as missing key features of sport. For example, the strategic or intentional foul in basketball is a violation of the rules of the game, so by formalism, it should not be allowed. And yet it is an accepted and common strategy in basketball. Something more than the formalist account seems needed. Conventionalism and broad internalism developed in large part to fill this need. Conventionalism, as the name suggests, emphasized conventional, nonformal features of sport. The rules of the game have to be applied but the application isn't something that can be formalized. The how and when of application is something to which the participants implicitly agree and accept. The intentional foul is allowable on this view because, though a rule-violation, it is an implicitly agreed upon acceptable strategy. Broad internalism, similarly, describes nonformal features of sport but argues that these are not merely or narrowly the social conventions of the participants. It is not just the acceptance of the intentional foul, according to broad internalism, that sanctifies it. It is that the foul in some way fits with a set of broad features or principles that while they are neither formal nor conventional, underlie and help constitute the game.

Francisco Javier López Frías argues that some form of broad internalism is the most accepted approach to sport. In "Broad Internalism and Interpretation: A Plurality of Interpretivist Approaches," he sketches out a taxonomy of theories of sport from the general distinction between internalism and externalism down the conceptual hierarchy to distinctive versions of interpretivism. Interpretivism is an account of sport rooted in an "appeal to the best interpretation of the game or an inference to the best explanation of its key elements."[7] López Frías argues that this approach is deeply informed and influenced by hermeneutical theories as developed by thinkers such as Alasdair MacIntyre, Ronald Dworkin, Richard Rorty, and Hans-Georg Gadamer.

López Frías fleshes these connections out and explains how these theories can be used to understand sport. Finally, he adds to the taxonomy by distinguishing two variations of interpretivism: realism and antirealism.

We return more directly to Suits' account of sport in "Hopscotch Dreams: The Cultural Significance of Sport." Kevin Schieman agrees with most of Suits' account but argues that it needs a corrective. To be a sport on Suits' account requires, among other elements, that the activity has a wide following and is stable over time. Schieman argues that while this is typically the case, these features are secondary to a more fundamental feature that explains why the activity has stability and wide following. Namely, this feature is that the activity is a *good game*, it is something worthy of the significant effort and time that we give to the activities regarded as sport. The wide following, stability, and institutional aspects that we see in sport are things that come about, he argues, because the physical game is a good game. Schieman then takes on the challenge of defining what counts as a good game.

The Olympics are highly esteemed and respected throughout the world (although the same probably cannot be said about the IOC). Many of the chapters in the book reference and discuss the Olympics. Often the reference is used as a sign of something reaching "sporthood." We see this in the attempt of many new "sports" looking for inclusion in the Olympics as a sign as having made it, as a sign of being a *real* sport. But what is it that makes something an Olympic sport? Heather Reid draws on the history of the Ancient Games and on the values and ideals of the modern Olympic Movement to provide an answer. By defining Olympic Sport in terms of the values of the philosophy of Olympism, Reid sets out to reclaim "Olympic" as an honorific term with moral import. To call something Olympic, argues Reid, ought to convey something about the value of that activity.

When talking with typical sports fans, there often seems be a big black hole between the ancient Olympics and the development of modern sports in the nineteenth century. Fans tends to know there were ancient athletic games like the Olympics and they are aware that most of today's popular sports are little more than a century or so old. There seems little awareness of the range of athletic contests that predated our modern sports. John McClelland fills in this gap in his "Early Modern Athletic Contests: Sport or Not Sport?" McClelland argues, through extensive examples and research, that there were many athletic contests in early modern Europe and that these contests can be made sense of using contemporary accounts of sport. He also puts sport into a broader conceptual relationship with work, play, and war.

Moving back to our own times, so much of contemporary sport is bound up with commercial media. In "The Impact of Mass Media on the Definition of Sport," Keith Strudler analyzes the ways that the media's coverage of and relationship with sport might be altering its very definition. From the early days of newspaper coverage up through ESPN and YouTube, Strudler looks how the goals of sports, participants, and spectators have changed and how that is affecting the way we think about the concept of sport.

The first three chapters of part II evaluate popular contemporary activities to determine whether they are sport or what the impact of the development of these activities has had on our conceptions of sport. Pam R. Sailors, Sarah Teetzel, and Charlene Weaving analyze the new emerging popular fitness trends of CrossFit, Tough Mudder, and Spartan Race. Using Suits' definition of sport, they set out to determine whether these borderline cases ought to be classified as sport.

In "Evolution of the Action Sports Setting," Chrysostomos Giannoulakis and Lindsay Pursglove examine how commercialization has transformed nonmainstream sports, such as BMX and board sports, into more mainstream sports. They argue that this transformational process also is affecting the way we conceive of and consume sports.

While Giannoulakis and Pursglove discuss skateboarding, Brian Glenney has a different spin on what the case of skateboarding shows us about our ideas about sport. In his "Skateboarding, Sport, and Spontaneity: Toward a Subversive Definition of Sport," he argues that the definition of sport must include rule-breaking aspects that reflect the inevitability of cultural evolution and change. Sport as a rule-governed activity is key to almost all theories of sport. Glenney upends this traditional way of setting the debate and argues that subversion of the rules is essential to understanding and playing sport. And though sport as subversion might sound like a license to cheat, Glenney is looking more at cases of creative spontaneity that push the sport to evolve rather than instances of mere cheating for individual advantage.

Bullfighting and the bullfighter are significant cultural symbols in Spain. Teresa González Aja tackles the history and nature of this controversial activity in her "Bullfighting: The Mirror and Reflection of Spanish Society." She argues that we have to see bullfighting as at the same time art, a game, a spectacle, a rite, and a sport. It doesn't fit neatly into any of these categories individually, but has elements of all these at once.

Bullfighting is just once example of sport that involves animals. Many popular sports and activities, such as horse racing and dog agility competitions, also involve nonhuman animals. Joan Grassbaugh Forry explores the question of whether and to what extent we should consider activities in which nonhuman animals are involved in sports. Her argument centers on the role of voluntariness in the concept of play and games. She extends this key feature to animal involvement in sport. Although we cannot look for actual consent from the animals, we can look for signs of voluntariness from the animals engaging in sport. She argues that when these signs are lacking or absent, the activity fails to meet a meet minimum threshold for what rightly can be considered sport. Her analysis also gives us conceptual tools to criticize the state of minimally acceptable animal sports.

Fantasy sports are big, *really* big. Something like thirty-five million North Americans play fantasy sport in some manner: that's more than the numbers of people who play golf, watch the American Idol finale, or own iPhones.[8] In "The Mainstreaming of Fantasy Sport: Redefining Sport," Brody J. Ruihley, Andrew Billings, and Coral Rae explore the impact of these fast growing and popular games on sport. They argue that while fantasy play is not actually itself a sport, it is altering the ways we think about sport. Fantasy sport participation cuts across many demographic boundaries and is upending many traditional ways fans consume and engage with sport—and this is not likely to change. Ruihley, Billings, and Rae convincingly show that fantasy is mainstream and will be an inescapable part of sport and how we conceive of it for a long time.

In the last chapter (Chapter 13), Joey Gawrysiak looks at what might be the fastest growing and most popular of the borderline cases. Though many might currently scoff at the idea, Gawrysiak makes a persuasive case for the inclusion of e-sport, video game competitions, as sport. E-sport, as he shows, is already consumed and marketed like traditional sport. Furthermore, by drawing on some of the standard accounts of what makes something a sport, Gawrysiak makes the case that there are sufficient needs for the development and use of physical skills—albeit vastly different from traditional sports—in video game competitions to meet the threshold of what is needed for something to be a sport.

ONLY THE BEGINNING

This work is not meant to be definitive or exhaustive. There are definitions, borderlines cases, and approaches not raised or discussed here. The definitional inquiry is not, in many ways, about the goal of defining the given concept. It is that, of course, but it is also just as much about what can be learned along the way. That may sound like some trite self-help advice, but my hope is that the chapters here inspire more thought and debate on just what sport is, how it relates to other activities and human endeavors, and what we can learn about ourselves through the study of sport.

NOTES

1. "Sport," *The Free Dictionary*, accessed July 1, 2016, http://www.thefreediction-ary.com/sport.

2. English, Spanish, Italian, Swahili, Japanese, and Hebrew, respectively.

3. Robert Nozick, *Anarchy, State, and Utopia* (New York: Basic Books, 1974), 240.

4. Cheese-rolling is a real annual event in the village of Brockworth, England. It involves competitors chasing cheese down a hill.

5. For the use of Grasshopperian as adjective to describe Suits' view, see Deborah P. Vossen, "A Grasshopperian Analysis of the Strategic Foul," *Journal of the Philosophy of Sport*, 41, no. 3 (2014): 325–346.

6. Bernard Suits, "Tricky Triad: Games, Play, and Sport," *Journal of the Philosophy of Sport,* 15, no. 1 (1988): 1–9.

7. Robert L. Simon, "Internalism and Internal Values in Sport," *Journal of the Philosophy of Sport,* 27 (2000): 8.

8. See Matthew Berry, *Fantasy Life: The Outrageous, Uplifting, and Heartbreaking World of Fantasy Sports from the Guy Who's Lived It* (New York: Penguin Group, 2013), 2; and Brody J. Ruihley and Andrew C. Billings, *The Fantasy Sports Industry* (New York: Routledge, 2014), 5.

Part 1

CONCEPTIONS OF SPORT

Chapter 1

A Three-Pointer

Revisiting Three Crucial Issues in the "Tricky Triad" of Play, Games, and Sport

Chad Carlson

Sport philosophers have spent a great deal of time and effort working through metaphysical issues central to the field. Indeed, questions about the nature of play, games, and sport have generated much philosophic inquiry. In the 1980s, sport philosophers Bernard Suits[1] and Klaus Meier[2] engaged in a published discussion on these issues—the "tricky triad" of relationships between the distinct but related phenomena of play, games, and sport. Suits and Meier seemed to agree on most discussion points regarding the nature of play and games. These phenomena, they agreed, can be depicted on a standard Venn diagram. The addition of sport into the pictorial description, however, became the source of their disagreement. Is sport simply another circle on the Venn diagram whereby it can be instantiated as play, as a game, as both, or as neither of the other two phenomena? Or is sport simply a circle on the diagram within the games circle—one that always is a game and sometimes is play?

In this chapter, I will revisit the "tricky triad" that spurred such lively debate during the early decades of the International Association for the Philosophy of Sport. I believe that there are three issues within the existing literature related to the triad that deserve more attention. Therefore, after reviewing the literature on the triad, I will describe these three issues. The first is the relationship between sports and games. The second is defining sport. And the third—a postscript of sorts—is whether professional athletes—that is, those whose "work" is "playing" games—can ever truly be at play in their work.

REVIEWING LITERATURE ON THE METAPHYSICS OF PLAY AND GAMES

The proliferation of philosophical literature on play underscores the innumerable ways in which scholars have identified the phenomenon.

Roger Caillois and Johan Huizinga wrote oft-cited books on the nature of play that have served as anchors of sorts as the winds of time have pulled play scholarship in divergent directions. In *Man, Play and Games*, Caillois identified a four-part typology of play.[3] *Agōn* is competitive play, or that in which winning or some other good is at stake; *alea* is play based on luck or chance; *mimesis* is mimickry or make-believe play; and *ilinx* is vertiginous play, or that which alters sense perceptions.[4] These are categories of play activities. Coursing throughout this typology is a continuum that delineates both the structure and the player's intentionality within agonistic, aleatory, mimickry, and ilinxial activities. *Paidia* is at one end of the continuum and is the term used to describe playful, spontaneous, or unstructured play. *Paidia* is the ancient Greek word for play. Children and beginners often take part in this kind of experience.[5] *Ludus*—Latin for games—lies at the other end of this spectrum and denotes mature and structured play within the typology. Caillois argues that the natural tendency is for an individual's play experiences to include less *paidia* and more *ludus* over time.[6]

In certain ways, Caillois' book serves to overcome deficiencies in Huizinga's definition of sport. In *Homo Ludens*, Huizinga described play as:

> A free activity standing quite consciously outside "ordinary" life as being "not serious," but at the same time absorbing the player intensely and utterly. It is an activity connected with no material interest, and no profit can be gained by it. It proceeds within its own proper boundaries of time and space according to fixed rules and in an orderly manner. It promotes the formation of secrecy and to stress their difference from the common world by disguise or other means.[7]

Caillois argued that this definition is both too broad and too narrow. It is too broad, he contends, in that it includes and even requires that which is secret or mysterious. Caillois believes, on the contrary, that play tends to expend or remove the mysterious. On the other hand, Caillois argues that Huizinga omits games of chance and those that lead to material gains, making the definition too narrow.[8]

Bernard Suits also criticized Huizinga, lamenting that the latter "began to find play under nearly every rock in the social landscape."[9] Suits explained, "There is little now that someone or other has not called play."[10] Thus, he sought a definition that would include limitations to the inclusiveness of Huizinga and Caillois' descriptions.

Suits' definition, then, is much more restrictive. He argues that, "x is playing if and only if x has made a temporary reallocation to autotelic purposes of resources primarily committed to instrumental purposes."[11] As such, Suits has listed two conditions necessary for an experience to be play. First, x must be playing with something. And second, for x to be playing with some resource, x must be temporarily reallocating that resource from instrumental to autotelic purposes. For example, if a child has mashed potatoes on a plate before her, the instrumental purpose of such resources is to eat them for nourishment. However, if the child starts building lakes, rivers, and mountains with her mashed potatoes, then she has temporarily reallocated them to autotelic purposes.

This definition is very tidy for resources like mashed potatoes, balls of yarn, and water in the bathtub, but it becomes problematic when thinking about baseball bats, chess pieces, and playing cards. Such resources were created for the purpose of autotelic pursuits. When x plays baseball with a bat, chess with finely crafted pieces, or poker with a deck of cards, x is not temporarily reallocating these resources from instrumental to autotelic purposes. Instead, they were created for autotelic pursuits. However, Suits' rejoinder broadens our understanding of resources. While baseball bats are not being reallocated from instrumental to autotelic purposes during baseball games, x's time is being reallocated.[12] X could be doing the dishes, finishing homework, or working to make money with this time that has been reallocated to play. Accordingly, baseball and chess are play when the player has reallocated her time from instrumental to autotelic purposes to participate in the game.

Although most scholars have been more normatively impressed with play than games, Suits was not. He mentioned that in studying play there is "less than meets the eye,"[13] and published little on the phenomenon. He was more intrigued by games. Accordingly, he published prominently on game metaphysics including his magnum opus, *The Grasshopper*, where he argues that:

> To play a game is to attempt to achieve a specific state of affairs, using only means permitted by rules, where the rules prohibit use of more efficient in favour of less efficient means, and where the rules are accepted just because they make possible such activity. I also offer the following simpler and, so to speak, more portable version of the above: playing a game is the voluntary attempt to overcome unnecessary obstacles.[14]

This definition includes four elements: goals, means, rules, and the lusory attitude. Game goals are two in form: prelusory and lusory. Prelusory goals include the achievable state of affairs that signify victory or completion, without regard to any limiting means. It is the state of affairs that occurs at the end of the game. The lusory goal, then, is the state of affairs that occurs at the end of the game having been achieved by the prescribed means and rules. The means, second, are the permissible ways of reaching the goal, and they are determined by a game's third element—the rules. Finally, the lusory attitude is "the acceptance of constitutive rules just so the activity made possible by such acceptance can occur."[15] In other words, the game-player accepts the fact that in games there are rules limiting more efficient in favor of less efficient means toward the goal. While normally it would be irrational to follow such excessive codes, the nature of games is such that the player participates just to be experiencing the inherent inefficiency.

This four-part definition and the rest of Suits' arguments regarding games have been the starting point for most subsequent academic forays into game metaphysics. Many have found great clarity in the tidiness of Suits' necessary and sufficient conditions. Much like in his essentialist definition of play, he is very willing to draw lines in the sand to demarcate what is and what is not game-playing, and he argues forcefully for the merits of his demarcations.

Many others have found fault in Suits' essentialism. Supporters of Wittgenstein's early work—a group to which Suits refers tongue-in-cheek as "terminally" plagued by poor theory[16]—take issue with his stipulations. This bloc of philosophical opposition has, in Suits' mind, no common ground by which it might understand and appreciate his arguments. Still others not opposed to Suits' metaphysical theories have argued that he needlessly rules out performances as games and "games" of chance. Yet even those who sling arrows at Suits' scholarship continue to find merit in referencing his publications to provide credibility to their analyses and bibliographies.

THE TRICKY TRIAD

It is from this context in the literature on play and games that Suits penned his 1988 article entitled, "Tricky Triad: Games, Play, and Sport." This essay is more than the sum of Suits' publications on each element of the "triad" (his article, "Words on Play" and book, *The Grasshopper* were preceded by a 1973 article called "The Elements of Sport"). Indeed, Suits begins "Tricky Triad" by stating, "I have changed my views in some important ways about play and sport."[17] He adds, "(I am) more interested in this inquiry in relations among the three than I am in distinctions between them."[18]

Suits' pictorial description of the relationship between the phenomena shows three overlapping but unique circles that depict seven different areas of focus.[19] Area 1 of figure 1.1 shows those experiences that are play and not games or sport. Suits calls this Primitive Play, an area that includes babies splashing in bath water. An activity is Primitive Play when the feedback the player receives is the payoff or pleasure of the activity. Area 2 is where the games and play circles overlap within the diagram to indicate when skill development occurs alongside play. Suits calls this Sophisticated Play and it includes play experiences that are games but not sports (puzzles, Monopoly, etc.). Area 3 includes Professional Nonathletic Games—puzzles, Monopoly, or poker, for example, done for an instrumental purpose.

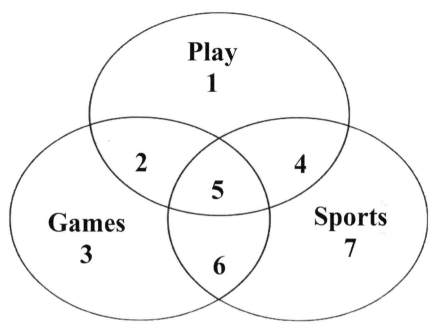

Figure 1.1 Relationship between sport, play, and games, showing Suits' seven areas of focus.

The rest of the areas in the diagram include sport, and these are the sections for which Suits received the most resistance. He calls Area 4 Amateur Performances. There are two kinds of sports, Suits argues: those activities that are athletic games and those that are athletic performances. The former are refereed activities and the latter are judged activities. Within the Olympics, both of these types of activities are present. Thus, Area 4 includes autotelic engagement in judged sports such as diving or gymnastics. Area 5, constituting the center of the diagram, consists of Amateur Games—autotelic experiences in which one is participating in a game that is also a sport (sandlot baseball or playground basketball, for example). Area 6 is the intersection of games and sport but not play, and Suits calls it Professional Athletics. It includes those who participate in games that are also sports for instrumental reasons (a child forced to play baseball or a professional football player). Last, Area 7 is the portion of the sport circle that does not overlap play or games. Suits calls this Professional Athletic Performances, and it consists of instrumental participation in those sports that he argues are performances and not games such as diving or gymnastics.

Klaus Meier responded to Suits' "Tricky Triad" in "Triad Trickery: Playing with Sport and Games" that is a direct critique of Suits. "Despite the auspicious achievement attained in (Suits') delineation of the concept of

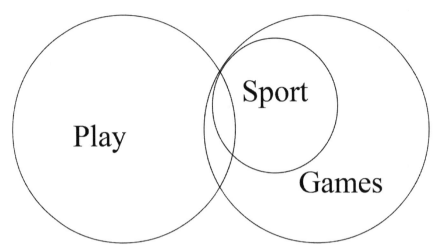

Figure 1.2 Meier's revised representation of the relationship between sport, play, and games.

game," Meier argues, "when he turns his attention to sport problems arise rather quickly."[20] Meier makes it clear that he will "wholeheartedly accept and adopt (Suits') definition of 'game,'" and believes that he and Suits have "conceptions of 'play'" that "are sufficiently similar."[21] "The concept of sport," however, "is the source of (their) greatest differences."[22]

Specifically referring to Suits' Venn Diagram, Meier argues that both Areas 4 and 7 are "untenable."[23] These two areas, in which sports but not games are present, prove problematic for Meier because he believes that all sports are a species of the genus games. Not all games are play and not all sports are play, but according to Meier, all sports are games.

POINT ONE: THE RELATIONSHIP
BETWEEN SPORTS AND GAMES

This area of disagreement spurred response articles in the 1989 *Journal of the Philosophy of Sport* in which Suits and Meier further clarified their disagreement. Suits elucidated his "Tricky Triad" claims in "The Trick of the Disappearing Goal" arguing that athletic performances are different from athletic games.[24] Athletic performances, including such activities as diving and gymnastics, for instance, are sports but not games because, as Suits argues, they have no prelusory goal. A prelusory goal was a part of Suits' original definition of games as "a specific, achievable state of affairs" without any necessary connection to rules.[25] Diving, Suits argues, has no specific, achievable state of affairs in the way of a goal the achievement of which would indicate that the game has been complete.

One of the arguments Suits uses in this line of reasoning is that diving has no rules that prohibit more efficient in favor of less efficient means. If, in a race, the prelusory goal is to cross the finish line first, then a racer might decide to use a jet propulsion pack to achieve such a state of affairs. Rules, however, prohibit this type of efficiency. Suits argues that there is no comparison in diving. The diver catapults off the board and gravity takes over without any agency on the part of the participant. The diver will, without any doubt and without any constraints, enter the water. Without rules to create artificial difficulty, diving cannot be a game. The diver always enters the water and rules do not prevent more in favor of less efficient entry into the water.

Meier disagrees, arguing that diving indeed has proscriptive rules, which means that a prelusory goal, at least in theory, exists. Indeed, Meier argues that Suits has a very narrow description of rules that proscribe behavior to make an activity a game. While a diver always enters the water by gravity without any reduction of efficient means, a diver must adhere to rules that determine aesthetics and compulsory movements within each dive. Such necessary elements, Meier argues, constitute rules that prohibit more efficient or easier means and, thus, provide a prelusory goal. A sport such as diving, then, does in fact constitute a game.

The basis of this issue is for Meier and Suits to determine whose depiction of the metaphysical landscape is more accurate—Suits' Venn diagram or Meier's Venn/Euler diagram. If diving—an activity that both philosophers seem to agree is a sport—is not a game, then Suits can claim that his Areas 4 (sport that is play but not a game) and 7 (sport that is neither play nor a game) are not null sets. Indeed, if diving is not a game but is a sport, then it and its peers such as gymnastics and figure skating constitute activities that are sports but not games.

However, if diving is a game, then Meier's diagram that depicts all sports as games becomes a better choice. Suits indicates, though, that even if Meier does not agree with his example of diving, there still might be examples of sports that are not games. Specifically, he mentions sailing a sailboat for fun or demonstrating to someone how to sail by actually doing so. In these examples, the sailor does not undertake the lusory attitude—thereby excluding game-playing—and is still engaged in activity that people refer to as sport.

Meier responds to this argument in two ways. The harshest of these is the way in which Meier rejects Suits' employment of "term usage" as a reason why sailing as such might be a sport but not play. Suits says that sailing is one of "a number of examples of activities that seem generally acknowledged to be sports, but which do not seem generally to be acknowledged as games."[26]

Meier responds that this is inconsistent with Suits' overall body of work. Indeed, he argues that Suits has advanced arguments dampening the relevance of language use toward making metaphysical claims. In *The Grasshopper*, Suits describes his views as such: "I grant that (language) usage must not be ignored in definitional inquiry ... but such usage cannot be finally decisive, can it?"[27] And in his article on play, Suits tells a story to explain that just because we call something play or a game, does not make it such. He refers to this type of stipulated definition or language arrangement pejoratively as "Humpty-Dumptyism." Stipulating that x is a sport can be "intellectually permissible ... for the sake of expository simplicity." The problem, then, is when "it is forgotten that a stipulation one has made is not a statement of fact."[28] Meier, then, concludes that, "despite Suits' current assertions to the contrary and despite the fact that the common usage of terms must receive some acknowledgment, the latter criterion is not necessarily the ultimate indicator or arbiter of legitimate entrance into a particular, rigorously defined category."[29]

Meier also concludes, "Suits' major difficulty is that he has no clear, defendable understanding of the concept of sport."[30]

POINT TWO: DEFINING SPORT

Suits argued in 1973 (and later reputed, leading Meier to repudiate Suits' own self-repudiation) that there are "four requirements which, if they are met by any given game, are sufficient to denominate that game a sport."[31] These four elements are: "(1) that the game be a game of skill, (2) that the skill be physical, (3) that the game have a wide following, and (4) that the following achieve a certain level of stability."[32]

Suits never refers to this as a definition of sport. Indeed, his other articles include definitions of game-playing and play, but he only refers to these as "elements of sport."[33] This uncharacteristically timid argument reveals Suits' interests. "I have no theory to support the list," he admits, "except the theory that the features are more or less arbitrary, since they are simply facts about sport. Finally, I have little to say about them aside from presenting them, except as regards the question of skill."[34]

Thus, the presentation of Suits' "elements of sport" serves only as an entrance into philosophic study of skill. And, by 1988, Suits found a better entrance by muting his four elements and instead dividing the realm of sport into those activities that are games and those that are performances. The four elements thus had no use, and have received only little attention in subsequent scholarship.

Meier referred to the four elements in his 1988 article, but only after Suits created his new description. Therefore, Meier attempts "to salvage at least one important characteristic (from the four elements), and to discard the rest."[35] He agrees with the first two—that sport be a game of skill and that the skill be physical—but he believes they can be condensed into one element: physical skill. Meier discards Suits' other two elements—that the game have a wide following and that the following achieve a certain level of stability—by arguing that these are not in fact elements of sport as much as they are "simply a comment on the changing social conditions" that institutionalize forms of sports or games. "Any recourse to institutionalization, as an integral, necessary component of the essential nature of sport," Meier argues, "is arbitrary, as well as erroneous and counterproductive; consequently, it should be actively rejected."[36]

This declaration is couched within Meier's broader arguments against Suits' characterization of the relationship between play, games, and sport. And yet it stands out among Meier's article as one of the better-crafted descriptions of sport. Indeed, despite its succinctness, Meier's description of sports as games that include physical skills whereby the participants who are most successful are those who demonstrate the most success in the physical skills required of the game seems to be among the more intuitive accounts of the phenomenon.[37]

In Meier's intuitive reconfiguration of Suits' elements of sports, the former has taken the cultural influences out of the picture. For all of Suits' airtight logic regarding metaphysical descriptions of games and, to an extent, play, the social influences that he allowed to be tied to our understanding of sport seems rather uncharacteristic. But is it helpful?

Meier's negation of social influences in determining what is and is not a sport helps this discussion in important ways. Popular discourse on what is and is not a sport often centers on social factors. When asked whether activities such as automobile racing or cheerleading are sports, many discussants respond in ways that rely on social or institutional decisions rather than logic: are these activities shown on television networks that feature sports; do sports magazines or websites report on these activities; are they included in sporting competitions such as the Olympics or Commonwealth Games?

While answers to these questions provide for entertaining discussion and offer descriptive sociological insight, they do little for the normativity we seek in determining the nature of sport. Meier's account, then, also helps to return the discussion's focus to normative features. Although cultural features may play a role in our understanding of sport, scholars seem to differ on whether they matter toward definitional efforts.

The *Journal of the Philosophy of Sport*—the discipline's most central and established academic publication—includes a rather unconvincing and disparate discussion on the definition of sport. Frank McBride started the dialogue on the nature of sport in a rather somber tone in his essay, "Toward a Non-Definition of Sport," in the journal's second volume. He wrote that his "purpose is to discourage attempts at defining the concept of sport."[38] McBride offers four claims to serve his purpose. First, "neither the intension nor the extension of the concept sport is concise." The intension is "the property or properties a thing must possess to belong to the class of things designated by that word." The extension, then, is "the class of things to which that word refers."[39]

Second, McBride argues, "attempts to limit concisely the intension of the concept sport will either fail or end up as stipulative."[40] This claim shows McBride's anti-essentialist slants. Third, "the concept sport is ordinarily employed in a wide variety of ways, i.e. has a wide variety of usages, or meanings."[41] This type of language argument has and continues to be part and parcel of the discussion. And fourth, "philosophers of sport ought not waste their time attempting to define 'sport.'"[42] Sport is "highly ambiguous and extremely vague."[43] Thus, McBride says that it cannot be defined, meaning not that it is too hard a task to be defined but that "it is logically impossible to define the concept."[44]

William J. Morgan argued much more optimistically in "On the Path Towards an Ontology of Sport" in which he draws "a line of thought leading from Huizinga [*Homo Ludens*] to Gerber ['Arguments on the Reality of Sport']."[45] Morgan attempts to make sense of the seemingly incompatible claims that these two authors make regarding play. Huizinga discusses play as an esoteric experience that is pervasive but different from normal life—a non-reality. Gerber, on the other hand, attempts to describe the reality of our lived experiences of sport. Morgan makes sense of these two seemingly contradictory arguments by describing Huizinga's ontic allegiances as a historian and anthropologist that differ from Gerber's ontological quest. Understanding this backdrop provides the basis for future ontological quests to understand the nature of sport.

Also in 1976, Duane L. Thomas penned an essay, "Sport: The Conceptual Enigma." Thomas asks many broad questions about sport's ability to be studied from many different disciplinary viewpoints, and how it relates to similar concepts. He concludes that sport "can be defensibly regarded as regulated competitive effort in physical activity, the outcome but not the existence of which depends on some degree and combination of physical skill, strategy, chance, and participant motives."[46] This definition, Thomas admits, is "generic," but it "would appear to include the entire spectrum of professional contests, school athletics, intramurals, sandlot occurrences, and conquest sports, as well as yet to be conceived activities."[47] While this definition is vulnerable to criticism that it allows sport to become ubiquitous, Thomas prudently argues that, "the cultural and evolutionary nature of sport combined with the elementary status of investigative attention would favor erring in the direction of inclusive as opposed to rigorously certain or exacting definitive statements."[48] New findings, then, can result in "more precise definitions" that derive from this "operational base."[49]

In 1977, Morgan composed "Some Aristotelian Notes on the Attempt to Define Sport." This article is written "to disarm the non-essentialist argument ... that 'sport' cannot be defined because of the multiple meanings it carries as a concept."[50] Morgan argues twofold: that non-essentialists use an inappropriate "conceptual apparatus" for defining sport and that following Aristotle's "focal meaning" will result in understanding the "systematic interconnections of (sport's) various meanings" in a way that is "nonambiguous."[51] Clearly, this essentialist argument counters McBride and others of such bent, and yet it is a much different type of optimistic approach than Thomas expressed in his article.

In 1980, Sheldon Wein offered a rebuttal to Morgan. Wein argues forcefully that Morgan was mistaken. Sport does not need to search beyond "standard manner" for definition as Morgan suggested.[52] Nor has Morgan accurately characterized Aristotle's description of genus and species in focal meaning. While sport can be described using "the 'focal meaning' approach,"[53] Wein's purpose is not to do so as much as it is to debunk Morgan's arguments.

The *Journal of the Philosophy of Sport* did not publish any articles focusing on the definition of sport between 1980 and the "Tricky Triad" discussion in 1988. Wein's article may have shut down discussions about the definition of sport or any related metaphysical discussions regarding the nature of sport. Or, philosophers may have taken more time to develop different methods of presenting this discussion. Suits and Meier took the latter tactic. However, their discussion did not focus on definability so much as it did on metaphysical relationships. The "Tricky Triad" discussion set a new, analytic tone within the journal's metaphysical articles. The tidiness of each author's arguments and the robustness of the debate make it a memorable part of the journal's dialogue.

S. K. Wertz kept his distance from this analytic slant when he published a 1995 paper provocatively titled, "Is Sport Unique? A Question of Definability." In it, Wertz says no. There are characteristics that may identify something as sport, but those are not unique to sport. Indeed, sport overlaps with dance, religion, art, and the like. Thus, essentialist definitions of sport are problematic, he argues, but definitional inquiry into sport is certainly not.[54]

Wertz, like Thomas, Morgan, and others they cite, seem to be optimistic yet humble about definitional inquiries. And yet Wertz and Thomas also hold fast to healthy extra-philosophical awareness. "There is no final and exhaustive statement of the defining properties of sport that would render the concept closed," Wertz argues, followed by a rhetorical question: "How could we make such a claim when we are talking about a historical, institutional process?"[55]

Sports are culturally and socially constructed activities that constantly evolve as humans do. Thus, the definitions and observations that Wertz and Thomas consider and put forth can accommodate changes.

This type of socio-biological awareness is what brought Suits and Meier to battle. Most of these scholars' philosophy shows no regard for social/ external factors altering or changing phenomena in the metaphysical landscape. And yet, in describing sport, Suits alludes to language use and cultural popularity.

Although Suits continued his arguments in published discussions related to metaphysical relationships between play and games, questions related to the definitions and definability of sport have not been asked in the *Journal of the Philosophy of Sport* since Wertz's 1995 article. Why is this the case? Did Wertz's article carry the day? Potentially, yes, based on the strength of its content. But it has not been sufficiently cited or built upon to make it a cornerstone publication in the field—if it was the slam-dunk culmination of the discussion, then one would guess that it would be championed much more in future literature.

The reasons for the recent lack of literature in this area may be manifold. Sport philosophy scholars may see this topic as sacred—the "text" inside the tabernacle of the discipline. Thus, scholars have acted humbly. Putting forth a definition of sport is so central to the field that any definitional attempts might be seen as self-aggrandizing and would certainly be put to great criticism.

Scholars in the field, on the other hand, might be comfortable with an intuitive sense of sport's nature. After all, more than forty years' worth of scholarship has come forth within the field without one prominent, critically approved and time-tested definition of sport. This might demonstrate the fact that sport is a term relatively well understood that seems to be the best descriptor of the content that the discipline has congregated around. And yet, philosophers rarely settle for vague, intuitive understandings—our intuitions instead are calls to action and reasons for deep, philosophical thought as we reflect, at times, *ad nauseum*. Philosophers are rarely accused of accepting ideas without critical analysis.

Another possibility is that the dearth of recent literature on the topic demonstrates an insurmountable philosophical stalemate on the question of definability. Is essentialism the best way to define such pervasive phenomena as play, games, and sport? Did Wittgenstein have it right in his early writings with the concept of family resemblances? Does Aristotle's "focal meaning" provide the best way to define things? And how much should language use direct our thinking? This debate in broader philosophy may have provided enough literature to dissuade scholars from even trying to define sport. Any attempts, then, have to hold up to criticism from those who disagree with the content and from those who disagree with the methodology.

Further, Wertz, Thomas, and Suits have all alluded to yet another facet of the difficulty in defining sport—socio-biological factors. Sport, as a concept, may be a moving target, evolving with the forces of culture, history, and humanity. Dennis Hemphill argues as much in his 2005 article entitled, "Cybersport." According to Hemphill, technology changes how we play games and may even be changing what it means to be an athlete or sport participant.[56]

From the existing literature, the development of two streams of thought might help us develop a more concise understanding of sport, if not an actual definition. Front and center to all discussions about the nature of sport is the necessity of physical skill demonstration as among the determining factors of success or lack of success. The focus has also been on sport's extension—its activities, which all happen to be games or game-like. The two streams of thought that may help us, then, are looking at the intentionality of sport activities and understanding the unique place of physical skill and its development.

Many discussions on the nature of sport focus on sports as activities—that is, those things we do or participate in. Sports are objects in this world, and we participate in them. However, this might be short sighted. Discussions of play and game metaphysics have found some favor in expanding their scope. Play, for instance, is usually best understood as a mindset, an attitude, or a spirit. We experience things and objects in this world playfully or with autotelic intentions. And yet we can also describe play objects or things. A baseball bat and a swing set are objects created for the purpose of invoking play. Thus, play is an intentionality, but it is one that is always intended toward a particular play object.

Our understanding of games is inverted. We usually best understand games as things, activities, or objects that we use or participate in. Suits describes as much in his definition of game-playing. The first three parts of his definition—that games must have goals, means, and rules—describe games as objects or things. However, when he introduces his fourth part—the lusory attitude—he has to change what he has defined. Since an activity cannot itself have an attitude, he then ascribes to his four-part definition the term "game-playing."[57] Thus, certain objects, activities, or things are games when people participate in or with them while adopting the "lusory attitude"—the game mindset or intentionality.

The hybrid nature of play and games depicts what Husserl refers to as the noetic and noematic factors in his phenomenology.[58] The noetic element is the intentionality. For an experience to be play, an individual must have the play attitude or spirit in which one is focusing on the experience as its own end. This play spirit or attitude is always attached to the noematic element—the object or activity. Games, relatedly, are activities or objects of our focus. And yet we are only game-playing when we experience them with the lusory attitude or spirit—accepting the limited means toward reaching a goal just so the activity as such can occur.

In ontological discussions of sport, we have not utilized Husserl's theory. Are there noetic and noematic elements of sport? We often focus on the noematic. Is baseball a sport? Is synchronized swimming? Is dancing? These are the extensions. We rarely focus on the noetic. Is there a particular sporting spirit or attitude like the lusory attitude of games or the autotelic spirit of play?

By dividing up our intentional landscape in such a way, we are forced to follow it to its natural end. If play experiences include taking the play spirit toward a particular object or activity and if game-playing includes taking the lusory attitude toward a particular object or activity, then it means that we are willing to ascribe to the category of play or games any activity to which one can or does take the play spirit or lusory attitude. This has not been problematic except that it has allowed critics, for example, to "find play under nearly every rock in the social landscape"[59] and to equate gaming to life itself.[60] The extension of these two concepts, then, has been vast, but the concepts remain relatively comprehensible.

Based on popular discussions, though, it seems that we are much more possessive of how far we are willing to extend the concept of sport. Unlike play and games, we seem to treat sport as an honorific, giving it privileged status. To call something a sport is to bestow it with an honor given out only after great deliberation. This seems to be underlining the noematic debate. What activities are sports? And, if we can determine the noetic element of sport, are we willing to consider a sport any activity toward which we can take this intentional act?

If all sports are games, as Meier argues, then the solution to these questions is simple: sport's noesis is the lusory attitude. If the participant takes the lusory attitude toward backgammon, then that is game-playing but probably not a sport because the proficiency of physical skill is not central to the outcome. If the participant takes the lusory attitude into soccer, then it is game-playing and it is a sport.

If Suits is right, though, and not all sports are games, then what is the intentionality that an athlete takes into a sport that is not a game? Is it an interest in doing one's best? Is it an interest in best displaying one's physical skills? Does it have to do with the aesthetics of an activity? Suits argues for the possibility of sport experiences that might not be games. If this is the case, what is an athlete trying to do when participating in a sport activity that is not a game? Improve one's skill? Practice? Learn a new skill?

Meier rightly argues that any sport activity that is a competition must be a game, for it necessarily includes each of Suits' four conditions. However, Suits considers sport more broadly. Any example of sporting behavior that is not part of a competition is generally focused on developing, utilizing, or autotelically performing one or more skills. As a basketball player spends time in a gym shooting because her coach told her to and a soccer player spends time on a field to practice his passing, the question arises whether they are engaged in sport or not. Suits' example of a sailor guiding a sloop along the water in a demonstration to others on how to sail presents an even more controversial example. Are the basketball player, soccer player, or sailor engaged in sport?

None of these three cases as described seems to be a game and none of them seem to be engaged in sport competition. Yet all of them are working on the development of skills or are displaying skills that are central to success in their respective sports. In other words, all of them are practicing or demonstrating one or many skills utilized in their sports. So if they are not participating in games and they are participating in activities that focus on one or more sport-specific skills, what are they doing?

Gordon Reddiford described pre-sport behavior as that which is or has been created by the rules of a particular sport but is not officially the instantiation of a game.[61] Shooting a basketball, passing a soccer ball, or demonstrating how to sail a sloop are not in themselves games, and may not be examples of sport as such, but Reddiford describes them as still within respective "institutions" of the sports or games.[62] Shooting a basketball is not in itself a game or a sport competition, but basketball is a sport, and shooting is clearly basketball behavior.

These examples demonstrate the second stream of thought regarding the nature of sport—that the focus on physical skills in sport is central. As much as these examples can help describe the importance of nongame behavior within particular sport institutions, they fail to give us definite answers regarding what is and is not a sport. However, the focus on physical skill helps us better conceptualize sport's intension and extension.

The extension of topics within the existing literature in the field of sport philosophy reveals a bit about the perceived extension of sport. Journals, chapters, books, and presentations have focused on Olympic events, traditional physical activities, physical education, extreme physical activities, martial arts and activities, recreational physical activity, and dance. While not every instantiation of each activity within each of these realms may be colloquially considered sport, each of them prominently displays physical skill and requires the execution or development of physical skill to at least a large extent for victory or success. Physical skill, sport philosophers seem to have intuitively understood, is a foundation for our academic content. In other words, activities that feature physical skill in comparative, competitive, developmental, or achievement settings seem to be, broadly, the content that brings together philosophers of sport.

POINT THREE: THE PERCEIVED PARADOX
OF PROFESSIONAL SPORT

Based on the previous discussion, we might be able to help navigate a notoriously popular and fundamental sport philosophy debate: can professional athletes—those whose work it is to participate in sports—be at play while they are at work?

An intuitive answer seems to be that, indeed, a professional athlete certainly can engage in play while participating in the job of sports. It is potentially the minority intentionality that an athlete has during much of the experience, but the play spirit probably forces its way into becoming the majority intentionality at times, too. In other words, a professional athlete has to show up to each game while trying to win because it is part of the job requirement. Therefore, nonplay is always looming in a professional athlete's intentionality, no matter how prominent play is. And being in the moment includes subverting thoughts of requirements and work tasks for the intrinsica of the experience. The challenge can be engulfing, the movements can be inspiring, and play can take over as the dominant mindset.

The previous description is focused on games or competitions within a professional athlete's career. These are, however, only a small part of the work a professional athlete puts in during a full career. Countless hours are spent practicing, scrimmaging, breaking down skills, learning new skills, watching film, conditioning, and the like—behaviors that fall within the institutions of sport even if they are not examples of sport games or competitions.

Scott Kretchmar's work is helpful here to embrace some of the complexity of majority and minority intentionalities regarding play or work experiences. Kretchmar argues that this "might be more helpfully discussed as a complementary pair (play~work) that (exhibits) greater and lesser degrees of intrinsic satisfaction."[63] This is a radical shift that may be a more appropriate framework for our experiences with these phenomena. "Work ... tends to have lesser amounts of *intrinsica* while play has more," Kretchmar argues, "but that does not exclude the intrinsic from work or the extrinsic from play." Games, then, he describes as having "roots in both work and play."[64]

It seems that sport has roots in both work and play, too. Thus, the question of whether professional athletes are at play or at work when participating in their competitions has an even simpler answer: yes. Professional athletes are engaged in a complementary pair of play~work that is an ever-changing mixture of the two phenomena.

We can describe sporting behavior within the institutions of sport by this same complementary pair framework. Is practicing one's shot in basketball, one's passing in soccer, or sailing to show others how to do so play or work?

Yes. Are these examples of games? As I have described them, probably not. Are they examples of sport? Because they are activities focusing on physical skills and because the intentionality is similar to what one would have at play and in a game, we can certainly say that these types of experiences are well within the main stream of sport behavior—sporting institutions.

NOTES

1. Bernard Suits, "Tricky Triad: Games, Play, and Sport," *Journal of the Philosophy of Sport* 15, no. 1 (1988): 1–9; and Bernard Suits, "The Trick of the Disappearing Goal," *Journal of the Philosophy of Sport* 16, no. 1 (1989): 1–12.

2. Klaus V. Meier, "Triad Trickery: Playing with Sport and Games," *Journal of the Philosophy of Sport* 15, no. 1 (1988): 11–30; and Klaus V. Meier, "Performance Prestidigitation," *Journal of the Philosophy of Sport* 16, no. 1 (1989): 13–33.

3. Roger Caillois, *Man, Play and Games*, trans. by Meyer Barash (Chicago: University of Illinois Press, 2001), 12.

4. Ibid., 12.

5. Ibid., 13.

6. Ibid., 13.

7. Johan Huizinga, *Homo Ludens: A Study of the Play Element in Culture* (Boston: The Beacon Press, 1955), 13.

8. Caillois, *Man, Play and Games*, 4–5.

9. Bernard Suits, "Words on Play," *Journal of the Philosophy of Sport* 4, no. 1 (1977): 117.

10. Ibid.

11. Ibid., 124.

12. Ibid., 125.

13. Ibid., 117.

14. Bernard Suits, The *Grasshopper: Games, Life and Utopia* (Boston: A Non-Pareil Book, 1978), 41.

15. Ibid., 40.

16. Suits, "Words on Play," 117.

17. Suits, "Tricky Triad," 1.

18. Ibid.

19. Suits, "The Trick of the Disappearing Goal," 7–9.

20. Meier, "Triad Trickery," 14.

21. Ibid., 27.

22. Ibid.

23. Ibid., 24.

24. Suits, "The Trick of the Disappearing Goal."

25. Suits, *The Grasshopper*, 41.

26. Suits, "The Trick of the Disappearing Goal," 9.

27. Suits, *The Grasshopper*, 91.

28. Suits, "Words on Play," 119.

29. Meier, "Performance Prestidigitation," 16.

30. Ibid., 13.

31. Bernard Suits, "The Elements of Sport," in *Philosophic Inquiry in Sport*, 2nd Edition, edited by William J. Morgan and Klaus V. Meier (Champaign, IL: Human Kinetics, 1995): 11.

32. Ibid.

33. Ibid., 8.

34. Ibid., 11.

35. Meier, "Triad Trickery," 14.

36. Ibid., 17.

37. Ibid., 14.

38. Frank McBride, "Toward a Non-Definition of Sport," *Journal of the Philosophy of Sport* 2, no. 1 (1975): 4.

39. Ibid.

40. Ibid.

41. Ibid.

42. Ibid.

43. Ibid., 9.

44. Ibid., 10.

45. William J. Morgan, "On the Path Towards an Ontology of Sport," *Journal of the Philosophy of Sport* 3, no. 1 (1989): 32.

46. Duane L. Thomas, "Sport: The Conceptual Enigma," *Journal of the Philosophy of Sport* 3, no. 1 (1976): 40.

47. Ibid.

48. Ibid.

49. Ibid.

50. William J. Morgan, "Some Aristotelian Notes on the Attempt to Define Sport," *Journal of the Philosophy of Sport* 4, no. 1 (1977): 15.

51. Ibid.

52. Sheldon Wein, "A Reply to Morgan," *Journal of the Philosophy of Sport* 7, no. 1 (1980): 40.

53. Ibid., 46.

54. Spencer K. Wertz, "Is Sport Unique? A Question of Definability," *Journal of the Philosophy of Sport* 22, no. 1 (1995): 89.

55. Ibid.

56. Dennis Hemphill, "Cybersport," *Journal of the Philosophy of Sport* 32, no. 2 (2005): 195–207. See also Joey Gawrysiak, "E-sport: Video Games as Sport" in this volume.

57. Suits, *The Grasshopper*, 41.

58. See Edmund Husserl, *Ideas: General Introduction to Pure Phenomenology*, trans. by W.R. Boyce Gibson (New York: Collier Books, 1972): 235–259 and Edmund Husserl, *Ideas Pertaining to a Pure Phenomenology and to a Phenomenological Philosophy*, trans. by F. Kersten (The Hague: Martinus Nijhoff Publishers, 1982): 211–235.

59. Suits, "Words on Play," 117.

60. See Suits, *The Grasshopper,* and James P. Carse, *Finite and Infinite Games: A Vision of Life as Play and Possibility* (New York: Free Press, 1986).

61. Gordon Reddiford, "Constitutions, Institutions, and Games," *Journal of the Philosophy of Sport* 12, no. 1 (1985).

62. Ibid., 45.

63. Scott R. Kretchmar, "Why Dichotomies Make it Difficult to See Games as Gifts of God," in *Theology, Ethics, and Transcendence in Sport*, edited by Jim Parry, Mark Nesti, and Nick Watson (London: Routledge, 2011): 187.

64. Ibid.

Chapter 2

Broad Internalism and Interpretation

A Plurality of Interpretivist Approaches

Francisco Javier López Frías

In the first section, I provide an overview of the main theories of sports within the arena of the philosophy of sport. To do so, I address them at three different theoretical levels: (a) theories of sports, (b) internalist philosophical accounts of sports, and (c) broad internalist proposals. By drawing this threefold distinction, I am able to define the limits and differences between the various philosophical ways to approach the study of sports. This provides an interpretivist framework vis-à-vis this philosophical approach to sport, which I refer to as the "hermeneutic theories of sports."

INTERPRETIVISM: BEYOND FORMALISM AND CONVENTIONALISM

Interpretivism is arguably the most broadly adopted philosophical account of sport. Cesar R. Torres, John S. Russell, Robert L. Simon, and William J. Morgan are the foremost proponents of this approach.[1] This interpretivist philosophical account of sports is part of a broader one that Simon calls "broad internalism."[2] However, according to Simon, we find two approaches in the philosophy of sport located on an even broader theoretical level than broad internalism, namely: internalism and externalism. The former appeals to some intrinsic values and goods in order to understand the very nature of sports, whereas the latter refers to principles imported from outside the realm of sports. An example of such external principles are those economic structures and mechanisms that determine our social reality, which Karl Marx calls "*the economic infrastructure* of society."[3]

According to Simon, as I will show in figure 2.1, we can differentiate among three theoretical levels: a first one composed by the twofold distinction

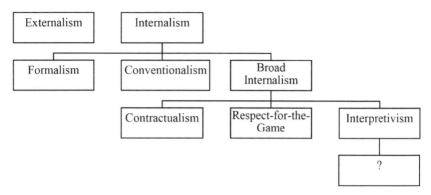

Figure 2.1   Theories of Sport: three theoretical levels.

between internalism and externalism. A second level where we find the three diverse and more specific types of internalist theories of sports, namely: formalism, conventionalism, and broad internalism. Finally, a third theoretical level formed by the different types of broad internalist theories. Here is where interpretivism should be placed, along with two other broad internalist proposals called "the contractualist approach" and "the respect-for-the-game approach." By revising Simon's categorization of sports theories,[4] I will argue that there is a fourth theoretical level to be taken into account: the one formed by multiple and diverse interpretivist approaches.

Formalism emerged from Bernard Suits' attempt to criticize Wittgenstein's claim in the *Logical Investigations* that "we cannot define the term 'game'."[5] In contrast to Wittgenstein's anti-definitionalist proposal, Suits defines games and sports in terms of their formal structure. According to this philosophical theory of games and sports, the essential feature of these activities is what Suits calls "constitutive rules." The main goal of these rules is to introduce unnecessary obstacles to the achievement of one end, namely, "the pre-lusory goal," in Suits' terms.[6] If constitutive rules create the gratuitous and artificial world within which the game takes place, then it could be argued that constitutive rules are the primary condition for the existence of a game or sport. For instance, the so-called pre-lusory goals of (a) introducing a ball into a bucket, (b) going to a neighboring city, and putting a ball into a hole become the sports of basketball, long-distance running, and golf, respectively, by means of a certain set of rules that introduce unnecessary obstacles to achieve these ends. In basketball, for example, one such rule is that participants can only run with the ball while bouncing it on the ground, whereas in endurance races rules prohibit runners from taking shortcuts or using means of transport other than their legs.

A second type of internalist theory of sports is conventionalism.[7] According to this approach, rules might be necessary for the existence of sports, but they are not their ultimate and most defining feature. In this sense, the conventionalist philosophical account of sports, first proposed by Fred D'Agostino, was raised as a critique to the reductive notion of sports provided by formalists. For conventionalists, formalism ignores the importance of what D'Agostino calls "the ethos of games."[8] This ethos is composed by a set of implicit conventions accepted by the participants, which shows how to apply the rules to the actual practice in specific events. For a conventionalist, rules are important but secondary to the set of conventions that tells us how rules should be applied and understood. For instance, in basketball, referees apply the no-contact rule in different ways depending on the level of competition or the age of the participants.

The third type of internalist theory of sports is broad internalism. According to Simon, broad internalism should be regarded as broader in comparison to the narrower internalist theories of sports such as formalism, and conventionalism because it "is the view that *in addition* to the constitutive rules of sports, there are other resources connected closely—perhaps conceptually—to sport that are neither social conventions nor moral principles imported from outside."[9] Simon calls this approach "broad" because it appeals to a broader set of resources connected closely to sport. According to Simon, depending on the nature of what he calls "other resources connected closely to sports," we can distinguish among three types of broad internalist conceptions: "the contractual approach," the concept of sports referred to the interests of the game, which I will call "the respect-for-the-game approach," and "interpretivism."[10]

The contractual approach in philosophy of sports holds that the sporting practice is built upon an implicit "social contract" among the participants, mostly hypothetical, by which they agree to abide by the rules. The "respect-for-the-game" theory resembles contractualism in that it argues that, participants have to agree on respecting the interests of the game, which are the ultimate grounds for formal rules and unofficial conventions. Participants should act in a way that they always promote and safeguard the interests of the game; that is, they have to take into account the game's interests as well as their own. Finally, interpretivism, in Simon's words, "derives the principles and theories underlying sport [...] from an appeal to the best interpretation of the game or an inference to the best explanation of its key elements."[11]

The three abovementioned approaches share the idea that in order to make sense of sports, we should appeal to certain features underlying constitutive rules and implicit conventions. After all, like games, rules and conventions are human artifacts created to fulfill certain human needs or goals. Therefore, there should be some ultimate principles or features according to which rules and conventions are built. This ultimate element could be either a social agreement, the interests of the game, or the normative principles underlying sports. Each of these three approaches appeal to some theoretical principles in addition to rules and conventions in order to approach the sporting phenomenon from a philosophical standpoint.

MACINTYRE'S HERMENEUTICAL ETHICS

As I argued in the previous section, interpretivism is nowadays the prevailing philosophical account of sport. Thus, the concept of "interpretation" lies at the very core of today's philosophy of sports. This has enormous consequences that have not been sufficiently addressed in the literature. "Interpretation" is the key concept within hermeneutics. It plays an essential role in interpretivist accounts of sports because the main proponents of such a theory of sports grounded their proposals in hermeneutical philosophers such as Alasdair MacIntyre, Ronald Dworkin, Richard Rorty, and Hans-Georg Gadamer.

According to Shaun Gallagher,[12] interpretation provides us with a way to attain understanding which is based on the idea that everything is conditioned by a number of factors, such as present and past, and society and circumstances. For hermeneutics, nothing exists in an isolated manner. Thus, hermeneutics are built upon the assumption that "different factors, including the epistemological, sociological, cultural, and linguistic factors"[13] are always involved in our process of interpretation. However, this does not mean that interpretation is always contextually determined. For instance, the so-called "critical hermeneutics" hold that if we provide us with the right method, we can escape the constraints of our finite and historical factors to reach an objective level of interpretation.

By emphasizing the relevance of contextual factors in understanding, hermeneutic philosophy situated interpretation at the core of philosophical reflection. This is essential to my argument, since the "discovering" of the relevance of interpretation produced what has been called "the hermeneutic turn" in contemporary philosophy, which has in turn had an influence on many relevant philosophical approaches in contemporary philosophy.[14] For instance, the use of interpretation as a point of departure for philosophical reflection is equally fundamental to hermeneutics, pragmatism, and communitarianism. Moreover, these three philosophical approaches are those that shaped the philosophy of sport into its current state. Their influence drew the attention of philosophers of sports to the analysis of practical and concrete problems instead of to questions related to the ontology of sports or the definitions of the basic terms in the debate, such as those forming the so-called "tricky triad": play, game, and sport.[15]

The hermeneutic turn in philosophy has also been regarded as very influential to the "applied turn" in contemporary philosophy. This is key to our topic. Owing to the applied turn most of the problems that concern philosophers of sport all over the world are those of practical nature, that is to say, ethical problems.[16] The philosophy of sport nowadays is essentially synonymous with sports ethics. Even purely theoretical debates, such as those on the concept of nature or on the "essence" of sports, are aimed at clarifying some practical problem like the implementation of new technologies or the commodification of sports. This extreme relevance of applied problems in sports philosophy reaches its peak, for instance, in Graham McFee's statement that, "The point here is just that, for sport, the philosophical questions will be ethical ones—the topic might, on a parallel with 'medical ethics,' be called 'sports ethics.'"[17]

Although the three approaches, hermeneutics, pragmatism, and communitarianism, played an important part in the transformation of the philosophy of sports into a more practically oriented discipline, the applied turn in this discipline was mostly a consequence of the introduction of MacIntyre's concept of "practice," which changed the paradigm of the philosophy of sports in the mid-80s. The later contribution of Richard Dworkin's interpretivist philosophy of law and Richard Rorty's philosophy as edification motivated the tendency to look at practical problems philosophically—from a hermeneutic perspective. However, MacIntyre must be located at the very beginning of the "hermeneutization" process of the philosophy of sport. As Mike McNamee shows,

> During the 1990s more eclectic writings emerged. Inspired by MacIntyre's writings in After Virtue, many philosophers came to conceive of sport as social practices and moved away from the ahistorical/asocial analytical accounts of the elements of games and sport.[18]

According to McNamee, MacIntyre's philosophy was so successful due to the, "sterility of analytical accounts of sport with respect to their ethical nature."[19] The goals and methods of an analytic philosophy of sports, which is aimed at clarifying disciplinary language use and fixing its meaning, was at odds with a philosophy of sports turned into a practical—or applied—discipline. Thus, the ahistorical/asocial analytical approach had to be abandoned in favor of a theoretical framework that could adequately adjust to the constantly changing nature of the practical issues raised within contemporary sports understood as MacIntyrean social practices.

The main goal of MacIntyre's philosophy, as he states at the very beginning of *After Virtue,* is to solve endless moral arguments—that is to say, the ambiguities in our moral vocabulary. Although this might seem to be an analytic task, MacIntyre draws on Gadamer's hermeneutics and his project of reviving Aristotelianism.[20] In so doing, he takes moral philosophy to a different level, namely, a level widely influenced by hermeneutics. This does not mean that most of the philosophical approaches in the arena of the philosophy of sports are hermeneutical. But it means that most of the philosophical proposals use hermeneutic tools to approach the sporting phenomenon. One such tools is, of course, interpretation, which is intrinsically linked to Aristotle's idea of "phronesis." By turning interpretation into a key to contemporary philosophy, hermeneutics also recovered the Aristotelian way to understand phronesis. This is one reason among others why hermeneutics played a relevant role in the applied turn in contemporary philosophy.

According to MacIntyre, Gadamer progressed the field by "characterizing hermeneutic practice in terms drawn from Aristotle's account of practice [phronesis]."[21] For Aristotle, phronesis or "prudential comprehension," as has commonly been translated, is always situated and forces us to find an application of our understanding to our specific situation. In this way, understanding is not something theoretical, but eminently practical. As Heidegger claims, practical concerns are there from the very beginning since we are always part of social practices and practical contexts that provide us with standards to act. This is why social practices are so relevant for our practical understanding. If we pay careful attention to them, they provide us with the means to solve our current endless moral disputes.

For MacIntyre, as mentioned above, engaging in a practice is not an act of sovereign subjectivity, but of becoming involved in the spirit of the thing—that is to say, of devoting one's full attention to the matter at hand. Gadamer illustrates this attitude by using the metaphor of the game.[22] When we enter a game, we do not play with it, we are not autonomous; we just accept the rules and play by them.[23] In fact, it could be said that it is the game which plays with us by taking us into its spirit. We are inside the ludic world as long as we abide by its rules; if we break them, the game is over:

> The person who «sees through» his playing partners to something beyond the understandings involved in their relationship—that is, does not take the game seriously—is a spoilsport.[24]

This does not imply that games are static and their rules do not change. Participants and games engage in a constant dialogue,[25] which ends up with changes in both rules and participants' attitude and experience. However, this is not possible without the initial act of abiding by the rules to enter the game. We change the rules by actively engaging in it.

Social practices follow the same logic. Participants must allow themselves to be immersed into the practice's spirit and become fully oriented in their conduct by such an internal logic. In so doing, participants abide by the same set of standards to delineate the appropriate conduct.[26] As they now share a common orientation toward collective goals, moral disputes should eventually come to an end.[27] Social practices are thus the cornerstone of ethics and its practical thinking.

As Kelvin Knight argues,[28] this idea can also be traced back to another author with whom MacIntyre was quite familiar: Wittgenstein and his notions of "language games" and "following a rule." Thus, it is worth pointing out that Wittgenstein's influence on philosophy was pivotal in both the emergence and decay of the analytic era in the philosophy of sports. Whereas this era was born out of Suits' rejection of Wittgenstein's philosophy,[29] MacIntyre's revival of Wittgenstein's approach initiated the applied era in the philosophy of sports at the expense of the analytic one inspired by Suits' formalist proposal.

According to Wittgenstein, we can only understand the other and communicate with him by following the publicly shared rules of language. We have to become part of a system of rules—that is, a language game, and abide by it to interact with others. A private language makes no sense,[30] since the rules governing the use of such language would depend on its creator's will instead of a public agreement. Private rules could never be fixed. Likewise, a game in which participants change the rules constantly and voluntarily would be impossible to play. Publicly shared rules provide a criterion to identify what is acceptable and what is not.

In alignment with this idea, for MacIntyre, social practices' intrinsic ends and standards of excellence act as publicly shared regulative principles. They become the public standards by which all the members should abide. We can see this clearly in his definition of the "social practice":

> Any coherent and complex form of socially established cooperative human activity through which *goods internal* to that form of activity are realized in the course of trying to achieve those *standards of excellence* which are appropriate to, and partially definitive of, that form of activity, with the result that human powers to achieve excellence, and human conceptions of the ends and goods involved, are systematically extended.[31]

MacIntyre regards intrinsic ends and excellences as those elements that make possible and regulate the functioning of social practices. Many of the so-called "fathers of the philosophy of sports" took these concepts of internal goods and excellences into account in order to understand the nature of sports as social practices. This being so, the goal of a philosophy of sport built upon MacIntyre's concept of practice is to identify the criteria that are already implicitly operative within the sporting practice.

According to Simon, this has to be done from within the practice, not from outside. The importing of external principles into the sporting practice would distort and radically transform sporting practice into something else, for example, into a strategic form of behavior. This is the main reason interpretivism is regarded as an internalist account of sports in opposition to externalist accounts of sports. As Simon states,

> Contrary to . . . externalist approaches, internalists argue that sport involves a set of principles and values inherent in and perhaps conceptually tied to sporting activities and practices. On the internalist view, we can best understand and evaluate sport by attending to its internal features or characteristics rather than its connection to broader social practices, institutions or values.[32]

Therefore, a philosophy of sports conceived in internalist terms uses hermeneutic tools and has a twofold aim. First, it describes what individuals are doing when they engage in a practice—that is to say, it identifies what differentiates a certain practice from the others. And, second, it provides a critical perspective on the way the practice should be carried out. In Fairfield's words, by "giv[ing] an understanding of the ends towards which a practice is always already oriented, the [sports] theorist may fashion principles of critique."[33] In this sense, interpretivism resembles a critical hermeneutical approach, for it not only provides an understanding of the intrinsic logic of sports practices, but it also points out several essential features that function as critical standards against which to measure the reality of such practices.

This twofold interpretation of the main goals of hermeneutic interpretation applied to sports is in line with Simon's characterization of interpretivism. For him,

> One function of a theory of sport is to help us make distinctions between activities that are sports from those that aren't, even if the distinction is not always a sharp one. . . . There is [also] a normative or evaluative function served by theories of sport; to the extent that they help us identify salient features of sport, they provide material we can use to morally assess sport as well.[34]

The fact that Gadamer's hermeneutics, by means of MacIntyre's philosophy, is at the basis of the interpretivist account in the philosophy of sport explains the origin of the very name of this approach: "interpretivism." According to Gadamer, there is no difference between the concepts "interpretation" and "understanding"; both refer to the same thing and may thus be used interchangeably. It could be argued that Simon holds the same position, since he explains the specificity of the interpretivist approach in the philosophy of sports by appealing to the task of interpreting a picture, namely, *The Fall of Icarus.*[35] In this illustration, interpretation and understanding, as with Gadamer, are regarded as synonyms.

This being so, a theory of sports aimed at understanding the intrinsic nature of this social phenomenon could be called either "sports interpretivism" or "hermeneutics of sports."[36] However, rarely within the philosophy of sports has anyone acknowledged this dual sided nature of interpretivism. This downplays the key role that hermeneutic elements and concepts play in their philosophical approaches to sports. In a sense, it could be argued that philosophers of sports have been following a hermeneutic methodology unconsciously ever since the practical turn in their discipline occurred. Simon does acknowledges the existence of diverse interpretivist approaches within the philosophy of sports, but he does not provide any explanation for this diversity of theories.[37]

In the philosophy of sports, these theories have been commonly differentiated by means of the distinction between realist and antirealist philosophical accounts of sports,[38] that is, between those theories that defended the possibility of grasping a true nature of sports, and those that reject that such nature exists. This distinction is accurate in many senses, and can be explained by referring to two diverse interpretations of the hermeneutic process of interpretation that will be explained in the next section.

REALIST AND ANTIREALIST THEORIES OF SPORT

There have been different ways to comprehend the understanding process through the history of philosophy. For instance, Gadamer criticized modern philosophical hermeneutics, such as that of Schleiermacher and Dilthey, for trying to reduce interpretation to the seeking of a comprehensive meta-principle that would give meaning solely by applying the principle to the phenomenon to be understood. For Schleiermacher and Dilthey, the understanding of something is only possible in reference to the whole from which it originated. In this process of relating a part to a whole, we grasp the nature of both of them.

This is also the case, for example, of what we call "Marxist hermeneutics."[39] For this type of hermeneutics, every single event in the world needs to be viewed through an economic infrastructure to assign meaning to activities. Labor is the single principle at the basis of every hermeneutic explanation since it functions as a link between what we actually do and the economic infrastructure. It should be noted that Marxist theories of sports' reductive character is one of the main reasons Simon rejects externalism as an accurate philosophical approach.[40]

As "modern-style" philosophical hermeneutics was influenced by the successful eighteenth century natural sciences, its main goal is to understand something fully. For example, in the case of interpreting a novel, Schleiermacher argues that we have to understand the work better than its author did. Therefore, hermeneutics' goal is "to understand the text at first as well as and then even better than its author."[41] Likewise, Chladenius claims, "one understands something completely when one considers all of the thoughts that the words can awaken in us according to the rules of heart and mind."[42] For these authors, hermeneutics has a clearly defined goal: to provide a *complete* understanding of what is at stake.

This has a crucial point. As the hermeneutical process has a goal that is clearly defined: that of understanding something completely, then there must exist certain "paths" that we can follow in order to attain such a goal. These paths provide us with rules or criteria to guide our interpretation process. When criteria are provided, then we have the proper tools to evaluate the correctness of our interpretations. A correct interpretation would be the one which takes the right path. This is the reason Schleiermacher argues that hermeneutics and criticism are so intimately related that the practice of one presupposes the other: hermeneutics is essentially a critical task.[43] By following Karl Otto Apel's terms,[44] we will call this hermeneutics "principled hermeneutics."

On this view, interpretation is not all there is. However, there are also some conditions of possibility of interpretation that are transcontextual to every process of interpretation. For instance, in discourse ethics, every participant in a moral debate should abide by a set of ideal speech conditions so that they are more likely to reach an agreement by embodying the same communicative rationality. Such ideal speech conditions are beyond linguistic utterances because they are necessary for speech to be possible. Therefore, since interpretation is linguistically constructed, the ideal conditions of speech are also beyond interpretation.[45]

Morgan takes Dixon and Simon to be the main proponents of the discourse approach within the philosophy of sports.[46] According to this approach, in our deliberations over the nature of sport, diverse parties with different (even opposing) viewpoints can engage in a debate to construct a common definition of sports if they abide by the same set of presuppositions (rules) of speech. These rules set a discursive framework where rational agreement between the participants in the discussion is possible. Thus, the definition resulting from such a process of deliberation, which is regarded as an intersubjective process of interpretation, is regarded as rational and therefore as better than those definitions achieved through distorted processes of communication where the abovementioned argumentation rules are not met.[47] Thus, although Dixon and Simon, along with the main proponents of discourse ethics, accept that our definitions are the result of a dialogical process of interpretation, they are able to identify certain criteria to critically and rationally evaluate the outcome of the interpretive process.

Likewise, the proponents of what Morgan calls "creative theories of sports" argue that we can track and identify real features of sports on the basis of certain perfectionist and voluntarist principles.[48] This approach also uses the hermeneutic tool of interpretation to grasp the main principles underlying sports located beyond particular contexts. However, unlike discourse theories of sports, interpretation is understood here in a solipsistic way. That is to say, proponents of the creative theory of sports regard interpretation as a subjective activity realized individually in order to define sports by grasping their common objective elements. According to this theory of sports, the main critical criterion to evaluate such definitions is the idea that sports are perfectionist enterprises created to elucidate who the best participant is.[49] Interpretation, thus, is key in this theory too, but it is critically assessed by using certain objective principles.

In opposition to this type of critical hermeneutics, Gadamer argues that interpretation is more complex than the mere discovery of a single set of interpretive principles, that is to say, hermeneutics is more than a method or a mechanical procedure used to better understand something. Following Heidegger, Gadamer, who is widely regarded as the father of contemporary philosophical hermeneutics, argues that to understand entails an existential engagement.[50] This engagement is something that cannot be reduced or equated to a mere mechanic method of understanding. According to Heidegger's existentialism, we are always unconsciously embedded in a particular context or situation; we are always "beings-in-the-world," to use Heidegger's terms. This status precedes all cognitive tasks. Understanding is the defining activity of our human existence. The idea of objective reason is impossible, since the possibility of reaching a complete understanding, which is the dream of the modern individual who thinks that nature can be fully grasped by reason, is always dependent on the circumstances in which it operates.

If nature cannot be fully grasped by reason, then it could be argued that our reason is inevitably impure, since it is always influenced by our situation. For Gadamer, this influence occurs through prejudices; they constitute our reality by providing us with a pre-understanding of the world produced within a particular tradition. We can never stand outside the framework created by our tradition since our rational thinking is only possible in relation to the proxy of tradition. Objective knowledge, on this view, is thus impossible, since it is impossible to separate it from the ontological fact of being-there-thrown-into-the-world.

Hermeneutics, understood under this existential light, is not an autonomous methodology to better understand, as in Schleiermacher's and Dilthey's account of it, but an inquiry on and a statement of the very temporal and existential nature of understanding.[51] Hermeneutics, for Gadamer, is therefore not intertwined with criticism,[52] rather hermeneutics is aimed at explaining how tradition, which is understood as a text because it is constructed linguistically, is revalidated by the interpreter in his or her particular situation.[53]

Our societies and traditions evolve through this process. The elapse of time or, to put it in Gadamer's terms, "the effect of temporal distance" eliminate interpretative errors, that is to say, those interpretations of reality that have proven to be useless or incorrect:

> [Temporal distance] does not merely allow prejudices of a particular nature to die away, but also those which provide genuine understanding to emerge as such. Nothing other than this temporal distance is capable of making the genuinely critical question of hermeneutics resolvable, namely, to separate the true prejudices by which we understand from the false ones by which we misunderstand.[54]

In direct opposition to Schleiermacher and Dilthey, Gadamer argues that there is no better understanding. The end of the fusion of horizons is not to understand completely, but rather to understand differently through time.[55] There is not a clear goal at the end of the road, just an endless journey. This is perfectly illustrated in the title of Heidegger's book *Holzweg*,[56] which in colloquial German means "a path (normally in the woods) that leads nowhere."[57]

Morgan's conventionalism is in line with these hermeneutic proposals. He argues that certain "deep conventions" shape and mold sports into the various forms they have taken. Such deep conventions are not constructed through rational processes of interpretation. Rather, they "are normative responses to our 'deep psychological and social' needs for playing sports."[58] Thus, deep conventions arise intersubjectively as uncoordinated responses to the challenges and problems that participants in social practices face. This being so, deep conventions are in the background, influencing individuals' values and reasons without being explicitly noticed or perceived. Thus, they are not objective but related to their particular contexts.

Those hermeneutic philosophical approaches that defend the existence of a goal and end to interpretation are realists, whereas antirealists are those theories of sport in which interpretation is a never-ending process without any goal or criteria to guide our interpretation. For example, whereas Simon's mutualist approach is based on the idea that competition is the fundamental and structural element of sports, Russell focuses on the excellences exhibited in the prosecution of sports' lusory goal. Either competition or sports-related excellences constitute the criteria (or "factic" element, in hermeneutic terms) upon which the interpretation of sports should be built. In so doing, these two different theories of sports could be called "realist hermeneutics of sports."

AntiRealist Approaches

Although Morgan does not define himself as an interpretivist author, he should be regarded as such as well. This is something that I have proposed in a different work[59] and that Simon acknowledges when he analyzes Morgan's deep conventionalism, which I call "conventionalist interpretivism." This is the reason Simon argues that, "broad internalists should ask if the deep conventions cited by Morgan are substantially different from the principles cited by broad internalists."[60] Deep conventions and broad internalists' principles are not very far from each other in the sense that both play the same role in their respective hermeneutic approaches: deep conventions and principles are the criteria that always need to be taken into account when interpreting a certain sport or sporting context.

Moreover, Morgan's conventionalist approach is a clear example of an antirealist hermeneutic account of sports, which is the consequence of Morgan's use of Rorty's philosophy hermeneutic perspective. To show why both Rorty's and Morgan's philosophy draws on hermeneutics, we only need to take a look at Rorty's famous *Philosophy and the Mirror of Nature.*[61] In this work, Gadamer's "hermeneutic theory of knowledge" plays an important part, since Rorty's notion of philosophy as edification is inspired by Gadamer's hermeneutics: both theories go against the traditional way of envisioning philosophy as a search of truth. In this sense, both Rorty's edifying proposal and Gadamer's hermeneutics "are abnormal" or peripheral in comparison with the dominant position in philosophy.[62]

> One way to see edifying philosophy *as* the love of wisdom is to see it as the attempt to prevent conversation from degenerating into inquiry, into a research program. Edifying philosophers can never end philosophy, but they can help prevent it from attaining the secure path of a science [. . .] For the edifying philosopher the very idea of being presented with "all of Truth" is absurd, because the Platonic notion of Truth itself is absurd. It is absurd either as the notion of truth about reality which is not about reality-under-a-certain-description, or as the notion of truth about reality under some privileged description which makes all other descriptions unnecessary because it is commensurable with each of them.[63]

According to Rorty, edifying philosophers' goal cannot be achieved in the, *de novo,* void of abstract principles or ideas,[64] such as those of the philosophers who look for the essence and intrinsic nature of things. Rather it must start by "enculturation [that is to say by] finding out a lot about the descriptions of the world offered by our culture."[65]

Morgan's theory of sports is based on Rorty's ideas exposed above. For instance, he does not use the term "edifying philosopher," but his concept of "moral entrepreneurs," borrowed from R. Posner, refers to the same type of individual or intellectual figure, as can be seen in the following quotation:

The way forward is to divine altogether new normative conceptions of sport and try to get the warring parties to see their attractive possibilities, the preferred path sought by what Posner called moral entrepreneurs. One thing they won't be able to do is to contend theirs is the only rationally defensible account of sport, since such a claim would require what any particular normative account of sport cannot, per impossible, plausibly claim, namely, that their normative take on sport is not a particular, historical one at all, but a transcultural one that can rationally defeat all comers.[66]

Regarding Morgan's notion of truth, we can see that he also draws on Rorty's epistemological claims. For Morgan, rational debate over sports is dependent on the acceptance of certain rational principles that he calls "deep conventions." Morgan borrows this concept from the philosopher of law Andrei Marmor, in order to refer to a particular type of conventions that creates the logical space in which rational discussion is possible; it is impossible to rationally adjudicate controversial claims outside such a space.

For example, in ancient Greek society, people thought of and reflected on sports, such as cheating and sportsmanship, within the framework provided by the laws and structure of the polis and the principles of the Olympic religion, to which sports we intimately linked. In so doing, the ancient Greeks came up with the following solution to deter cheating: if participants in the Games were caught cheating, either they or their city should pay for the construction of golden statues of Zeus called "zanes." These statues should include an inscription in the base with the name of the cheater, and be placed just before the entrance of the stadium in a "wall of shame," where everybody could see them. This was probably the worst punishment that somebody could suffer in ancient Greece, since by placing their names in such a shameful place they would never be able to achieve excellence (*aretē*) and recognized as such by their equals. The achievement of *aretē* was the previous step to immortality. Therefore, the punishment for a sporting foul such as cheating would be the denial of immortality. It is obvious that a religious solution like this would not succeed in recent times in cases such as those of Ben Johnson's and Lance Armstrong's doping offenses.

For Morgan, the assessment of recent controversial sporting cases is possible only by means of our particular deep conventions regarding the nature of sports. Therefore, in line with Rorty's proposal, for us to be able to discuss sports rationally, we first have to start by adopting the deep conventions of our culture and stay "inside the walls" of the logical space that they create. This is the reason Morgan calls his proposal an "intramural theory of sports."[67] In such a theory of sport, contrary to principled-interpretivist accounts of sports, there are no fixed (trans-contextual) principles or final goal common to all possible interpretations of sport, such as that of conceiving all sport as essentially "a contest for bodily excellence" for example.

> I have been arguing all along that there is no such neutral rational standpoint that can bail us out when conflicts like this arise, and that the only candidate that interpretivists offer, sport conceived as a test of bodily skill, won't do because it is too far removed from the fray in which such conflicts germinate to have anything of substance to say about how to rationally adjudicate them.[68]

Realist Approaches

The negation of the existence of a goal and certain criteria to guide our interpretations contrasts with the basic point of realist-interpretivist accounts of sport, and can be linked to Gadamer's idea that hermeneutic knowledge never ends but goes back and forth, leading to different interpretations every time. It could be said that, according to this proposal, a certain interpretation of sport cannot be compared as being better or worse than another; they are simply different interpretations. However, the distinction between realist and antirealist hermeneutics of sport is not black and white, but rather, there are nuanced interpretations situated between both extremes. For example, Morgan's philosophical proposal resembles that illustrated in John Rawls' idea of the reflective equilibrium. Nonetheless, some of the most famous realist interpretivists' accounts of sport draw on this idea.

According to Georgia Warnke, Rawls' theory is a "hermeneutic political theory."[69] This hermeneutic interpretation of Rawls' theory can be grounded by taking a look at some of his latest texts like "Kantian Constructivism in Moral Theory" and "Political Liberalism." Therein, Rawls offers an interpretation of his Theory of Justice which abandons the search for foundations for his political theory. In contrast, he contends that to justify our ethical theories we need,

> to articulate and to make explicit those shared notions and principles thought to be already latent in common sense; or, as is often the case, if common sense is hesitant and uncertain, and doesn't know what to think, to propose to it certain conceptions and principles congenial to its most essential convictions and historical traditions.[70]

In line with this idea, his two prominent principles of justice are not based on some set of atemporal moral bases, but rather they stem from what we the current citizens of the world—or at least of modern liberal societies—regard as fair for—free and equal—human beings. Philosophy thus should not search for an ultimate justification or principle, but rather, in a Hegelian way, it should articulate the principles already inherent in our own traditions.

An example of a "mixed theory of sport," that is to say, a theory that is located somewhere in between realism and antirealism, is Cesar Torres' interpretivist account. This interpretivist theory of sport is based on the methodological assumption that: "interpretivists infer the best explanation of a sport's key elements, and [. . .] articulate its most cogent version."[71] The goal of this hermeneutic theory of sport is thus not the one of grasping the true nature of sports, but rather the formulation of the most cogent and widely accepted explanation of sport.

In such a mixed type of sport hermeneutics, there is a certain appeal to criteria that guide interpretation, but such criteria are temporal since the acceptance of their truth is based on wide acceptance. In line with this idea, Simon's theory of sport holds that interpretivist authors

> need not be committed to . . . an ahistorical or transcendent approach . . . we can start from discourse in a particular historical context with the goal that continued discussion among interlocutors with diverse viewpoints might promote a consensus among advocates who were at one time in disagreement. Thus, discussion starts in a particular historical context but can also transcend it towards universality.[72]

Simon's last words, "discussion starts in a particular historical context but can also transcend towards universality," show us, first, that his interpretivist theory of sport is also grounded in Jürgen Habermas' Kantian-inspired hermeneutics, and, second, how far his proposal is from Morgan's conventionalist account where no claim to universality is possible. For a Habermasian theory of sport, the grasping of truth is impossible, but the ongoing debate between free and equal human beings is the way to get closer to it. Truth is thus a "counterfactual assumption."[73]

Cogency is Cesar Torres' counterfactual assumption, whereas Simon's is the possibility of a free-speech situation where everybody can engage in public discussions equally and freely. Another possible counterfactual assumption found in the philosophy of sport is coherence. According to Paul Fairfield's interpretation of Gadamer's hermeneutic philosophy,[74] the criterion to solve interpretative conflicts is that of "the harmony of all the details with the whole."[75] For Gadamer, the process of hermeneutics resembles that of a circle—the hermeneutical circle—thus he regards both reality and interpretation as having a circular structure. They are defined by a constant back and forth relationship between the whole and its parts. Reality and knowledge are always changing according to this process. This is the reason Gadamer argues that there are no better interpretations, but rather only different ones. However, despite not being a criterion for deciding which interpretation is better, the coherence criterion tells us whether a given interpretation is valid or not by referring to the logic of the hermeneutical circle. An interpretation is valid only when it, acting as a part of a more comprehensive whole, coheres with the whole. In Fairfield's words, "when coherence is wanting, we say that understanding is deficient."[76]

To make this claim stronger, Fairfield, by following Gadamer, identifies the whole that gives meaning to our interpretations as the set of social practices within which we, as social beings, are embedded. Social practices orient and configure us as cognitive and acting beings by providing us with a common set of goals, rules, and a context for agreeing or disagreeing on these matters—that is to say, a context for using our communicative capacities. We recognize ourselves as linguistic and interpretative beings through our embeddedness in social practices. Owing to this, Fairfield argues that, "lifeworld practices constitutes the alpha and omega of philosophical [hermeneutics] theorizing."[77]

This proves how influential Gadamer has been on the recent philosophy of sport. For instance, Dworkin's interpretive philosophy of law grounds John S. Russell's philosophical account of sports, which he calls "coherentism."[78] In Dworkin's *Law Empire,* we can read that,

> the interpretative situation is not an Archimedian point, nor is that suggested in the idea that interpretation aims to make what is interpreted the best it can seem. Once again I appeal to Gadamer, whose account of interpretation as recognizing, while struggling against, the constraints of history strikes the right note.[79]

In this quotation, Dworkin is drawing on Gadamer's critique of modern hermeneutics. He realizes, through Gadamer, that for our interpretations (of law) to be accurate, we need to take into account their historicity. However, acknowledging the crucial role played by historicity, Dworkin still claims that, as Russell shows in his paper "Are rules all an umpire has to work with?," we have at our disposal certain criteria to critically evaluate interpretations.

> Interpretation can . . . be understood to involve three stages. We interpret social practices, first, when we individuate those practices. . . . We interpret, second, when we attribute some package of purposes to the genre or subgenre we identify as pertinent, and, third, when we try to identify the best realization of that package of purposes on some particular occasion.[80]

As Russell's reading of Dworkin's best known work shows, the criteria that shows us when an interpretation is closer to the truth are coherence

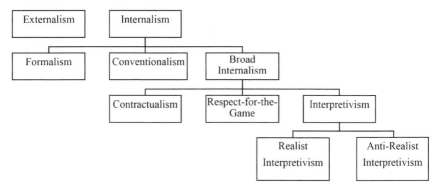

Figure 2.2   Theories of Sport: four theoretical levels.

and integrity regarding, in Dworkin's words, the package of purposes of a given activity, that is, sports in our case. This means, for Russell, that the cornerstone of our interpretations of sport is the group of purposes pursued through our participation in sports:

> Dworkin's notion of integrity come into play as a guide for the weight and role various principles will have in a legal system. That is, we might try to understand and interpret these the rules of a game, say, baseball, using these principles, to generate a coherent and principled account of the point and purposes that underlie the game, attempting to show the game in its best light.[81]

As shown in the quotation above, Russell's proposal is realist since it is aimed at understanding the game in "its best light," which is a similar purpose to Schleiermacher's goal of understanding the author better that he understood himself. This demonstrates that the debate on the nature of the different theories of sports is a reproduction of the general debate in hermeneutics regarding the two different ways to conceptualize the term "understanding." Thus, by differentiating between those hermeneutics aimed at a goal and those focused solely in the interpretation process, we could argue that this very difference is that which explains the distinction in the philosophy of sport between realist and antirealist interpretivist theories of sport. We can thus complete the four theoretical levels as seen in figure 2.2.

THE PHILOSOPHY OF SPORTS MIMICKING
THE DEBATE ON PHILOSOPHICAL HERMENEUTICS

In this chapter, I have shown first the state of the work in the philosophy of sports in terms of what the most important theories of sports are in our time. In so doing, I pointed out that the most prominent approach nowadays is interpretivism. Second, I showed how interpretivism is linked to hermeneutics: first, by analyzing the term "interpretation" and the role that it plays in interpretivists' accounts of sports, and second, by showing how these accounts resulted from the introduction of Gadamer's hermeneutics into the philosophy of sports, especially, through MacIntyre's, Dworkins', and Rorty's works. I further demonstrated that the diverse interpretation of Gadamer's hermeneutics through these authors resulted in two different types of interpretivist approaches: "realist" and "antirealist." Finally, to conclude, I claimed that this reveals that the debate between the different theories of sports reproduces the more general debate on hermeneutics between "principled hermeneutics" and "historicists hermeneutics."

NOTES

1. Robert L. Simon, "Theories of sport," in *The Bloomsbury Companion to the Philosophy of Sport,* ed. Cesar R. Torres (London: Bloomsbury Publishing, 2014); William J. Morgan, "Broad internalism, Deep Conventions, Moral Entrepreneurs, and Sport," *Journal of the Philosophy of Sport* 39, no. 1 (2012): 65–100; Cesar R. Torres, "Furthering Interpretivism's Integrity: Bringing Together Ethics and Aesthetics,*"* *Journal of the Philosophy of Sport* 39, no. 2 (2012): 299–319; and John S. Russell, "Are Rules All an Umpire Has to Work With?," *Journal of the Philosophy of Sport* 26, no. 1 (1999): 27–49.

2. Robert L. Simon, "Internalism and Internal Values in Sport," *Journal of the Philosophy of Sport* 27 (2000): 1–16.

3. Karl Marx, *A Contribution to the Critique of Political Economy* (Chicago: Charles H. Kerr and Company: 1904), 11–12.

4. Simon, "Theories of Sport," 83–98.

5. Ludwig Wittgenstein, *Philosophical Investigations* (New York: Macmillan, 1953).

6. Bernard Suits, *The Grasshopper: Games, Life and Utopia* (Peterborough, Ont: Broadview Press, 2005).

7. Drawing on Simon, I argue elsewhere that there is also an externalist version of conventionalism. The fact that a conventionalist proposal in the philosophy of sport is externalist or internalist depends on the origin of the conventions widely accepted in the sporting community: some come from the wider society, and other from the intrinsic nature of sport. An example of an externalist convention widespread in sport is the assumption that we should always seek to increase the profitability of our activities by increasing efficiency. This idea is widely accepted in our societies, especially, in the managerial spheres. In fact, this is the reason the modern individual has been defined as *homo economicus.* Francisco Javier López Frías, *La Filosofía del Deporte Actual. Paradigmas y Corrientes Principales* (Roma, Qua.Pe.G, 2014).

8. Fred D'Agostino, "The Ethos of Games," *Journal of the Philosophy of Sport* 8, no. 1 (1981): 7–18.

9. Simon, "Internalism and internal values in sport," 7. (cursives are mine)

10. Ibid.

11. Ibid., 8.

12. Shaun Gallagher, *Hermeneutics and Education* (Albany: State University of New York Press, 1999), 4.

13. Ibid., 5.

14. Theodore R. Schazki, *The Practice Turn in Contemporary Theory* (New York: Routledge, 2001).

15. Bernard Suits, "Tricky Triad: Games, Play, and Sport," *Journal of the Philosophy of Sport* 15, no. 1 (1988): 1–9. See also Chad Carlson, "A Three-Pointer: Revisiting Three Crucial Issues in the 'Tricky Triad' of Play, Games, and Sport" in this volume.

16. Mike McNamee, "Ethics and Sport," *British Philosophy of Sport Association Website,* http://philosophyofsport.org.uk/resources/ethics-sport/

17. Graham McFee, "Normativity, Justification, and (Macintyrean) Practices: Some Thoughts on Methodology for the Philosophy of Sport," *Journal of the Philosophy of Sport* 31, no. 1 (2004): 15.

18. McNamee, "Ethics and Sport," 4.

19. Mike McNamee, *Sports, Virtues and Vices: Morality Plays* (London: Routledge, 2008), 45.

20. Alasdair MacIntyre, "On Not Having the Last Word: Thoughts on Our Debts to Gadamer" in *Gadamer's Century: Essays in Honor of Hans-Georg Gadamer,* ed. H. G. Gadamer, J. Malpas, U. Arnswald, and J. Kertscher (Cambridge: MIT Press, 2002), 167. See also Kelvin Knight, *Aristotelian Philosophy: Ethics and Politics from Aristotle to MacIntyre* (Maiden, MA: Polity Press, 2007).

21. MacIntyre, "On Not Having the Last Word," 167.

22. Randolph Feezell, *Sport, Philosophy, and Good Lives* (Lincoln: University of Nebraska Press, 2013), and Hans-Georg Gadamer, *Truth and Method* (New York: Seabury Press, 1975).

23. Jacobo Muñoz and A.M. Faerna, *Caminos de la Hermenéutica* (Madrid: Biblioteca Nueva, 2006).

24. Kurt Mueller-Vollmer, *The Hermeneutics Reader: Texts of The German Tradition from the Enlightenment to the Present* (New York: Continuum, 1988), 291.

25. Andrew Edgar, "The Aesthetics of Sport," *Sport, Ethics and Philosophy* 7, no. 1 (2013); Kenneth Aggerholm, *Talent Development, Existential Philosophy and Sport: On Becoming an Elite Athlete* (London, Routledge, 2015).

26. However, participants do not always fully agree to abide by the same set of basic principles and standards. This is the reason why moral debate is, and will always be, inevitable in every social practice. For instance, as William Morgan has rightly pointed out, whereas amateur participants understand participation to be the main goal of sports, professional athletes take victory and prestige to be their main goal. Both participants try to engage in the same social practice but disagree on the standards and goals of the practice. This is an example of a moral disagreement (or debate) within sports that produces a change in the rules and configuration of the social practice.

27. Paul Fairfield, *Philosophical Hermeneutics in Relation Dialogues with Existentialism, Pragmatism, Critical Theory, and Postmodernism* (New York: Continuum, 2011), 110.

28. Knight, *Aristotelian Philosophy*.

29. Suits, *The Grasshopper,* 11.

30. Wittgenstein, *Philosophical investigations*, §243

31. Alasdair MacIntyre, *After Virtue: a Study in Moral Theory* 3rd ed. (Notre Dame, Ind: University of Notre Dame Press, 2007), 187 (emphasis added).

32. Simon, "Theories of Sport," 85.

33. Fairfield, *Philosophical Hermeneutics,* 113.

34. Simon, "Theories of Sport," 83.

35. Ibid., 89–90.

36. If we agree with Kurt Mueller-Vollmer's concept of interpretation, and analyze further the distinction between interpretation and understanding, we should argue that the correct name for the interpretivist theory of sports is "the hermeneutical approach to sports" or "hermeneutics of sports." According to Mueller, although both interpretation and understanding are part of a same continuum, they refer to different processes. Understanding is more a purely cognitive task, and interpretation refers to the verbal and discursive explication of what has been understood. In line with Mueller's definition of interpretation, Eric D. Hirsch argues that the terms "understanding" and "interpretation" refer to two separate functions, which are often confused. Like Mueller, he contrasts understanding (*subttilitas intelligendi*), which is concerned with the intellectual grasp of a certain meaning, and interpretation (*subtilitas intelligendi*), which refers to the strategies used to convey such a meaning. Thus, for Hirsch, "understanding is prior to and different from interpretation." Therefore, by following this interpretation, we can infer that a theory of sport aimed at making sense of the nature of sports should be called "sports hermeneutics" and not "sports interpretivism." However, some classical hermeneutic authors, such as Schleiermacher and Gadamer, use the terms interpretation and understanding in the same way, that is to say, interchangeably. For them, there is no distinction between interpretation and understanding. The reason for this is that, our mind—or the horizons of meaning we are part of, in Gadamer's terms—is linguistically constructed through dialogue, to isolate the process of comprehending as something different from the process of explaining what we have understood is highly unlikely. Non-differentiation between the two terms is the most widely accepted way of understanding their relationship nowadays.

Mueller-Vollmer, *The Hermeneutics Reader*, 40. Eric D. Hirsch, *Validity in Interpretation* (New Haven: Yale University Press, 1967), 129.

37. Simon, "Theories of Sport," 91.

38. John S. Russell, "Moral realism in sport," *Journal of the Philosophy of Sport* 31, no. 2 (2004): 142–160; Robert L. Simon, "From ethnocentrism to realism: Can discourse ethics bridge the gap?," *Journal of the Philosophy of Sport* 31, no. 2 (2004), 122–141.

39. Ernesto Laclau and Chantal Mouffe, *Hegemony and Socialist Strategy: Towards a Radical Democratic Politics* (London: Verso, 1985).

40. Simon, "Theories of sport."

41. Mueller-Vollmer, *The Hermeneutics Reader*, 83.

42. Ibid., 56.

43. In line with this idea, Schleiermacher argues that we have to understand something, first, as an expression in terms of the language of which it is part and, second, as a part of the speakers' life-process. These two moments of interpretation provide us with two criteria for guiding our understanding. By following these rules, we can get closer to the goal of completely understanding something. The closer we get, the bigger part of the whole picture we will see. This is how we can distinguish a good interpretation from a bad one. However, Schleiermacher introduces one caveat: whereas the goal of criticism supposedly ends, the goal of hermeneutics is endless. Complete understanding is the goal, but we know in advance that completeness is impossible to attain. We have to go back and forth in order to get as close as possible to it. Thus, the task of hermeneutics moves constantly. It involves a circle. However, this is not a vicious circle, as many critics have argued, but a virtuous one.

44. Karl Otto Apel, *Towards a Transformation of Philosophy* (Boston: Routledge & Kegan Paul, 1980).

45. Saral Jhingran, *Ethical Relativism and Universalism* (Delhi: Motilal Banarsidass Publishers, 2001), 325.

46. William J. Morgan, "Conventionalism and sport," in *Routledge Handbook of the Philosophy of Sport,* ed. Mike J. McNamee and William J. Morgan (New York: Routledge, 2015), 45.

47. Jürgen Habermas, *On the Logic of the Social Sciences* (Cambridge, MA: MIT Press, 1988).

48. Morgan, "Conventionalism and Sport," 35.

49. Ibid.

50. Karl Otto Apel, "German philosophy," in ed. D. Moran, *The Routledge Companion to Twentieth Century Philosophy* (New York: Routledge, 2010).

51. In Gadamer's words: "Understanding is in truth not understanding-better: neither in the sense of factually knowing better by means of clearer concepts nor in the sense of the fundamental superiority that conscious production possesses over unconscious. It is enough to say that one understands differently, if one understands at all." Gadamer, *Truth and Method,* 296–297.

52. Hirsch, *Validity in Interpretation.*

53. Apel, "German philosophy," 748.

54. Gadamer, *Truth and method,* 298–299.

55. Apel, "German philosophy," 751.

56. Martin Heidegger, *Country Path Conversations* (Bloomington: Indiana University Press, 2010).

57. This also brings to mind the following words of the Spanish poet Antonio Machado: "Wanderer, your footsteps are the road, and nothing more; wanderer, there is no road, the road is made by walking. By walking, one makes the road, and upon glancing behind, one sees the path that never will be trod again. Wanderer, there is no road. Only waves upon the sea."

58. Morgan, "Conventionalism and Sport," 39.

59. Francisco Javier López Frías, "William J. Morgan's 'Conventionalist Internalism' Approach. Furthering Internalism? A Critical Hermeneutical Response," *Sport, Ethics and Philosophy* 8, no. 2 (2014).

60. Simon, "Theories of Sport," 94.

61. Richard Rorty, *Philosophy and the Mirror of Nature* (Princeton: Princeton University Press, 1979).

62. Ibid., 360–61.

63. Ibid., 372 and 377–78.

64. Ibid., 366.

65. Ibid., 365.

66. Morgan, "Broad Internalism," 67.

67. Ibid.

68. Ibid., 78.

69. Georgia Warnke, "Social Interpretation and Political Theory," in ed. K. Wright, *Festivals of Interpretation: Essays on Hans-Georg Gadamer's Work* (New York: State University of New York Press, 1990), 138.

70. John Rawls, *Collected Papers* (Cambridge, MA: Harvard University Press, 1999), 518.

71. Torres, "Furthering Interpretivism."

72. Simon, "Theories of sport," 95.

73. Jürgen Habermas, *Between facts and norms: Contributions to a discourse theory of law and democracy* (Cambridge, Mass.: MIT Press, 1996), 163.

74. Fairfield, *Philosophical hermeneutics.*

75. Gadamer, *Truth and Method,* 291.

76. Fairfield, *Philosophical Hermeneutics*, 76

77. Ibid., 99.

78. John S. Russell, "Moral Realism in Sport," *Journal of the Philosophy of Sport 31*, no. 2 (2004), 154.

79. Ronald Dworkin, *Law's Empire* (Cambridge, Mass.: Belknap Press, 1986), 62.

80. Ronald Dworkin, *Justice for Hedgehogs* (Cambridge, MA; London: Belknap Press of Harvard University Press, 2003), 131.

81. Russell, "Are Rules All an Umpire Has to Work With?" 35.

Chapter 3

Hopscotch Dreams

Coming to Terms with the Cultural Significance of Sport

Kevin Schieman

The English word "sport" owes its etymology to the Old French word *desport*, meaning leisure, pastime, recreation, or pleasure.[1, 2] Given the seriousness we often attribute to athletic competition, the historical origins of our present use of the word "sport" have been rendered somewhat ironic. Bill Shankly, late manager of England's iconic Liverpool Football Club, once quipped, "Some people believe football is a matter of life and death, I am very disappointed with this attitude. I can assure you it is much, much more important than that."[3] While Shankly is clearly poking fun at fanaticism, it would be difficult to overstate the cultural significance of sport. Consider, for example, that soccer's 2014 World Cup Finals generated nearly 300 million viewers in the United States, across a population of just less than 320 million people.[4,5] Given that sort of interest, it should hardly be surprising then that our investment in sport is lucrative by other measures as well. Based purely on its domestic following, the National Football League generates better than nine billion dollars in annual revenue and maybe most revealing is the frequency with which athletes are able to parlay the celebrity of athletic achievement into political influence.[6,7] Whatever the etymology of the term, our investment in sport is much, much more than leisurely.

The focus of this argument, however, is not the sort of definition one might expect to find in a dictionary, be it English, French, old, or new. Instead, this argument focuses on understanding the conceptual basis for such a definition. Conceptual analysis seeks to understand concepts in terms of their necessary and sufficient conditions, as opposed to their use in language. Philosopher Thomas Hurka explains, "The necessary and sufficient conditions for a concept X are those properties shared by all Xs that make them Xs, whether or not people who talk about Xs know what they are."[8] By way of example,

I can claim without contradiction that people frequently describe video games as "sports," but that those games lack some requisite feature to actually count as sports.[9] Call it what you like, the argument might proceed, but Halo just doesn't require the right sorts of physical skills to actually be a sport. While the use of a word might vary from time to time or from place to place, the essential properties of the concept remain relatively constant since they describe the essence of the thing language seeks to capture. Of course, we should hope the definition of a word tracks our conceptual understanding of the thing it refers to, but that obviously isn't always the case. Faced with that reality, there is considerable benefit in understanding the concepts that underwrite our use of language.

My principal aim in this paper is to argue that the seriousness we attribute to sport reflects a central feature of our conceptual understanding of the term. Bernard Suits argues that in order for an activity to count as a sport, it must be a game, require physical skill, and necessarily enjoy a wide following and stability over time. To the contrary, I claim that widespread following and stability are not constitutive of sport, but bear more than accidental relation to a property that is (see figure 3.1). Sports enjoy a certain level of social esteem because, among other necessary qualities, they are essentially good games.[10] That is to say, some games are better than others in that they are better able to satisfy our reasons for playing them in the first place. Sports are necessarily the sorts of activities that warrant a significant investment of time and effort because they are able to yield the benefits of game-play to a greater degree than other similar activities.[11] It is because sports are necessarily good games that they often develop a popular following, but that popularity itself is not what makes them sports.

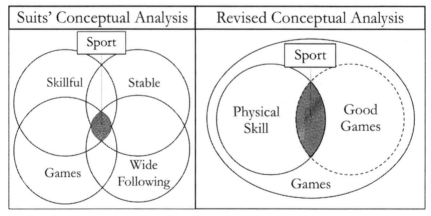

Figure 3.1 On the left is a visual representation of Suits' conceptual analysis of sport. On the right is the proposed revision to Suits' view.

I will present this argument in five sections. The first section describes Suits' conceptual analyses of games and sport, focusing on his characterization of widespread following and stability as necessary properties of sport. The second section considers a brief thought experiment involving the popular children's game hopscotch, suggesting that there may be some intuitive reason to doubt Suits' claim that games like hopscotch could ever become sports. The third and fourth sections of the paper explicate Suits' view of the role of play as a human ideal and suggest a rough framework for understanding the qualities that distinguish good games from mere games. Finally, I consider several cases suggesting that our judgments about what constitutes a sport track a game's quality, rather than its popular following. Sometimes, relatively bad games grow to be quite popular; others still are very good, but lack popularity for a number of contingent reasons. Although popularity is often a reliable indicator of a game's quality, it is that underlying quality that distinguishes a game of physical skill as sport, rather than related properties like widespread following or stability. Much like the properties that identify games as physical or skillful, the qualities that distinguish games as good are inherent to the structure of the games themselves. Ultimately, sports constitute a class of games that share the necessary properties of being physical in nature, skillful, and good with respect to games. Like certain nonphysical games, sports often—but not always—achieve stability and widespread following because they are simply good games. In addition to being games of physical skill, sports are necessarily the sorts of activities that are worthy of more than mere leisurely pursuit.

HARDLY SUITABLE

Recent attempts to provide a theoretical framework for understanding games have varied significantly. In contrast to Suits' own efforts, Ludwig Wittgenstein, one of the most influential philosophers of the twentieth century, argued that games deny reduction to a series of necessary and sufficient conditions.[12] In his posthumously published, *Philosophical Investigations*, he insists that the meaning of a word is no more than "its use in the language."[13] Wittgenstein doubted it was possible to characterize a word like "game," whose usage varies across such a wide range of activities, according to a single set of essential properties.[14] Notwithstanding his broader doubts about the usefulness of conceptual analysis, it isn't difficult to appreciate some skepticism about the possibility of subsuming such diverse phenomena as games under a single set of necessary and sufficient conditions. After all, what properties could we reasonably expect the Olympic Games to share with card games? At any rate, I believe Suits' analysis presents significant challenge to Wittgenstein's skepticism.

Arguing contra Wittgenstein, Suits claims that all games share three basic structural properties. At his pithy best, he defines games as "the voluntary attempt to overcome unnecessary obstacles."[15] According to Suits, all games have a goal, restrict the means available in achieving that goal, and require players to willingly accept the absurdity of so limiting themselves for sake of the game. That is to say, games require players to adopt a certain sort of attitude in voluntarily conforming to the rules and inefficiencies that constitute a game as such. He describes these essential features of games as the pre-lusory goal, rules, and lusory attitude. Beyond offering a basis for understanding games that fares well across a wide range of cases, this conceptual analysis forms the foundation of his understanding of sport. Suits claims that, "sports are essentially games," but that, "the difference between sports and other games is much smaller than the difference between humans and other vertebrates."[16] Sports are not merely a category or type of game, as "the distinguishing characteristics of sport are more peripheral, more arbitrary, and more contingent than are the differences required to define a species."[17]

In addition to being games, Suits argues that all sports require physical skill, have a wide following, and that their popularity must achieve a certain level of stability. In claiming that sports are necessarily games of physical skill, Suits offers two distinct insights into the nature of sport. First, sports can't simply be games of chance; sports require skillful performances. Second, the physical skills that define a game as sport must necessarily factor in the outcome. For example, even though the game of chess traditionally involves players manually moving pieces around the board, this modest physical capacity says very little of how good one is at chess. To the contrary, one could play chess by simply dictating moves and still play quite brilliantly. In fact, playing chess doesn't technically even require a board or pieces. John Haugeland once imagined particularly skillful players engaging in "esoteric chess," where they simply play through commands by reference to an imagined chessboard.[18] Sports, on the other hand, require physical performances that bear directly on one's ability to affect outcomes within the game. Although each of these insights offers something significant in elucidating our understanding of the nature of sport, neither is particularly controversial in the context of this essay.[19]

More problematic, however, is Suits' characterization of sport in terms of a widespread and stable following. Echoing Kierkegaard, he imagines a game called sweat-bead, whereby students delight in causing a particularly irascible professor to perspire according to a peculiar set of restrictions. Despite the oddity of the game, there is something strangely familiar about its object. The professor that no doubt inspired Kierkegaard's musing is an iconic feature of the college experience. A decided lack of physical skill notwithstanding, Suits claims that sweat-bead isn't a sport, although it could be. He reflects, "if there were a great many people who shared the constitutional peculiarity of [the professor], and if there were a great many people equipped with the kind of sadism to which this game appeals, and if the rules were clearly laid out and published, and if there were to grow up a body of experts whose concern was to improve the game and its players, then sweat-bead would become a sport."[20] Sweat-bead isn't a sport, according to Suits, on account of a series of contingent facts, largely independent of its weirdness as a game.[21]

The first point in distinguishing sweat-bead from sport, on Suits' view, is that not many people know about the game on account of its being a philosopher's contrivance. Since so few people know about the game of sweat-bead and even fewer participate, Suits recognizes the reality that "it is simply a highly idiosyncratic game."[22] To even entertain the possibility of sweat-bead being anything more than an unusual game between friends, it would have to be relatively well known. Sports aren't just the sorts of games we enjoy with a small group of friends; they are the sorts of games that span large groups of people. Sports are cultural phenomena by their nature.

A second point in distinguishing sports is that their following must be persistent. It isn't enough for a game to find sudden, fleeting popularity. It must be stable in sustaining that popularity. Suits proposes that fads like Hula-hoop and subsequently Wii Hula-Hoop enjoyed a short-lived popularity that resembles sport, but are not actually sports. In addition to longevity, he argues that stability is marked by "the birth and flowering of a number of attendant roles and institutions which serve a number of functions ancillary to a sufficiently popular game of physical skill."[23] In particular, he points to coaching, training, research, criticism, and archivism. Not all sports require each of these ancillary functions, "but at least some of them will be associated to some degree with every game worthy to be called a sport."[24] Suits' word-choice here though seems to reveal an underlying tension in his view. If some games are worthy of sustained popularity, then it seems odd to characterize the features that distinguish sports from games as arbitrary. On my view, some games are worthy of being called sports because our judgments about what gets to count as a sport respond to features inherent in the games themselves. With all due regard to Kierkegaard and Suits, above all else, sweat-bead isn't a sport because it isn't a very good game. One might make the same argument about hopscotch.

THE CURIOUS CASE OF HOPSCOTCH

It turns out hopscotch has surprisingly deep historical roots. There are rumors that Chinese texts refer to the game better than two thousand years before the birth of Christ. Still, others claim Roman soldiers played the game to stay fit on courses that were up to one hundred feet long. The first documented reference to the game was made in *Poor Robin's Almanac* in 1677.[25] Whatever its ultimate origins, the game, which requires skipping across a pattern of numbered squares, has enjoyed robust popularity among children. Because of that popularity, it offers an interesting case study for Suits' conceptual analysis.

Aside from his very particular understanding of popularity and stability, hopscotch fares well by evaluation according to Suits' list of essential properties. First, hopscotch satisfies the requisite criteria to count as a game. The pre-lusory goal of hopscotch is to complete the patterned course as quickly as possible according to a series of restrictions on the efficient means of doing so, with winning times recorded in the same fashion as any other race. The Guinness Book of World Records even lists the fastest game of hopscotch as an official record.[26] Second, hopscotch obviously requires physical skill. Most prominently, the game requires players to bound, often on a single leg, from square to square, rather than running or walking. Although the layout of the course varies somewhat, navigating the course, let alone doing so quickly, requires a player to demonstrate speed, balance, and agility. Whatever its failings with respect to sport, hopscotch is at least a game of physical skill. It is far less obvious whether hopscotch has a sufficiently widespread following to count as a sport and it seems a foregone conclusion that it lacks the necessary attendant institutions almost entirely. (I mean, the Guinness Book will record a record for nearly anything. I'm pretty sure there is even a world record for creepiness measured by fingernail length.)

Despite hopscotch's wild popularity among children and persistence over two millennia, it seems a stretch on Suits' analysis to characterize it as having a widespread following or stability. The game is tremendously popular across schoolyards, but it clearly lacks following in the way Suits defines the term. While children play the game all the time, there aren't formalized competitions or leagues as there are for clear cases like soccer or basketball. Many people are familiar with the childhood game of tag by way of comparison, but it would be a stretch to say any of them follow it. Familiarity and even widespread participation aren't sufficient to indicate the popularity Suits uses to characterize sport. Despite its long history, hopscotch has never enjoyed the emergence of stable institutions like coaching, research, or governing bodies. Suits claims that for an activity to count as a sport, it must be a game, require physical skill, and enjoy a widespread and stable following. Since hopscotch is a game of physical skill, it is worth imagining what hopscotch might look like adorned by the robust institutional support Suits thinks characteristic of sport.

Imagine for a moment, the game of hopscotch supported by the attendant institutions Suits suggests are characteristic of sport. Consider a friend explaining that her hopscotch dream is to win the upcoming World

Championship Tournament. She explains that she recently completed a rigorous offseason training regime designed to maximize explosiveness and balance while bounding on a single leg. Moreover, she is investing considerable resources in an expensive, top-flight coach and the latest hopscotching shoes designed by Reebok (presumably the sponsor of our hypothetical Hopscotch World Championships). If the conversation seems absurd, it isn't because there aren't enough other people that share your friend's aspiration. Likewise, it isn't absurd because the lack of world-class hopscotch coaches makes hiring one a practical difficulty. On the contrary, we would be surprised by the very fact that the game was sufficiently popular to support such institutions. It would probably surprise us because hopscotch doesn't seem like the sort of game capable of supporting that level of continued interest. Even in an imagined world where hopscotch is both a game of physical skill and wildly popular, it is odd to think it a sport. To the contrary, the development of such widespread following and stability would seem quite curious. But if hopscotch seems no more a sport with a popular following and attendant institutions, that seems reason to doubt whether those features are in fact constitutive of sport.

It's fair to concede that one might make similar claims about other controversial sports as I've made about hopscotch (e.g., curling, which is an Olympic sport). Admittedly, there is some disparity in people's intuitions about what ought to count as a sport. However, there is a substantive difference between hopscotch and curling, which I will describe more fully in the following sections. In general terms, there is sufficient reason to think curling is distinct from hopscotch in the degree to which it requires us to perform skills that are difficult to master in an activity that is strategically complex. Plainly put, there is good reason to think curling is a better game than hopscotch. In any case, the argument doesn't rest on converging intuitions about hopscotch. Quite the contrary, the functional understanding of sport proposed here provides some substantive basis for adjudicating conflicting intuitions, even if consensus ultimately proves impossible.

Hopscotch, like Kierkegaard's sweat-bead, doesn't lack attendant institutions according to some bizarre cosmic coincidence. These games lack such institutions because they aren't good enough games or, to quote Suits, they aren't "worthy to be called a sport."[27] Although hopscotch is a good game in the sense that it is able to absorb hours upon hours of child's play, it isn't good enough to justify a significant investment of time and effort beyond that.[28] Among other things, good games are differentially able to provide a sustainable, competitive venue that encourages the pursuit of physical and athletic excellences. People are willing to invest considerable time and effort into good games specifically because they can expect that investment to continue to bear fruit over the long-term. As anyone that has toiled in pursuit of sporting excellence can attest, athletic success often comes at substantial costs in time and sweat. Playing a sport is often enjoyable, but the requisite practice and conditioning tend not to be. Hopscotch is hardly the sort of game that would warrant such efforts. It might make for an enjoyable diversion with friends, but one would grow bored of it rather quickly.

TO PLAY'S THE THING

In one of the more under-appreciated works in contemporary philosophy, *The Grasshopper: Games, Life, and Utopia*, Suits argues that play constitutes an ideal of human existence. In a utopian world, he explains, all we would do is play. Suits cleverly argues from the point of view of Aesop's fabled Grasshopper. According to the fable, the Grasshopper spends the whole summer playing, while a diligent ant works in preparation for the impending winter. Left unprepared for the harsh winter months, Suits' Grasshopper appears content to meet his fate. Reflecting on his looming demise, the Grasshopper explains, "My death is inevitable in any case. For if I am improvident in the summer, then I will die in winter. And if I am provident in summer, then I will cease to be the Grasshopper, by definition."[29] Were it not for the contingent necessity that he prepare to survive winter, all the grasshopper would do is play. The Grasshopper continues, "if there were no winters to guard against, then the Grasshopper would not get his comeuppance nor the ant his shabby victory."[30] The moral of Suits' imagining of the fable is that we only work because it is necessary, strictly speaking. Suits explains that play constitutes an ideal of existence in that it is, "that thing or those things for the sake of which we do other things whose only justification is that they justify everything else; or, as Aristotle put it, those things for the sake of which we do other things."[31]

It is one thing to argue that we do all other things for the sake of play, but Suits' argument about the role of games in the good life rests on two further claims. First, in order to constitute an ideal of existence, play must be chosen for its own sake.[32] In practice, not all game-play constitutes play. A professional athlete, for example, might play hockey to earn a living or, to use the Grasshopper's words, "prepare for winter." Many of the things that constitute work in the world we live in might likewise count as play in Suits' Utopia, but whatever else it is, play is necessarily noninstrumental.[33] Even a baby, splashing around a bath is engaged in play in the sense that, "it is not engaged in an instrumental enterprise." Nevertheless, play isn't necessarily frivolous. So long as it is chosen for its own sake, one might even engage in play by reading and writing about philosophy. In a utopian world devoid of instrumental challenges, play allows us to invent obstacles to overcome.

Second, Suits argues that, "game playing performs a crucial role in delineating that ideal—a role which cannot be performed by any other activity, and without which an account of the ideal is either incomplete or impossible."[34] Play that isn't game-play lacks certain qualities of games that make them indispensable to the pursuit of the ideal Suits has in mind. At face value, this claim hardly seems implausible. In a world without necessity of labor, activities like playing catch or casually jumping rope would make welcome diversions, but they would hardly be sufficient to fill the whole of the time we normally dedicate to instrumental pursuits—pursuits that have grown unnecessary in Suits' Utopia. The problem as the Grasshopper describes it, "is that there does not appear to be anything to *do* in Utopia." Games are uniquely able to satisfy the quandary in that, "Game playing makes it possible to retain enough effort in Utopia to make life worth living."[35] My argument is that Suits' Utopia doesn't just require games; it requires *good* games.

Primitive play can certainly challenge and entertain us, but only for relatively short stretches. For example, I might spend a few minutes juggling a soccer ball. I might even spend a whole afternoon if I find some immediate success. However, there is a limit to the amount of entertainment most people might expect to derive from that sort of play. One would likely find that juggling quickly ceases to be play at all in that we would grow bored of it and cease to choose it for its own sake. If you've ever observed small children at play, you've noticed that they usually move quickly from one type of play to the next. As a rule, they play with each toy just long enough to leave *every* toy on the living room floor, regardless of how much time or how many toys they have. This is as much a feature of play as it is of children. The value of games is that their rule-bound, goal-directed structure makes them capable of sustaining play for long periods of time—a feature most evident in the best of games.

Somewhat paradoxically, games are valuable despite the fact that the pre-lusory goal of any game is completely trivial. For example, outside the context of game-play, what value could there be in driving a small, six-ounce disc of vulcanized rubber into a rectangular opening that measures a relatively expansive four feet tall by six feet wide? Described strictly in those terms, hockey hardly seems a challenge at all. However, good games have value exactly because they challenge us. In addition to requiring players to compete against a team of six other players trying to accomplish the same goal with a single puck, they have to do so while ice-skating. Hurka, in an interview about Suits, explains that, "To play [a] game you have to aim at a trivial goal, and you haven't succeeded in the game unless you achieve the goal, but the value of the activity is independent of the value of the goal."[36]

Playing games has value through the process of striving to attain an otherwise trivial goal in competition with others directed toward the same end. It isn't *just* whether you win or lose, it's *that* you choose to play the game.

PUTTING THE GOOD IN GAMES

Aristotle's functional understanding of conceptual analysis is particularly helpful in further developing Suits' argument. He argues that in order to understand the essence of a thing, one must first understand its function.[37] For example, we understand the essence of what it is to be a heart in terms of its function as a pump. Considered across the breadth and scope of nature, hearts look very different depending upon the organism each inhabits, however, they are essentially alike in that they serve to pump blood. One could make the same argument about a human artifact like a hammer. I understand what it is for a thing to be a hammer in terms of its ability to drive nails into wood. This functional approach also serves as a basis for evaluating quality: good hearts pump better than bad hearts, good hammers drive nails more effectively than bad hammers, and good games allow us to play more than bad games.

Normative judgments follow intuitively from Aristotle's functional approach. The difference between something that performs its function well and something that performs its function poorly is a set of excellences characteristic of the thing itself. For example, since good hearts are able to pump blood more effectively than bad hearts, they achieve excellence through volume. Any pump can achieve volume either by pumping more blood per cycle (capacity) or by pumping more frequently (rate). Heart rate and capacity, then, are excellences or virtues of hearts. Simply put, good hearts are better than bad hearts because they have a greater capacity, higher heart rate, or both—they demonstrate the excellences of hearts to a greater degree. Of course, not all good things are good in the exact same way. One heart might achieve functional excellence with a massive pumping capacity despite a lumbering pace. Another might pump very rapidly, moving relatively little blood with each contraction. Nevertheless, each moves a certain volume of blood relative to the size of the organism, thus satisfying its function. It is important to note that while all good hearts share a relative functional advantage, the excellence of any heart is limited to a particular range of conditions (e.g., a good heart for a creature on Earth at sea level, might not work very well for that same creature on the moon). Likewise, games admit of excellences or virtues. Good games, like good hearts, are distinct in the degree to which they are able to contribute to the life well lived.

Good games are distinct in at least three ways that make them better able to contribute to the life well lived: they are difficult to master, strategically complex, and aren't too pointlessly painful. I will explain each of these characteristics in the next several paragraphs, but my aim is not to offer a comprehensive analysis of the excellences of games; games may admit of other excellences as well. Instead, I only wish to suggest that understood in the context of game-play as an important feature of human life, there are properties that provide a reasonable basis for judging the quality of games. As mentioned previously, Suits explains that with respect to institutions like coaching and training, "Not all sports . . . require all of these ancillary functions in order to be accepted as sports, but at least some of them will be associated to some degree with every game worthy to be called a sport."[38] I wish to offer a similar understanding of the excellences characteristic of good games.

Above all, good games are able continually to challenge us and they typically do that in two ways. First, they require us to perform tasks that are difficult to master. Excerpted from the game of baseball, for example, it is physically difficult to hit a pitched ball with a bat. Likewise, despite outward appearances to the contrary, it is extremely difficult to hit a stationary golf ball with a golf club—or at least it is difficult to intentionally hit it towards something. Good games require us to perform difficult skills. This might be most evident with physical games, but the same is true of good nonphysical games. Chess, for example, requires players to demonstrate a range of complex analytic skills. They must visualize the board, calculate risk, and evaluate the game in terms of the pieces and space available. Maybe unsurprisingly, there is some research to indicate that students receiving chess instruction at a young age outperform students that do not across a range of metrics measuring critical reasoning, spatial reasoning, and complex problem solving.[39] The point is that chess is a game of skill and its skills are difficult to master. Chess is a good game, in part, because it requires us to do things that are difficult even outside of the context of the game.

Second, good games are able to continually challenge us because they are strategically complex; that is, they don't admit of a dominant strategy. It isn't just that good games require us to perform difficult skills like hitting a baseball or a golf ball; they require us to do these things in competition, either against others or ourselves.[40] What allows a game to sustain competition over time is that players can choose different approaches within the rules of a game in order to realize the pre-lusory goal. There are many reasonable approaches to winning a game of chess and the effectiveness of each depends on a complex interaction with an opponent considered against the further complexity of the circumstances of the competition. Even more, these strategic choices must be sensitive to a player's strengths and weaknesses with respect to the skills required by the game. While there are principles common to many of the most fruitful strategies in any given game, those principles can be realized in a number of ways and tend to drive strategic choice as much as define it. For example, in chess it is considered generally advantageous to control the middle of the board. Such principles help distinguish good strategy from bad strategy, but one can obviously win a chess game without controlling the center of the board. For example, I can direct my efforts toward controlling the center of the board or figure out how to win without it. Either way, the variables that influence the success or failure of a particular strategy in chess are as complex as they are dynamic. All of that is to say that one reason chess is such a good game is that its strategic landscape admits of both breadth and depth.

Finally, in addition to creating a stable, competitive venue, good games shouldn't be too pointlessly painful or destructive. We choose games for their own sake because they allow us to test ourselves against the skills constitutive of the game and test ourselves against others in a strategic exchange, but is probably equally as important that the games not be tremendously destructive. As much fun as people seem to derive from playing paintball, they don't seem inclined to engage in real gunplay as play. The basic similarities between paintball and an actual firefight are obvious, but we don't play paintball with real guns because it would be outrageously destructive, even fatal, to do so. The example is obviously absurd in a sense, but that is to illustrate the point exactly. Recognition of the long-term health risks from repeated head injuries has affected the popularity of certain contact sports like football and hockey, particularly among children. Whether these concerns have a major impact on the popularity of these sports remains to be seen, but there seems considerably less appetite for games likely to cause death or severe disability. Whatever the case, part of choosing a game for its own sake is that the ennobling effects of testing oneself against unnecessary obstacles isn't likely to come at too steep a cost.

HOCKEY AND AN INCONVENIENT TRUTH

In characterizing sport, Suits explains, "[he has] no theory to support the list, except the theory that the features are more or less arbitrary, since they are simply facts about sport."[41] The properties characteristic of sport are not arbitrary, though there is a sense in which they are contingent. In this section, I want to consider two types of interesting cases in order to both clarify my account and suggest that it offers theoretical support in the spirit of Suits' broader project. Specifically, I want to consider the cases of bad games with wide following and good games without wide following.

One potential peculiarity of Suits account is the oddity of sports coming into being. Presumably, there was a period shortly after James Naismith invented the game of basketball at a YMCA in Massachusetts when basketball was no more than an idiosyncratic game between friends. It seems odd a century later to characterize the game in much the same vain as sweat-bead, maybe in part because basketball's popularity has erupted. Even when they lacked popular institutions in equal share, there is a sense in which basketball was always a better game than sweat-bead. It was always more likely to develop a popular following because it is more strategically complex and its skills are more difficult to master. It is in that light that I wish to examine the emerging popularity of CrossFit.

CrossFit, which has experienced a nearly unprecedented surge in popularity over the past decade, requires competitors to complete a diversity of strenuous physical exercises, generally for time. CrossFit's popularity has exploded over the past decade, growing from thirteen affiliated gyms in 2005, to more than nine thousand gyms today.[42] It supports a range of attendant institutions including coaching, a World Championship Tournament (which claims to crown the "World's fittest man and woman"), and even research and sponsorship. Reebok is not only the hypothetical sponsor of our hypothetical Hopscotch World Championship, but also the official licensed sponsor of the CrossFit Games. Given this recent explosion in popularity, there is a question on Suits' account whether we should think of CrossFit as a sport or a fad.[43] That is to say, is CrossFit more like basketball, or hula-hoop, to use Suits' own example? Maybe somewhat unsatisfyingly, the answer is that it's too soon to tell.

Frustratingly, our judgments about which games of physical skill are good enough to count as sports may require considerable patience and observation over time. It may become evident over time whether CrossFit is a good game in the manner I've suggested, but its rule-bound structure makes it one or the other long before that fact is obvious to us. Independent of whether it retains a popular following or ever develops one, CrossFit is either more like sweat-bead or basketball. It is either a good game or it isn't and correspondingly, it is either a sport or it isn't. Whether CrossFit is ultimately a good enough game to count as a sport remains to be seen, but it is certainly possible to imagine a good game that lacks popular following.

Previously, I suggested robust institutional support would do little to affect our impressions about the potential of hopscotch to count as a sport. Here, we should engage in another thought experiment very much the reciprocal of the first. Imagine for a moment the game of hockey in some dystopian future where the climate has grown much hotter and ice much more sparing. That is to say, imagine a world in which our worst fears about the environment and climate change have been realized. Let's call this hopefully very distant reality Dune. In Dune, people don't play hockey. They don't play hockey because sweltering heat makes natural ice a rarity and the challenges of refrigerating large sheets of artificial ice in such a world are prohibitive. Along with the game's following, whatever institutions once supported ice hockey withered under Dune's oppressive heat. On Dune, hockey is very much a good game without a wide following. At least, it is very much the same game it is now, save for its popularity, and hockey as presently constituted is certainly a sport on Suits' account. What should we think of the game on Dune? Should we really think hockey has ceased to be a sport somewhere between here and Dune?

On Dune, hockey is the same great game it has always been, even if people no longer find much occasion to play. The relationship between the rules and pre-lusory goal of hockey remains unchanged. Ice-skating is still difficult enough on its own terms and the challenge of scoring goals against a worthy opponent is no less daunting. Hockey is every bit the good game of physical skill that it ever was, so is it possible that changes in the world around it could change the sort of thing it is? We might understand the relationship between games and their surrounding circumstances in the spirit of Aristotle's ethics. In the *Nichomachean Ethics*, Aristotle argues that a lack of certain external goods can impeded the exercise of virtue. "It is impossible, or not easy," he explains, "to do noble acts without the proper equipment."[44] Even if one intends to act in accord with virtue, that is, to do virtuous things, "in many actions we use friends and riches and political power as instruments."[45] Similarly, playing sports requires time, suitable facilities, and willing competitors. On Dune, where such external goods are lacking, our attempts at play fail not for the sort of activity hockey is, but for the sort of place Dune is. We might fail to invest in certain games for either reason, but only one speaks to the sort of thing a game is by its nature.

Like our imagined postapocalyptic world, similar external considerations have shaped the precipitous growth of hockey's popularity over the past century. In its modern form, the International Hockey Federation claims the game dates back to the late nineteenth century, when the first indoor game was played in Montreal, Quebec.[46] For much of the intervening century, hockey has been most popular in American northeast and the Great Lakes region, where the climate is relatively similar to that of Canada. However, over the past decade, amateur participation in hockey has experienced the most growth in the relative warmth of the American southeast.[47, 48.] One possible explanation for this sudden explosion of popularity is that improvements in technology have made year-round ice affordable even in climates where natural ice is infrequently.[49] What should we say of the game's status as a sport then? At least in theory, hockey was a sport even before it found its way onto ice in Montreal better than one hundred years ago.[50] Like basketball a century prior, hockey was always likely to develop a popular following because its rule-bound structure creates a sustainable challenge for competitors. Suffice it to say, Dune is a step further removed from Suits' Utopia than even the barren, frozen wilderness of nineteenth-century Canada. In the harsh dystopian desert of Dune, the necessities of work have likely increased considerably. Although our investment in hockey might wane relatively more than other games in such an arid climate, I doubt we find very much time for sports of any kind in Dune. Sports and other good games may give us something to do in Utopia, but there is plenty of necessary work on Dune to leave little time for noninstrumental pursuits. In the relatively hospitable climate of North America, however, hockey is exactly the sort of activity we choose for its own sake because it is has proven worthy of serious investment.

MUGGLE QUIDDITCH AND COMING TO A POINT

I'd like to conclude by offering one further obscure example at the fringes of sport; in for a penny, in for a pound, I suppose. Quidditch, the game made famous by J. K. Rowling's Harry Potter novels, may well be a sport. The wild game combines something like polo with an elaborate game of tag; all while players navigate a three-dimensional course on flying brooms. Sans flying brooms, a game very much like Quidditch (Muggle Quidditch, if you will) has become quite popular with students on college campuses. That may well be a sport too, I suppose. Part of what makes Rowling's Quidditch such a spectacle is the speed of the players, flashing around the expansive course like fighter planes in a dogfight. Quidditch might well be a sport, but unfortunately, our world doesn't admit of many flying brooms, so much like hockey on Dune, opportunities to play the game are sparing. However, if we can imagine a world in which technological advancements have made flying brooms a reality (for all we know, Elon Musk may already be working on it), Quidditch might well be a sport. It may well be structured in such a way that it would present the very challenges Rowling imagines in her books. Unfortunately, until flying brooms become a reality, we can only speculate as to whether the rules of Quidditch would make for a very good game. Even then, it might not be readily apparent for some time whether Quidditch gives us good reason to continually choose it for its own sake.

Wittgenstein's skepticism about the possibility of describing games in terms of a single set of necessary and sufficient conditions appears largely unwarranted. Still, there are significant challenges in knowing which games actually get to count as sports. Since good games are distinguished by their ability to provide a sustainable venue for play, judgments about a game's quality require great patience. By way of example, football's viability has come under recent scrutiny on account of players suffering serious, debilitating injuries owing to the game's violent nature, despite the game's wild popularity over the past century. Increasing awareness of the serious-ness of repeated traumatic brain injuries, the competitive advantage afforded by training players to become bigger, stronger, and faster, and ironically, the development of better protective equipment that allows players to weather more severe collisions, have all conspired to undermine perceptions of the game as a suitable athletic pursuit. The latter two factors might even be seen as natural strategic developments, given the nature of the skills required by the rules and goal of football. Although football was a good game before, it has become so destructive that it is no longer worth choos-ing for its own sake. Football was a very good game in 1945, but given considerable increases in the speed and size of the players, it might not be any longer. Whether or not a game challenges us depends in large part on the capabilities and limitations of human beings, broadly speaking. Should we change in significant ways, as one might argue is the case with football, our corresponding judgments about which games are good and bad will likewise change.

According to Suits, games fill a unique and essential role in realizing play as an ideal of human existence. Some games, however, do this much more effectively than others. Good games are important because they are differen-tially able to contribute to play as an ideal of human existence; they are able to continually challenge us. Although many sports have a widespread and popular following, that popularity tends to track, somewhat reliably, a more essential feature of sports. That is to say sports, in addition to being games of physical skill, are necessarily good games. Sports, like many good, non-physical games, are worthy of our continued investment because they are necessarily the sorts of games we will continue to choose for their own sake. Suits summarizes the relation between work and play through Aristotle's observation that, "to exert oneself and work for the sake of playing seems silly and utterly childish. But to play in order that one may exert oneself seems right."[51] Sports, properly understood, allow us to make sense of Aris-totle's dictum.

NOTES

1. I extend special thanks to Shawn E. Klein, Richard Schoonhoven, and Tim Leone for their guidance in developing my argument and their comments in revising this essay.

2. "Sport," *Oxford Dictionaries*, accessed January 20, 2014, http://www.oxford-dictionaries.com/us/definition/american_english/sport.

3. Robert Ellis, *The Games People Play: Theology, Religion, and Sport* (Cam-bridge: The Lutterworth Press, 2014), 165. In a footnote, Ellis includes a nice

discussion of the origins of the quote and the fact that it is somewhat apocryphal in its most common form. Nevertheless, it suits the discussion well and largely captures Shankly's intended meaning.

4. Seth Vertelney, "TV Viewership Hit Record Highs in U.S. and the District for the World Cup," *Washington Post*, last modified July 18, 2014, https://www.washingtonpost.com/express/wp/2014/07/18/tv-viewership-hit-record-highs-in-u-s -and-the-district-for-the-world-cup/.

5. "United States and World Population Clock," *United States Census Bureau*, accessed March 8, 2015, http://www.census.gov/popclock/.

6. Monte Burke, "How The National Football League Can Reach $25 Billion In Annual Revenues," *Forbes*, last modified August 13, 2013, http://www.forbes.com/sites/monteburke/2013/08/17/how-the-national-football-league-can-reach-25-billion-in -annual-revenues/.

7. Among others, Steve Largent, Bill Bradley, Tom Osborne, and Jack Kemp spring to mind. Maybe more prominently, Ronald Reagan and Arnold Schwarzenegger both enjoyed great success in athletics, but there is good reason to think that subsequent Hollywood success played some role in explaining each man's star in politics.

8. Thomas Hurka, Introduction to *The Grasshopper: Games, Life, and Utopia,* Bernard Suits (Toronto: University of Toronto Press, 1978), xi.

9. For a different view, see Joey Gawrysiak, "E-sport: Video Games as Sport" in this volume.

10. I believe there is necessarily overlap between the conceptual analysis of sport (and hence, on my view, the normative evaluation of a sport) and corresponding social evaluations. Since I am claiming that a game must be good in order for it to count as a sport, we should expect some correlation between our conceptual evaluation of an activity and the corresponding social evaluation. In this case, the normative claim is grounded in a functional account of games. Games describe a class of activities that perform a particular role in human life and good games are those that perform that function to a greater degree than other games. A good game is just more likely to develop a popular following than a bad game because it is more fruitful. Still, as I will argue, good games sometimes lack popular following and vice versa.

11. It is worth pointing out on this view that sports share much in common with good nonphysical games. For example, many of the properties that make chess such a wonderful game and explain its massive popular following are evidenced across the breadth of sport. It is little wonder that by manner of speaking, spectators will refer to the strategic exchanges within a game of baseball or football as a "chess match."

12. Ludwig Wittgenstein, *Philosophical Investigations* (New York: Macmillan, 1953), 66.

13. Ibid., 43.

14. Ibid., 66.

15. Bernard Suits, "The Elements of Sport," in *Ethics in Sport* 2nd ed., ed. William J. Morgan (Champaign, IL: Human Kinetics, 2007), 14.

16. Ibid.

17. Ibid.

18. John Haugeland, "Truth and Rule Following," in *Having Thought: Essays in the Metaphysics of Mind* (Cambridge, Mass.: Harvard University Press, 1998), 327.

19. Some have argued that Suits is wrong to characterize all sports as games. See Klaus Meier's essay "Triad Trickery: Playing with Sport and Games." Of particular concern are sports whose scores are judged aesthetically like gymnastics or figure skating. Such activities seem more like competitions or performances according to such arguments and certainly don't seem to fit as neatly under Suits' characterization of games as the voluntary attempt to overcome unnecessary obstacles. I will remain agnostic about that debate in this essay, but I will say that I think the point is not substantive to my argument that sports are necessarily good games. That might seem counterintuitive, but I think the qualities that distinguish good games from bad games are the same as the qualities that distinguish good competitions from bad competitions. Ultimately, even if CrossFit (an example I will use in my penultimate section) is a competition, rather than a game, it is good because it is difficult to master, strategically complex, and entertaining. That is to say, I think this argument stands independent of the related question of the relation between sports and games.

20. Suits, "The Elements of Sport," 16.

21. Kierkegaard's Sweat-Bead also reflects a curious choice in the context of Suits' argument since it seems to clearly lack the appropriate physical skills to count as a sport, independent of its other idiosyncrasies. Nevertheless, it demonstrates Suits' concerns about following well enough that I think its use appropriate here.

22. Ibid.

23. Ibid.

24. Suits, "The Elements of Sport," 17.

25. "Proceedings of the Association, March 27th," *Journal of the British Archaeological Association*, Volume 26 (1870): 242, accessed March 8, 2015 http://www.google.com/books.

26. According to the Guinness Book of World Records, American Ashrita Furman holds the record, completing a course in 1 minute, 1.97 seconds.

27. Suits, "The Elements of Sport,"17.

28. Shawn E. Klein has suggested that there may be room on this view to accommodate various subclasses of sports, like kid-sports. As I will argue, sports have to be good enough games that they are a worthy source of serious investment over the long term. While a physical game like hopscotch might not satisfy this requirement taking the long view, it might in a much more limited context. Specifically, a kid-sport might satisfy a lesser requirement, like being good enough to provide fruitful game-play for children. I certainly find considerable divergence between the sorts of pursuits that engage my two young children and those that engage me. It's even possible that the criteria that distinguish a good game from a bad game vary slightly from those that distinguish a good kid-sport from a bad kid sport. For example, maybe competitive sustainability is less critical to a good kid-sport than the challenge posed by the game's constitutive skills. I won't develop the idea any further in here, but it suggests an interesting area for further development.

29. Bernard Suits, *The Grasshopper: Games, Life, and Utopia* (Toronto: University of Toronto Press, 1978), 11.

30. Ibid., 11.

31. Ibid., 182.

32. Ibid.

33. Bernard Suits, "Tricky Triad: Games, Play, and Sport," *Journal of the Philosophy of Sport*, No. XV (1988), 2.

34. Ibid.

35. Ibid., 189

36. Nigel Warburton, "Tom Hurka Interview on Bernard Suits's The Grasshopper," *Virtual Philosopher*, last modified December 13, 2007, http://virtualphilosopher. com/2007/12/tom-hurka-on-be.html.

37. W.D. Ross, *Aristotle: The Nicomachean Ethics* (Oxford: Oxford University Press, 1998), 1097b22-1098a20.

38. Suits, "The Elements of Sport," 17.

39. Wendi Fischer, "Educational Value of Chess," *School of Education at Johns Hopkins University*, accessed April 7, 2015, http://education.jhu.edu/PD/ newhorizons/
strategies/topics/thinking-skills/chess/.

40. Golf is an interesting case in that one can play golf as a sport without competing directly against others. Of course, golf tournaments and leagues do allow for direct competition, but it seems that the rigid, rule-bound structure of the game allows one to compete just as easily against a personal best or a course record. Further, it seems an outstanding demonstration of strategic complexity. On a windy day, playing shorter clubs might be a good strategy. On a well-manicured course, it might be worth the risk of playing longer clubs and missing the fairway. There is no dominant strategy. Depending upon one's particular skills, the skills of one's opponent, and the conditions on the course, different approaches will yield different results.

41. Suits, "The Elements of Sport," 14.

42. Jon Friedman, "Success and the Bull's Eye," *The CrossFit Journal,* Last modified March 1, 2014, http://journal.crossfit.com/2014/03/success-and-the-bulls-eye-1.tpl.

43. For a more extended analysis of CrossFit as sport, see Pam R. Sailors, Sarah Teetzel, and Charlene Weaving, "Borderline Cases: CrossFit, Tough Mudder, and Spartan Race" in this volume.

44. Ross, *Aristotle: The Nichomachean Ethics*, 1099a20–1099b10.

45. Ibid.

46. "History, The Early Beginnings," *International Ice Hockey Federation*, accessed April 4, 2015, http://www.iihf.com/iihf-home/history/.

47. Jeff Klein, "Where Hockey Is Growing, State by State," *New York Times*, last modified February 20, 2011, http://slapshot.blogs.nytimes.com/2011/02/20/ where-hockey-is-growing-state-by-state/.

48. The District of Columbia, North Carolina, Georgia, Kentucky, and Florida have experienced the highest rates of growth.

49. It is also worth noting that the NHL recently awarded an expansion franchise to Las Vegas, Nevada. Kevin Allen, "NHL approves expansion to Las Vegas,"

USA Today, last modified June 22, 2016, http://www.usatoday.com/story/sports/nhl/2016/06/22/las-vegas-nhl-expansion/86239704/.

50. Of course, that might just be a post-hoc justification for all of the money I've spent on hockey tickets and club apparel over the years. It would add insult to injury if it turned out hockey weren't a very good game to begin with.

51. Suits, "The Elements of Sport," 17.

Chapter 4

Defining Olympic Sport

Heather L. Reid

On the face of it, defining "Olympic sport" may seem simple: it is a sport practiced in the Olympic Games.[1] But this superficially acceptable definition raises important philosophical questions, including what we mean by "sport" in the first place. Since that topic is discussed extensively elsewhere in this book, I will focus here instead on the modifier "Olympic," seeking to understand what distinguishes Olympic sport from the greater class of sporting activities of which it is, presumably, some kind of a subset. I will also refrain from the method of listing the activities already practiced in the Olympic Games and trying to find common features among them because I don't want to beg the question that every sport ever included in the Olympic Games is automatically, much less equally, "Olympic." The Roman Emperor Nero once "moved" the Olympic Games from its traditional time to coincide with his excursion in Greece and introduced novel events, such as a ten-horse chariot race, which he conveniently proceeded to win. Hardly anyone, ancient or modern, considers that to be authentic Olympic sport—though it would satisfy our superficial definition. How can we tell? The problem is not that chariot racing isn't a sport—it was one of the most important Olympic sports in antiquity. The problem is that Nero's contest seems to violate some higher ideal—the Olympic spirit, if you will.

Defining Olympic Sport in terms of the "Olympic spirit" is dangerous, however. As any historian of the modern Olympic Games can tell you— trying to define a spirit can destroy it. In the early twentieth century, the International Olympic Committee attempted to codify the spirit of amateurism—doing something out of love—into a set of eligibility rules. By trying to remove financial interest from the Games, however, they inadvertently placed it at the center. Every effort to define an amateur in terms of not making money ended up promoting efforts to make money without breaking

65

the letter of the rules.[2] As the Chinese philosopher Confucius wisely warned thousands of years earlier, most people respond to rules by looking for exemptions.[3] Defining Olympic sport in terms of the Olympic spirit need not be an exercise in trying to codify and legislate a particular set of ideals, however. For one thing, the Olympic spirit, or more precisely, the philosophical ideals that underpin the Olympic Movement, are already articulated in the Olympic Charter, especially the "Fundamental Principles of Olympism."[4] The International Olympic Committee also stipulates specific criteria for the selection and evaluation of Olympic sports.[5] Though useful, these criteria are too complex and pragmatic to pinpoint what makes a sport truly "Olympic." What we need is a succinct definition of Olympic sport that distinguishes it from other forms of sport by invoking the values of Olympism.

In this chapter I propose a definition of Olympic sport that reflects the enduring values of the Olympic Games as revealed by their ancient history and as articulated in the Fundamental Principles of Olympism. This will be a *prescriptive* rather than a merely *descriptive* definition in that it will seek through its usage to promote a particular set of values and behaviors worthy of Olympic ideals. It will not, however, be a *stipulative* definition seeking to attach a new meaning to particular word. Rather, I am proposing a *theoretical* definition of "Olympic sport"—one that seeks to attach the term to a wider intellectual framework already established in Olympic history and literature. The criteria that render a sport "Olympic" under this definition may also be applied to sports, athletes, coaches, and even behaviors. If we can change what people think about when they use the term "Olympic," we may promote a positive ethos within the community of language users. The values and goals of the Olympic Movement are clearly stated, let the definition and subsequent usage of the term "Olympic sport" faithfully reflect them.

SPORT VS. OLYMPIC SPORT

In order to modify the way people think about and use the term "Olympic," it may be useful to begin by observing the way people already use the term to distinguish among different forms of sport. One thing the modifier "Olympic" seems to imply immediately is a certain level of excellence. If I ride my bike around with friends or enter a local race, we may say that I am participating in the sport of cycling. We may also acknowledge that cycling is an Olympic sport. But the term isn't necessarily transitive. It doesn't seem quite right to say as I ride around the block with other enthusiasts that I am participating in an Olympic sport, and it is certainly incorrect to say that I am an Olympic cyclist or even an Olympic-level cyclist. On the other hand, people may use the term "Olympic" to describe something that is not a sport but is done seriously at a high level of excellence, as in "Olympic lawn mowing." The association between excellence and the term "Olympic" derives primarily from the Olympic Games being the most prestigious and competitive athletic event in antiquity. It also reflects a philosophy focused on human excellence, an effort to perfect oneself and better resemble the gods of Mount Olympus, especially Zeus, to whom the Ancient Games were dedicated. The ancient Greek concept of excellence, *aretē,* was closely linked with ancient sport and had a big influence on the founders of the modern Games and the ethos of modern sport, more generally.

Another thing that seems to distinguish Olympic from non-Olympic sport in common usage is a commitment to ideals beyond sport itself and especially beyond commercialism. In part, this is reflected in the opening and closing ceremonies, which are distinctive of the Olympic Games and other events specifically designed to imitate them. Again, these ceremonies derive from the religious rituals that surrounded the ancient Olympic festival, but in the modern Games they are intended to promote Olympic ideals. The Olympic flame and torch relay were not part of the Ancient Games, yet they symbolize the modern Games' connection to ancient Olympia and to the quasi-religious ideals that underpinned the contests there. It is also significant, though seldom noticed, that advertising is not allowed in and around Olympic venues, and that Olympic symbols may not be used for commercial purposes, except as authorized by the IOC for the benefit of the Games and their ideals.[6] People often complain about commercialism in the Olympic Games, but this is not because non-Olympic sports are not commercialized. Rather, it is because there is a public expectation that Olympic sports should differ from other sports by rejecting commercialism and focusing on higher ideals such as fair play. We can see, when comparing the Olympic and non-Olympic iterations of a sport like beach volleyball, that the ubiquitous advertising and antagonistic rhetoric from courtside announcers are replaced by more conservative uniforms and special emphasis on friendship and fairness in the Olympic version.

There is also an expectation in common usage that Olympic sport is international. American football is certainly a sport, but too regional to be Olympic. Indeed the exclusion of baseball and softball from the Olympic Games in 2005 had partly to do with its lack of international appeal.[7] It seems disingenuous to call Major League Baseball's championship the "World Series" when all of the eligible teams are based in North America. Baseball's Olympic internationalism is closely linked with the movement's emphasis on peace, which is not as widely recognized as it should be. Ancient Olympic history suggests that by coming together as equals under the rules of sport, rival tribes were able to interact peacefully and even work together for a common cause.[8] The modern Games were founded with a similar goal in mind and even when people have used the Games to trump up nationalism or exercise political rivalries, a sense that peace may at least be possible usually prevails. It has been argued that national teams should be eliminated from the Games, but even if athletes represented only themselves, the expectation of bringing together people who are culturally, linguistically, and religiously diverse seems central to the concept of Olympic sport.

Based on these observations about the contemporary use of the term "Olympic sport," along with a forthcoming analysis of Olympic history and philosophy, I would like to argue that what makes a sport Olympic are its values, goals, and philosophy. I therefore propose the following definition:

> An Olympic sport is one that focuses on human excellence, commits itself to justice, and promotes peace.

To argue for this definition, I will examine the philosophy of Olympism as stated in the Olympic Charter, the technical criteria used by the International Olympic Committee to evaluate Olympic sport, and events from Olympic history which have come to exemplify a distinctive Olympic spirit.

FOCUS ON HUMAN EXCELLENCE

The Olympic emphasis on human excellence is evident in the first fundamental principle of Olympism, which has changed little over the century-plus history of the modern Games. It states,

> Olympism is a philosophy of life, exalting and combining in a balanced whole the qualities of body, will and mind. Blending sport with culture and education, Olympism seeks to create a way of life based on the joy of effort, the educational value of good example, social responsibility and respect for universal fundamental ethical principles.[9]

The claim that Olympism is a philosophy designed to exalt all aspects of the human being hearkens back to the classical philosophers of ancient Greece whose ethical theories focused on *aretē*—virtue or excellence. In the *Apology,* Socrates admonished Athenians to care for *aretē* rather than fame or wealth,[10] and Aristotle went so far as to define human happiness (*eudaimonia*) as activity in accordance with *aretē*.[11] In fact, *aretē* had been associated with athletics long before the philosophers started promoting it. It is though athletic feats that Homer's Odysseus demonstrates his nobility and worthiness to lead. The rising phenomenon of the Olympic Games, however, taught ancient Hellenes that *aretē* was not just a matter of birth, but something trainable and within the grasp of even low-born people.[12] Achieving excellence in ancient Greece meant becoming like a god—not just in body but in will and mind. *Aretē* is the excellence of the whole human being, and it is expressed not just in athletics but in intellectual and political endeavors as well.

Olympism's vision of a holistic and balanced human excellence derived from a blending of sport, culture, and education may seem to be at odds with the purely athletic and results-oriented excellence suggested by the Olympic motto: *citius, altius, fortius* (faster, higher, stronger).[13] However, the aspiration for human excellence is neither incompatible nor identical with athletic achievement. Ideally, athletic performance is an expression of balanced *aretē*. This means that distinctively Olympic sports should challenge the mind as well as the body and that they should reward the effort and discipline of of training while penalizing techniques that improve performance without increasing *aretē*. What kind of educational example is set by an athlete who gains a winning advantage through expensive equipment or performance-enhancing drugs? The need for Olympic sports to focus on human excellence motivates the requirement that all Olympic sport federations adopt the WADA (World Anti-Doping Agency) code[14] and control the technological evolution of their sport.[15] They are also expected to assist athletes with studies, development of life-skills, and post-athletic career transitions.[16] The Olympic creed,[17] furthermore, which emphasizes participation over victory and struggle over triumph, is not opposed to the Olympic motto. Together the creed and motto show that the struggle to improve is what produces human excellence.[18] Distinctively Olympic sports should link results with human excellence as much as possible.

Memorable moments in Olympic history reveal the importance of human excellence to the Olympic ideal. It is not just a matter of winning and triumph, but paradoxically the emphasis on excellence comes from the distinctively Olympic practice of staying to cheer on the final finishers of a long race. In 1968, an injured John Stephen Akhwari of Tanzania finished the marathon more than an hour after the winner—to a huge ovation from the crowd and the glowing praises of journalists, one of whom said he "symbolizes the finest in the human spirit" and "gives true meaning to sport."[19] When 2014 gold medalist Dario Cologna waited nearly half an hour at the finish line to greet the last athlete in the race, he exemplified the Olympic idea of human excellence, which exalts not just the virtues of victory but also those of participation and struggle. Likewise marathoner Abebe Bikila made a much bigger Olympic impression by winning the 1960 race barefoot than cyclist Chris Boardman made by setting a world record in the 1992 Games with a super high-tech proprietary bicycle. Among the lowlights of Olympic history are contests falsified by drugs—notoriously the disqualification of sprinter Ben Johnson from the 1988 Games. It is not just victory that counts in Olympic sport, it is virtue.

Some people claim that the amount of money involved in the Games is what causes the privileging of victory over virtue, the sacrifice of human excellence for the sake of efficiency. Such concerns are only heightened by the IOC practice of evaluating sports according to "popularity" criteria, including public and especially youth appeal,[20] the number of tickets sold to spectators, the number of media accreditations granted, and the amount of coverage in the television, print, and social media—including YouTube, Facebook, and Twitter.[21] Sponsorship is also a criterion.[22] It will be remembered, however, that the Olympics' association with human excellence is precisely what draws sponsors and fans to the Games in the first place. Performance-enhancing technologies that diminish the role of human excellence run contrary to sponsors' interests as well. It was, in fact, Olympic sponsors such as John Hancock Mutual Life Insurance who pressured the IOC to get control of the doping situation in sports and found the World Anti-Doping Agency.[23] The popularity and economic viability of Olympic sport depends on its continued emphasis on human excellence.

COMMITTED TO FAIR PLAY

The fourth fundamental principle of Olympism says that fair play is essential to the "Olympic spirit" in which sport should be practiced.[24] As is clear from our previous discussion, an atmosphere of fair play is needed to cultivate human excellence. Although fair play is a modern concept, it may be profitably understood as the sporting manifestation of justice, which was conceived by ancient Greeks to be an excellence (*aretē*) of communities.[25] If, following Alasdair MacIntyre,[26] we understand sports to be practice communities, then a commitment to fair play is an essential characteristic of Olympic sport. Since sports are governed by rules and nations are governed by laws, fair play, like justice, demands the proper administration of a sport's rules and regulations. Fairness should not be reduced to rule adherence, however. As the adjective 'fair' suggests, there is an aesthetic element that can be sensed and judged by spectators.[27] Fair play demands equal opportunity and reward according to merit, but it should also celebrate athletes who go beyond rule adherence with gestures that indicate the other elements of the Olympic spirit: friendship, solidarity, and mutual understanding.

Unsurprisingly, ethical governance is prominent among the evaluation criteria for Olympic sport. International federations must have a code of ethics that aligns with the IOC's code, procedures to fight against competition fixing, rules to sanction members of an athlete's entourage involved in doping or sexual harassment, and efforts to promote transparency and fairness on the field of play.[28] In fact, the first item listed under "The Mission and Role of the

IOC" in the Olympic Charter is "to encourage and support the promotion of ethics and good governance in sport [and] to ensuring that, in sport, the spirit of fair play prevails and violence is banned."[29] Antidiscrimination is central to Olympism's concept of fair play. Fundamental principle #4 declares that "the practice of sport is a human right" and principle #6 specifically bans discrimination based on race, color, sex, sexual orientation, language, religion, political or other opinion, national or social origin, property, or birth.[30] Olympic sports are evaluated according to the criteria of gender equity and "sport for all"—an effort to encourage wide participation rather than focusing on the elite.[31] If fair play demands a commitment to equal opportunity as well as reward according to merit, Olympic sports should be structurally resistant to discrimination—allowing a variety of body- and character types to flourish—and they should challenge the status quo of socioeconomic privilege, rather than reinforcing it.

Many of Olympic history's most cherished moments involve the breaking down of racial and gender stereotypes. African-American Jesse Owens' friendship with German Luz Long in the face of Nazi propaganda at the 1936 Games in Berlin is a favorite example of the Olympics' ability to transcend injustice. More recently, the IOC has made huge strides toward gender equity in sport, achieving 50 percent women's events with 40 percent female athletes at the 2014 Winter Games in Sochi, and 47.4 percent women's events and 45 percent female participation at the 2016 Rio Games.[32] A more formidable challenge to fair play in Olympic sport is economic advantage in sports such as equestrian, sailing, skiing, and cycling, where participation is costly and a technological edge can be bought by wealthier athletes and countries. The problem is only exacerbated by the evaluation criterion that quantifies a sport's sponsors.[33] Sponsors value expensive sports such as equestrian and sailing because they attract a wealthy following, but the Olympic movement has larger concerns. Olympic sports must demonstrate their commitment to fair play by adopting rules that ban discrimination and diminish economic advantage, and by administering those rules ethically and transparently.

PROMOTES PEACE

After excellence and fairness, the third defining characteristic of Olympic sport is its promotion of peace. The second fundamental principle states that the goal of Olympism is "to place sport at the service of the harmonious development of humankind, with a view to promoting a peaceful society concerned with the preservation of human dignity."[34] That this peaceful society is global is made clear by principle three, which points out that the Movement covers all five continents, the unity of which is symbolized by the interlaced

Olympic rings.[35] The modern Olympics' internationalism contrasts with the ancient Olympics' ethnic homogeneity, but only in scope. The Hellenic tribes that came together on neutral ground for common worship in Olympia were diverse and often warring; indeed their safe travel had to be protected by a sacred truce called the *ekecheiria*.[36] The Games were credited with helping the Hellenes to overcome their enmities, to share ideas, and eventually to unite against their common enemy, the Persians.[37] The revival of the Games in the nineteenth century was partly inspired by this legacy of peace promotion through sport. Playing sports together seems to humanize "the other," by overcoming cultural and linguistic barriers and demanding mutual respect. Sometimes it even fosters unlikely friendships. To make it work, though, Olympic sport needs to bring together people culturally and politically diverse enough that they might otherwise be fighting.

It is difficult to quantify the contribution that the Olympic Games makes to peace in the modern world, but there have been important symbolic achievements, such North and South Korea's decision to march together under one flag in the opening ceremony of the Sydney Games. It was neither an athlete nor an Olympic official, but a young spectator named John Ian Wing who suggested in 1956 that athletes break national ranks for the closing ceremony and enter the stadium mixed together as one nation.[38] At those same Games in Melbourne, an ongoing political conflict between Russia and Hungary seemed to tarnish the water polo competition with violence and vitriol that was patently un-Olympic and required police intervention to prevent a riot.[39] However the 2006 documentary called *Freedom's Fury* on the match and its aftermath reveals that the politicized hype surrounding the match contrasted with the athletes' own experience. It also staged a fifty year reunion of athletes on both teams which showed that the Olympic spirit prevailed even in what may seem like the nadir of Olympic efforts at peace.[40] Since 1994, the United Nations has been urging its members to observe an Olympic Truce, and an Olympic Truce Resolution has officially been adopted for every Games since 2004.[41]

It is for the sake of peace promotion that Olympic sports are expected not only to have national federations and participants from all over the world, but also to award Olympic and world championship medals to athletes from a variety of continents.[42] Working against such "universality" criteria, however, are the "history and tradition" criteria, which consider how long a sport has been part of the Olympic Games and other multisport events, such as the Pan-American or Commonwealth Games.[43] The problem here is that the sports in the modern Olympic Games reflect the Movement's European origins. These sports are more likely to meet the universality requirements precisely because they have already been exported globally as part of the Olympic Games. Judo and Taekwondo, the only non-western sports on the Olympic program, were not added until 1964 and 2000, respectively.[44] If the Olympic Movement wants to place sport at the service of all humankind and thereby promote peace, it cannot define history and tradition in terms of its own biased past. It needs to choose sports that reflect the cultural diversity of the Movement rather than reinforcing the traditional domination of the west.

IMPLICATIONS

Defining Olympic sport in terms of excellence, fairness, and peace not only reflects the history and philosophy of the Olympic Movement, it implies that athletic practices should be critically evaluated and progressively improved according to this standard. Under this definition, a sport, an athlete, even a coach, official, or administrator can become more "Olympic" by better exemplifying these ideals. I would argue, for example, that the fledgling Youth Olympic Games are in many ways more "Olympic" than the regular Olympic Games. The balanced ideal of human excellence is expressed by the requirement that athletes stay for the duration of the festival and participate in "Learn and Share" activities with such themes as Olympism, skills development, well-being and healthy lifestyle, social responsibility, and expression. Exemplary Olympians also are invited to share their experiences and act as role models for the younger athletes.[45] In support of fairness and peace promotion, the Youth Olympic Games have been experimenting with mixed gender and international teams in archery, athletics, cycling, equestrian, fencing, judo, modern pentathlon, swimming, table tennis, tennis, triathlon, biathlon, curling, luge, ice skating, and skiing.[46] These events allow athletes from different cultures and even different genders to work together for common goals—an intentional promotion of Olympic ideals through sport.

The innovations achieved in the Youth Olympic Games show how sports can become more "Olympic" when they are consciously guided by the principles of Olympism. It also illustrates how some of the events in the Games may be more "Olympic" than others. A vision of excellence that engages body, will, and mind, for example, favors complex and strategic sports over simpler tests of strength and skill. A weightlifting event like the clean and jerk, which emphasizes speed, technique, and planning over sheer strength, is more "Olympic" than power-lifting events such as the bench press or squat. Likewise, the emphasis on "joy of effort" seems to point toward sports like running or cycling more than technical sports like shooting or popular activities such as computer gaming. Expensive sports like equestrian and sailing might be dropped in favor of less expensive activities such as ultimate Frisbee or tug-of-war. Meanwhile, disciplines that require less expensive facilities within a given sport might be favored, such as mountain biking over velodrome cycling. The Youth Olympic Games prohibits the construction of new venues for the Games[47]—a requirement that respects the environment and keeps financial demands under control, thereby promoting diversity.

Given the demands of promoting peace through diversity in a globalizing world, the Olympic Movement might even reconsider what counts as a sport, or more specifically, an event. In Rule 45, the Olympic Charter distinguishes sports (i.e., cycling) from disciplines (i.e., road racing) and events (i.e., the 1984 women's Olympic road race). It says an event is "a specific competition in a sport resulting in a ranking giving rise to the awarding of medals and diplomas."[48] Many athletic activities that may promote Olympic ideals are not set up to generate rankings and award material prizes. Many purists objected to the traditional Chinese martial art called *wushu* becoming part of the Olympic Games because its goal is the cultivation of an internal energy called *qi*, which cannot be easily quantified by judges and should not be reduced to a point system. Some say, likewise, that the established Olympic sport of figure skating has been ruined by judging scandals that gave rise to a rigid point system that upsets the balance between the sport's technical and artistic aspects. Defining Olympic sport in terms of values rather than structures opens the door to debate about the nature of sport itself.

FROM PRESCRIPTION TO DESCRIPTION

Defining Olympic sport prescriptively in terms of focus on excellence, commitment to justice, and promotion of peace may seem like little more than an exercise in idealism. But ethics, like language, is learned and exercised within a community. If we are able to imbue our use of the term "Olympic" with normative force, we may well inspire more normatively Olympic behavior within that community. It must not be forgotten that sport is not a natural phenomenon, like lightning or childbirth. Sport is defined and interpreted by human beings, and *how* we define and interpret sport impacts the ethics of its performance. Indeed the British already do this with their use of the term "sporting." The first definition of that term in the Oxford English Dictionary is simply, "Connected with or interested in sport." The second definition, however, is "Fair and generous in one's behaviour or treatment of others, especially in a contest."[49] Even more prescriptive is the use of the expression "It's not cricket" to describe morally questionable conduct, even outside of sport. Both expressions may hearken back to a gentlemanly ethos which raises its own moral questions today, but they are good examples of how a sport-specific term can take on normative force in usage that transcends sport.

The process of imbuing the term "Olympic" with a moral force derived from the enduring values of Olympism can begin with academics—especially those of us who write about ethical issues in the Olympic Games. Just because certain sports, athletes, and actions are part of the Olympic Games, we do not have to describe them as "Olympic." We should save that term to describe the sports, athletes, and actions that best exemplify the ideals of Olympism. Furthermore, we should use the term as a standard of evaluation. We might say, for example, that swimming is a more Olympic sport than shooting, that Jesse Owens was a more Olympic athlete than Ben Johnson, or that the cross-country ski coach who handed a spare pole to competitor who had broken his behaved more Olympically than one who tries to motivate an athlete by denigrating her competitor. We might say that FIFA behaved Olympically when they adapted the safety rules to allow Muslim women to wear head coverings when they play, or that National Olympic Committees behave Olympically when they help athletes pursue their educations and not simply medals. Those who understand the values of Olympism must be the first to use the term "Olympic" in a way that reflects them.

Normative usage of terms like "Olympic" has the potential to spread—especially if it starts being used by members of the media, who facilitate most people's experience of the Olympic Games. Like sponsors, members of the media generally understand that it is the distinctive Olympic values which make the Games so much more important than the non-Olympic versions of most sports. Indeed it is through the media's depiction of athletes' individual stories and their coverage of Olympic gestures such as crowds cheering on a last finisher, or athletes helping competitors to their feet, that most people get a feel for what Olympism is all about. Sponsors in "The Olympic Program" also devote part of their advertising to the promotion of Olympic values. Sports officials can help as well, as in the London Games of 2012 where athletes were disqualified for "not using their best efforts" in preliminary matches in order to gain advantageous matches in the finals.[50] Such penalties may grate against our analytical sense of justice since those athletes broke none of their sport's rules, but our aesthetic sense of fair play makes such disqualifications appropriate, even "Olympic."

CONCLUSION

From the point of view of Olympism, the first and vaguest criterion for the selection and evaluation of Olympic sport may be the most important. It is called the "value added" criterion—meaning the value that the sport adds to the Olympic Games and the value that the Olympic Games add to the sport. Value here should not be construed in terms of money or even exposure, but rather in terms of values—the values of Olympism. To be truly Olympic, sport must embody and reflect the values of Olympism. Succinctly put, Olympic sport should focus on human excellence, make a commitment to fair play, and promote peace.

NOTES

1. I acknowledge the National Endowment for the Humanities, the Andrew W. Mellon Foundation, and the American Academy in Rome for their support of this and other projects during my 2014–2015 fellowship year.

2. For a full account, see David Young, *The Modern Olympics: A Struggle for Revival* (Baltimore, MD: John Hopkins University Press, 1996).

3. Confucius, *Analects*, trans. E. Slingerland (Indianapolis: Hacket, 2003), 4.11

4. *The Olympic Charter* (Lausanne: International Olympic Committee, 2014), 11.

5. *Evaluation Criteria for Sports and Disciplines* (Lausanne: International Olympic Committee, 2012).

6. *The Olympic Charter*, Rule 7.

7. Ongoing drug problems and the fact that the sport's most excellent athletes didn't participate in the games were also factors, for an account see The Associated Press, "Secret Ballot Eliminates Baseball, Softball." *ESPN*, last modified July 8, 2005, accessed Aug. 28, 2015. http://espn.go.com/olympics/news/story?id=2103234.

8. For a full account, see Heather Reid, *Athletics and Philosophy in the Ancient World: Contests of Virtue* (Abingdon: Routledge, 2011).

9. *The Olympic Charter*, 11.

10. Plato, *Apology,* 29de

11. Aristotle, *Nicomachean Ethics,* 1098a.

12. For the full argument, see Heather Reid, *Athletics and Philosophy in the Ancient World: Contests of Virtue*, Chapter X.

13. *The Olympic Charter*, 23.

14. Ibid., Rule 45.3, 84.

15. *Evaluation Criteria for Sports and Disciplines*, #30.

16. Ibid., #26.

17. The Olympic Creed does not appear in the *Olympic Charter* or on the current IOC website, but it is frequently cited in discussions of Olympic history. In full, it states "The most important thing in the Olympic Games is not to win but to take part, just as the most important thing in life is not the triumph but the struggle. The essential thing is not to have conquered but to have fought well."

18. See Cesar Torres, "Results or Participation? Reconsidering Olympism's Approach to Competition," *Quest* 58, 243.

19. Bud Greenspan, *100 Greatest Moments in Olympic History* (Los Angeles: General Publishing Group, 1995) 180.

20. *Evaluation Criteria for Sports and Disciplines*, #14 and #15.

21. Ibid., #s 17-22.

22. Ibid., #23.

23. John O'Leary, *Drugs and Doping in Sport* (London: Routledge, 2013) 140.

24. *The Olympic Charter*, 11.

25. This is the main argument of Plato's *Republic*.

26. Alasdair MacIntyre, *After Virtue* (Notre Dame, IN: University of Notre Dame Press, 1981).

27. I have argued elsewhere that the ancient Olympics' success in settling competing claims to honor derived from setting up an impartial contest—a simple footrace to

the altar for the honor of lighting the sacrificial flame--that was observed by a crowd who peacefully accepted its result. See Heather Reid, *Athletics and Philosophy in the Ancient World: Contests of Virtue.*

28. *Evaluation Criteria for Sports and Disciplines*, #s 2, 5, 27, 33.

29. *The Olympic Charter*, 16.

30. Ibid., 11–12.

31. *Evaluation Criteria for Sports and Disciplines*, #s 31 and 32

32. *Factsheet on Women in the Olympic Movement* (Lausanne: IOC, 2016) 4–5.

33. *Evaluation Criteria for Sports and Disciplines*, #23.

34. *The Olympic Charter*, 11.

35. Ibid., 11.

36. See M.I. Finley and H.W. Plecket, *The Olympic Games: The First Thousand Years* (New York: Viking, 1976) 98.

37. Nigel Crowther "The Ancient Olympics and Their Ideals," in *Athletika: Studies on the Olympic Games and Greek Athletics*, edited by W. Decker and I. Weiler (Hildesheim, Germany: Weidemann, 2004), 21.

38. Greenspan, *100 Olympic Moments,* 206.

39. Ibid., 90.

40. *Freedom's Fury* directed by Colin Keith Gray (2006).

41. "Timeline," *International Olympic Truce Foundation*, www.olympictruce.org.

42. *Evaluation Criteria for Sports and Disciplines*, #s 10-14.

43. Ibid., #s 7 and 8.

44. Karate will debut at Rio 2016, along with golf and rugby sevens, but the Chinese martial art called wushu was again left out of the program

45. *The Youth Olympic Games Vision and Principles* (Lausanne: International Olympic Committee, 2014).

46. *The YOG – Sports Programme* (Lausanne: International Olympic Committee, 2014).

47. *The Youth Olympic Games Vision and Principles.*

48. *The Olympic Charter*, Rule 45.2.2, 84.

49. *Oxford Dictionaries*, "sporting," http://www.oxforddictionaries.com/us/definition/american_english/sporting.

50. "Olympics badminton: Eight women disqualified from doubles," *BBC Sport.* Last accessed May 8, 2013. http://www.bbc.co.uk/sport/0/olympics/19072677.

Chapter 5

Early Modern Athletic Contests

Sport or Not Sport?

John McClelland

"Sport" ranks as one of the most frequently used words in American English, occupying the satanical 666th position among all parts of speech (and 247th among the nouns) in the list established by the *Corpus of Contemporary American English,* ahead of such commonly used words as board, subject, rest, officer, behavior, and so on.[1] Despite this it has been notoriously difficult to define just what is and what is not "sport." English-language dictionaries usually limit themselves to something vague, like "athletic games" or "athletic contests," among the various meanings that "sport" has historically possessed (see part 2 below). Dictionaries of foreign languages, where the word is monosemic—it was imported from English starting about 1830—suggest a cumulative approach to definition, stressing the physicality of sport, its relation to play and games, its competitive dimension, its subjection to rules, to which they add—significantly—both prior (methodical) training and the pleasure that sport gives the participant.[2] An activity thus merits the label "sport" if it exhibits all the characteristics enumerated in the definition.

Like any noun with some history behind it, the semantic and referential boundaries of "sport" have evolved over time, but since the 1930s these have acquired a tendentious chronological dimension. According to some scholars, "sport" can be applied legitimately only to post-eighteenth-century athletic contests, while earlier forms are mere play or pastime.[3] The roots of this distinction may be found in the work of E. Norman Gardiner[4] and more especially in Johan Huizinga's *Homo Ludens.*[5] The former, a distinguished historian of ancient Greek athletics, saw increasing twentieth-century professionalism as an "evil" that was destructive of true sport.[6] Huizinga shared this view and deepened the negative image of sport by adding organization, systematization, and bureaucratization as further ills. Younger sports scholars reacted, using Roger Caillois's 1958 neo-Darwinian thesis of the evolution of games from the meaningless *ilinx* (self-induced disorientation) to the disciplined *agōn* (contest, sport), to positively connote professionalism and other twentieth-century "evils" as signs of sport's modernity, a feature of human progress. Since earlier forms of athletic competition had not exhibited these features, they were therefore not sport.

The underlying assumption of these definitions of sport is that it is a variant of, or an improvement on/deterioration in play. Play becomes sport either through a process of accretion—Huizinga's various -isms and -izations, or the progressive incorporation of specialized equipment, dedicated playing surfaces, rules, and accommodation of spectators;[7] or through a contrary process of subdivision, eliminating from the general concept of play those components that definitely do not belong to sport.[8]

These formulations also tend to treat sport as a phenomenon distinct from other human and social pursuits. Sport, however, is a multifarious physical and cultural reality constituted by a constantly evolving set of practices, and, I would argue first, not isolated from the larger set of humanity's major preoccupations but related to them. Second, I want not so much to define sport as to characterize it by identifying and enumerating features that seem to have been constant in autotelic ludic physical contests from earliest times.

SEMIOTICS

Using concepts formulated in Aristotle's logic[9] but most cogently explored and developed by A. J. Greimas,[10] semiotics affords us a model—the semiotic square—for understanding sport's significance by placing it within the larger nexus of concepts and phenomena with which it has been associated, either analogically or differentially.[11] Sport's semantic and substantive relationships are thus understood as the complex interplay of contraries, contradictories and complementarities, not just as the simple antagonistic juxtaposition of opposites.

In the present context we can begin to construct the square using the common dichotomy work versus play as our basic pair.[12] Though usually imagined as mutually contradictory, work and play do share the essential characteristic of cooperation among the players or workers. There is, however, a third form of human activity that overrides both work and play and that is the waging of war. Play and war are complementary in the sense that both are wasteful of time, resources, and energy (leaving aside the degree of relative magnitudes). And since war undoes what work has accomplished,

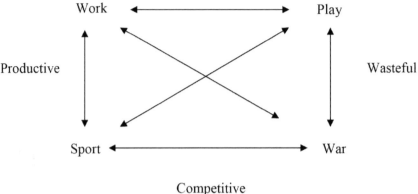

Figure 5.1   Semiotic Square of Opposition

it is not simply unproductive in the way that play is, it is destructive and therefore the contradictory of work.

By inserting sport in the fourth corner of the square we can begin to understand the complicated position it occupies within the set of human activities. Though it may be difficult to consider sport as the contradictory of play, there are obviously many situations—and not just those invoked by Huizinga—where sport negates play. Because sport occurs in the time of leisure (at least for the spectators and most of the participants), it is the contrary of work; and because it is not supposed to generate either destruction or death, it is the contrary of war. At the same time, it is complementary to work because at the highest level athletes are paid and sport generates various forms of economic activity. Sport is also complementary to war in that both are competitive and strategic and that many of the basic sports were, in fact, skills useful in warfare and in personal combat. More significantly, perhaps, is the fact that sport and war—though they both generate economic development (the fabrication of specialized implements, etc.)—are wasteful of the energy of both the athletes and the soldiers, since neither directly produces goods or services.[13] The final form of the square can be seen in figure 5.1.

Examined and situated in this way, sport is no longer relegated to being the irreconcilable opposite of work, but is understood as part—and not the end part—of a continuum that stretches from the innocent and the innocuous to the deadly serious. Moreover, this continuum is not a finite line but actually a square within a circle whose arcs (the set of complementarities), diameters (the set of contradictories), and chords (the set of cognitive axes) reveal that any point on the circumference is linked to the other three in a semantically complex relation. Sport cannot be defined simply as an "autotelic, ludic, physical contest" because it has many more dimensions than that.

DISTINCTIVE FEATURES

These dimensions can be further explored with the aid of a model derived from distinctive feature analysis, a linguistic hermeneutic first proposed by Morris Halle.[14] Its underlying principle is that meaning is generated by a set of often minute differences between two phenomena. Its methodology is thus empirical and pragmatic rather than theoretical and conceptual and relies on detailed examination and finely drawn distinctions. Its problematic is hence centered on the determination of which differences are significant (i.e., are signs) and which are simply non-signifying variants. Through the application of this model, one can identify some thirty distinctive features that are the connotative signs of the set of activities that in 2015 are generally agreed to be sports. These can conveniently be grouped in two categories: features characteristic of the athletes and features characteristic of the practice of sport.

The Athletes

Sport is both ostensibly pleasurable for the athlete and functionally gratuitous, since his/her gestures accomplish nothing durable except the expenditure of energy. It is also focused on winning—or wanting to achieve one's personal best or to establish a record—and is thereby necessarily competitive on the level of the individual. As correlatives to that, sport is also fixated on rewards, whether material (money, objects having real value) or symbolic (crowns of laurel, Olympic medals, all manner of rings, cups and trophies). And thus sport implies the athlete's constant effort to improve her/his proficiency in order to reap these rewards.[15] It also implies a high degree of specialization on the part of the athlete, who will normally not compete in more than one—or at most two—track and field events or play more than one position in a team sport.

Because sport is oriented toward victory, it requires physical training and psychological preparation, and more than that, tactics and strategies that take into account the strengths and weaknesses of the opponent. For that reason, sport encourages the athlete to be innovative and to imaginatively exploit situations using feats of prowess not originally conceived as being possible. Correlatively, sport, since ancient times, has implied pushing the body to or beyond the limits of normal physical capabilities, often using means deleterious to the athlete's health or exposing her/him to physical injury.

But it is precisely through the ostentatious display of physical excess and indifference to danger that the athlete evinces his/her passion, an emotion that is transmitted to teammates and spectators.[16]

Sport

First, then, sport is physical, gratuitous, competitive, and—through its focus on winning and ultimately championship at all levels of athletic competence—serious and teleological.[17] It is necessarily performed according to rules, regulations, and conventions—not by laws—and at set days or times of the year or at specified yearly intervals; it is thus also ritualistic. Some of the rules and regulations may be practical, but most are dictated by the logic of the game and are consequently arbitrary. However, sport, being human, is innovative, transitory, and evolutionary. Rules change to accommodate faster, more exciting forms of play (the forward pass, fewer players on the ice surface) or to reduce injuries (helmets, some body contact disallowed). New sports are created while others cease to be fashionable and hence disappear.[18]

Perhaps the chief characteristic of sport is its "possible world" autonomy with respect to the "real world." Its rules and regulations make no reference to any external ethical system and are applied absolutely; penalties are imposed, goals awarded, winners declared without the intervention of considerations such as self-defense or attenuating circumstances. In addition to being morally autonomous, sport is temporally autonomous. Its stop-clocks record only the time the puck/ball is in play; or the time the competitors are actually racing; or it is not temporally regulated at all.[19] It is however regulated by the abstract principles of mathematics. Achievements being most often expressed as numbers, sport performance is objectively measurable and quantifiable in arithmetical terms. Sport is also spatially autonomous. The playing surface is defined both arithmetically—precise numbers of feet or meters—and geometrically: circles, semicircles, and parallel lines intersecting with their perpendiculars are traced on the playing surface to represent boundaries that regulate play and symbolize targets to be reached. Nonplayers are not allowed into the playing space. Concomitantly, the playing surface is located within a larger structure or physically defined space that may be shared with other ludic activities but not, generally, with any practical pursuit.[20] This singularity is also marked by the resort to costumes and equipment that are peculiar to each sport and that are generally unused or even unusable outside the sport to which they belong.[21] Sport also, for the most part, either ignores or defies meteorological contingencies (by playing as if the weather was not there) and even the day/night dichotomy (by utilizing artificial light).[22] It is similarly indifferent to both inflicting and receiving physical injury (though enhanced protective gear is becoming more common in some sports). On the other hand, sports, being ideal worlds, are also conciliatory. Passionate competition ceases with the end of the event, and equilibrium, iconicized by the initial disposition of the athletes and the terrain, re-established. A sporting event—unlike war or work—is thus digressive, because it does not fundamentally alter the relations of force among the competitors.

Finally, western sport, from its very beginnings in ancient Greece, has implied the presence of spectators. And that—in addition to the fact that from the start athletes have competed for real monetary rewards[23]—has meant that sport, in sharp contradistinction to play, is significantly economic. At the point where play becomes sport, that is, at the point where the activity has taken on most of the features outlined thus far, the athlete either pays to participate—league fees, ice or court time, equipment—or is paid to play, either as a *Staatsamateur* or as a full or part-time professional. In addition, sport also implies paying groundskeepers, erecting facilities, charging admission, manufacturing equipment, attracting tourists, and selling souvenirs, goods and services whose price is linked to specific athletes and specific sports events. Given that the most spectacular athlete generates the most money, sport has become increasingly democratic, previously operative social and ethnic barriers having yielded to sheer talent. The meaning of sport, anthropologically speaking, is thus a function of the kinds of financial dealings that are its end product and its justification.

The thirty or so signs that have been identified here can be observed to varying degrees in the practice of almost all the forms of high-level athletics at the present, and less intensively in amateur sports as well. Taken together, they constitute a determinative paradigm of what we may call sport. However, any attempt to define "sport" as an activity displaying all these features is fraught with perplexity: swimming has many fewer of them than ice hockey, yet the swimmer is as much of an athlete as the hockey player. The absence of certain signs may thus be deemed inconsequential. What is consequential is not that in some athletic activity any of the foregoing features be reduced to the degree zero, but rather that they be negated; that the participants insist on not recognizing their obligatory character as a sign of sport and try to substitute some contradictory features in their place.

HISTORICAL USES OF "SPORT"

One argument invoked to deny the label "sport" to early modern athletic contests is that the word then did not mean what it does now. It first appeared in English in the early fifteenth century to denote a variety of physical and occasionally sexual pursuits, but always in opposition to what might be deemed serious activities. The word itself is an abbreviation of "disport," an

anglicized version of the Anglo-Norman French "desport." The *-port-* root of
the word means "to bear, to carry" and the *dis-/des-* prefix signifies "down"
or "away." Whatever sport is, it is at least a digression from the direct path.

In its original form, the word occurs some twenty times in Chaucer's *Can-
terbury Tales* (before 1400), always with the connotation of entertainment or
pleasure; and as "sport" 150 times in Shakespeare, where it denotes mockery,
amusement, or diversion (whether connoted positively or negatively).[24] There
are only three cases where it refers to sport in the contemporary sense: hunting twice: *Henry VI iii*, 4.5 and *Titus Andronicus* 2.2; and a fencing match
once: *The Merry Wives of Windsor* 2.1: "We have sport in hand . . . a fray
to be fought between Sir Hugh the Welsh priest and Caius the French doc-
tor."[25] The few instances of "sport" in the work of John Milton conform to
this earlier model.

Given the predominance of Chaucer, Shakespeare, and Milton in determining our historical understanding of English, one can hardly blame social historians and historians of sport for concluding that "sport," as we use the term
today, is exclusively coterminous with the "specific sports that originated in
England in the late-eighteenth and early-nineteenth centuries."[26] These new
phenomena needed a name and so the word was stripped of its extraneous
meanings and in its "narrower sense" converted into a specialized label. Consequently, one might be using "sport" anachronistically—or at least "indis-
criminately"—when one uses it to refer to the "game-contests and physical
exercises of all societies."[27]

But to make such a claim is to overlook the early examples of "sport" used
to denote precisely what is now meant by the term. In his 1595 translation
of Robert Garnier's 1574 French tragedy, *Cornélie*, the English dramatist
Thomas Kyd renders "aux jeux Olympiens" by "at th'Olympian sports."[28]
And in the same year, in *Astrophel*, a poem written on the death of sir
Philip Sidney, Edmund Spenser proclaims that his hero in "all the sports
. . . vanquisht everyone," the sports in question being "wrestling, running,
swimming, shooting [i.e., archery], striking, throwing, leaping, lifting."[29] In
1617 the Anglo-Scottish king James I issued his famous *King's Declaration
of Lawful Sports to Be Used*, specifying that those who attended Church of
England services on Sunday morning might legitimately practice "archerie
leapinge valtinge" in the afternoon.[30]

Five years earlier the lawyer Robert Dover had created an annual festival in
the Cotswold Hills involving competitive athletic games. By 1636 these had
become well enough known that the London publisher Matthewe Walbancke
printed a commemorative program, *Annalia dubrensia*, containing laudatory
texts by thirty-two poets. What is common to most of these texts is that they
baptize the games as "Olimpick" and constantly refer to them as "sports."[31]

And in the early 1660s the diarist Samuel Pepys labeled as "sports" both pall-mall and ninepins.[32]

Later in the century "sport" crops up twice as a synonym for hunting in Henry Purcell's 1689 opera *Dido and Aeneas*. And shortly after that in 1697 the English poet John Dryden, in translating/recasting Vergil's *Aeneid*, uses "sports" and "sportful" eleven times either to refer to the various Greek-style athletic contests that the epic narrates; or to translate specific words, notably "certamina," the Latin equivalent of "agōnai," the word the Greeks used to designate the Olympics and other "Crown" games.[33] As Dryden was sixty-six when he did this translation, it is safe to assume that his use of "sport" in its now accepted modern meaning was not an innovation but reflected what had become standard in English in the seventeenth century. In short, from the late-sixteenth century onward, English writers are using "sport" exactly the way we now do, to refer to strenuous, competitive athletic games and activities, all the way from the highest, most prestigious order—the revered ancient Olympics—to humbler, more local—but no less sporting—activities.

EARLY MODERN USAGES

Manuscript illuminations, murals, stand-alone paintings, legal and administrative documents, travelers' reports, memoirs, biographies, and works of history and literature, from the twelfth through the eighteenth century, attest to the variety of competitive games and contests that were widely practiced in early modern Europe.[34] The best known of these representations are the list of 217 games in chapter 22 of François Rabelais's *Gargantua*[35] and the eighty amusements depicted in Pieter Bruegel's 1560 painting, *Children's Games*.[36] Neither one of these was intended to be an authoritative account of contemporary athletic pastimes, but the ubiquity of the text and the picture made them the paradigm for understanding all early modern physical contests, which then were categorized as play, hence as radically different from the modern practice of sports.[37]

There were indeed many varieties of folk and street games and *ad hoc* imitations of more structured forms of play, though beyond graphic representations, our knowledge is generally limited to the locations and the occasions. The latter were largely Sunday afternoons, saints' days, and other religious holidays, since these were the only times the lower orders of rural and urban society were free of the obligation to work. The former were simply open fields between two villages or some relatively unencumbered space within the town or city. For the rest, we can only guess at how the game or match actually unfolded.

For the play contests of the bourgeoisie and the nobility we are, as might be expected, better informed. These can be roughly classified into three categories: military games and combats (including archery/shooting competitions), games with large (mostly inflated) balls, and games with small, solid balls. Each of these categories fits very nicely into the lower left corner of the semiotic square, first to the extent that their practitioners sought to have them recognized as legitimate recreation, thus as the counterpart to work. Second, these activities were also deliberately related to warfare, through the choice of implements and through the argument that the players would both harden their bodies for the rigors of the military life and learn tactics and strategy while playing.[38] The next sections explore the parallels and continuity of the early modern athletes and sports with their contemporary counterparts.

The Early Modern Athlete

To judge by the verbal and iconographical evidence, pre-1750 athletes found their play contests unquestionably pleasurable and participated with a high level of enthusiasm, expending their energy gratuitously and ostentatiously.[39] The players were certainly very focused because winning was the only thing that counted (the concept of second and third-place finishers was not yet a reality). As texts from the twelfth century onward tell us, competition was central to the events and the rewards were real: tourneying knights seized the horses and equipment of their defeated opponents and might even hold the latter for ransom. The notion of disinterested sport did however exist. The heroes of Chrétien de Troyes' Arthurian romances (1160–90) disdain any material reward for their tournament victories, wanting only to demonstrate their skill and valor.

Texts also tell us that knights trained in order to improve their skills and we can surmise that the professional ball players of the Renaissance did the same, since their livelihood depended on the quality of their performance. In his *Trois dialogues* of 1599 the famous sixteenth-century acrobat, Arcangelo Tuccaro outlines the physical training of the young gymnast and goes on to stress the psychological dimension of his sport,[40] as king Duarte of Portugal had done in his treatise on jousting, the *Livro da ensinança*.[41] Athletes seem also to have specialized within their sport, for example, playing one of the varieties of tennis or another, or a specific position on a twenty-seven-man *calcio* team.[42]

Early modern athletes also sought to innovate, seeking to change the rules to simplify play[43] or attempting new levels of achievement: contemporary writers thought that turning a somersault through eight hoops was the best an acrobat might do, but Tuccaro showed he could do it through ten. Passion, and its concomitant, indifference to danger, were also amply displayed by Medieval and Renaissance athletes. Deaths in jousting were not uncommon, but the sport showed no sign of abatement until the French King Henri II couldn't be bothered fastening his visor in a 1559 joust and received a mortal hit in the eye for his temerity.[44] With the invention of the rapier, a light sword with a long, fairly flexible narrow blade (useless in battle), fencing became more frequent and more dangerous. Fencers could slightly rip each other's clothes and the hits could thus be counted to determine the winner. But it was also easy to inflict dangerous puncture wounds. The fencing master Antonio Manciolino, writing in 1531, says that getting wounded by a friendly adversary is part of the game.

Ball games, whether played with large balls or small, also posed dangers to the players. Tennis was an indoor game using a hard ball that could hurt. Playing the net position (there were always two or four players to a side) could be dangerous and yet it was more prestigious and desirable. Players might lose an eye or even be killed if hit in the head by the ball. Tennis was also played with considerable emotional intensity and it happened that games led to dueling and even murder. As today, athletes took advantage of team games and the supposed inviolability of the playing surface to settle scores.[45]

Early Modern Sport

Early modern sports were certainly more physical and violent than most sports today (with some possible exceptions, for example, mixed-martial arts, hockey, or North American football). Jousting hits bore the combined energy of two large horses and two men encased in armor charging each other at a closing speed of about 25 km an hour, yet knights might run six courses, one right after the other. Indeed, the evolution of sport during the early modern period tended toward a reduction in the level of physicality. Competition was rife, both on an individual and a team basis, but was limited, seemingly, to single encounters. Even where they might occur repeatedly between different city district teams, there is no evidence of revenge matches or of champions being declared at the end of a playing season. This despite the fact that competition was necessarily local and rivalries might thereby be exacerbated.

On the other hand, rules, in the sense of an itemized list of do's and don'ts, appeared in the thirteenth century, though in their preliminary form they concerned chiefly the orderly conduct of events and the avoidance of violent confrontations. Point-based scoring systems for jousting—and shorthand methods for recording the different types of hits (head, body, shield, misses)—appeared in the mid-fifteenth century in both Italy and England; specimens of English score sheets from the sixteenth century have survived and attest to the rigorous precision of the marker. With the spread of printing in the sixteenth century rules ceased to be merely *ad hoc* and aspired to become more generally applicable. The *Vingt-quatre ordonnances du jeu royal de la paume* (twenty-four statutes for playing royal tennis) of 1599, the *Loix du paillemail* (eighty-three rules for pall-mall) of c. 1640 and the *Capitoli del calcio fiorentino* (thirty-three rules for playing Florentine *calcio*) of 1673 are recognizably modern in the style of their formulation.

Scheduling, on the other hand, was more aleatory. In the absence of leagues and any national or international bureaucracy, athletic contests were organized on the basis of external criteria. Noble weddings and treaty signings were always accompanied by jousts and tournaments, while other kinds of contests occurred on saints' days and other holidays or were determined by the season. In both cases these events were ritualistic in the sense that the occasion would not be complete without an athletic contest—like NFL games on Thanksgiving in the United States and college bowl games on January 1. More elaborate one-off events that required complex arrangements were widely publicized well in advance, that is, the jousts at St Inglevert in 1390, where three French knights announced that for a period of thirty days in May they would take on all comers. Generally speaking, in fact, the initiative to schedule a contest came either from the athletes themselves—as was the case for Florentine *calcio* or the *pallone* games played before a paying public every Sunday evening in the Campo Santo Stefano in Venice;[46] or it came from above: in the twelfth century local aristocrats arranged pick-up tournaments on short notice; England's Richard II mounted a lavish display of jousting in London in September 1390 because his rival, Charles VI of France, had done so in Paris earlier in the year;[47] in 1563 the grand duke of Florence, in emulation of the ancient Roman emperors and applying the "bread and circuses" principle, organized an annual chariot race in his own honor.

Rules and scoring systems imply a recognized and autonomous internal morality in sport, but these came late in the early modern period.[48] The only morality accepted (or avoided) by early modern sport was that imposed by civil and religious authorities, who condemned jousting because of the injuries inflicted, ball games because people bet on the result,[49] almost all other games because they were a waste of time that could be put to better uses. On the other hand, pre-1750 athletic contests did enjoy at least temporary spatial autonomy. No new arenas or stadiums were built, but fences were erected around public squares to keep spectators away from the tourneyers or the *calcio* players during the match. Some areas were permanently reserved for certain sports and the traces of this reservation survive in the name and configuration shape of the space: La Lizza (the lists) and the Via del Cavallerizzo (riding school) in Siena, the Via del Pallone in Verona, Pall Mall in London, and its French equivalent, the Rue du Mail in Paris. Monarchs constructed permanent jousting grounds within the confines of their palaces, while purpose-built tennis courts became a fixture of noble houses and modern cities (c. 1600 there were 200–250 pay-as-you-go tennis courts in Paris).[50]

In the absence of stop-clocks and readily available timepieces, temporal autonomy was impossible. Florentine *calcio* games began at some ill-determined time in the afternoon and ended when the sun set. Most other games lasted until the knights had run a fixed number of courses or when one side had beat the other by a pre-set number of points or games (a tennis team had to win at least four games and beat the other team by at least two); or, in the case of fencing, hits (cf. *Hamlet* 5.2). The game, in other words, lasted as long as it had to. On the other hand, from about the fifteenth century, when tennis became popular and point-scoring became general in jousting, winning in early modern contests was increasingly objectified, that is, quantified in arithmetical terms, replacing the old qualitative, that is, subjective, criteria. Geometrical criteria were also introduced when tennis court surfaces were marked so as to fix the point where the ball bounced the second time. When Antonio Scaino in 1555 gave precise measurements for the small, medium, and large tennis courts and when Giovanni Bardi in 1580 defined the *calcio* playing surface as being 172 *braccia* by eighty-six (i.e., about 100 meters by fifty), they were introducing genuine geometrical autonomy into sport. The space had to be created to accommodate the game rather than the game adapting itself to the space.

By the thirteenth century sports equipment had also become autonomous and distinct from the needs of practical life. The manufacture of tennis balls was a thriving industry in Paris before 1300; players needed special gloves for *jeu de paume* and later racquets, paddles, bats, and nets as further innovations were introduced. Jousting and tourneying knights required special lances and heavily padded armor designed to change direct hits into glancing blows, along with personal helmets decorated with large, extravagant symbols. Proto-golf and pall-mall were played with a variety of clubs for long shots, approach shots, and putting, while *calcio* players needed light-weight clothes and good running shoes and both *calcio* and *pallone* required inflatable balls; the latter game was also played with specially fabricated wooden armlets. By the seventeenth century, pall-mall courts were being surfaced by groundskeepers with a special mixture of ground sea shells.[51]

Meteorological autonomy seems also to have been part of early modern sport, although with some exceptions. Knights did not joust in the rain since the horses could slip on muddy grounds. But despite being encased in fifty pounds of armor and a helmet that admitted very little ventilation, they jousted in the hottest weather and suffered from heat exhaustion to the point of dying, the fate of some sixty or so knights and squires in a single day at a tournament in the summer of 1241.[52] Sports like *calcio* were thought of as winter activities because they were too strenuous to play in the summer, and cold weather generally did not deter early modern athletes. In the harsh winter of 1490–1491 Venetians jousted on the ice and young Florentines played *calcio* on the frozen Arno River. In the 1660s Londoners played soccer-football on ice-covered streets and pall-mall on the frozen Thames.[53] There are many depictions of people in the Low Countries doing the same on frozen canals and ponds.[54] Speed-skating was observed in Brussels in the fifteenth century and curling in Scotland at the same time.

Early modern physical contests were not conciliatory, even though they were thought to be a way of dissipating tensions and keeping civic peace. They did, however, have definite economic spin-offs in addition to the manufacture and sale of equipment. By the twelfth century, noninheriting younger sons of the nobility, trained in the feudal arts, made their living as professional tourneyers, and some of the knights amassed considerable fortunes. Professional tennis players appear in the early fifteenth century, either as freelancers taking a share of the winning bets or being employed in noble households to exhibit their skills. Professional sport was already international. Knights traveled the length and breadth of Europe to joust and tourney wherever an event was held. By the 1550s the duke of Ferrara had both French and Spanish tennis pros on his payroll. Italian acrobats, fencers and riding-masters were working in all the courts of northern Europe.

Spectatorship—with its companion, wagering—also increased in volume and was recognized as being essential to the success of the event. Again, as early as the twelfth century organizers were building temporary elevated structures to provide spectators with a close-up view of the action, and later—as in Henry VIII's palace at Hampton Court—such structures became permanent. Spectatorship also became international. English tourists crossed to France in 1390 for the express purpose of seeing the jousts at St Inglevert. Tourists went out of their way to watch competitions and paid to watch tennis matches in Paris, fencing in Germany, chariot races in Florence, and ball games in Venice. Cities and towns became aware of the revenue potential of hosting tournaments and competed with each other to hold the events, like modern bids for the Super Bowl, the Olympics, or the Pan-Am Games.

Early modern physical activities were also becoming more democratic. The appreciation of sheer athletic skill and of the money that might be made from it meant that the noble classes would employ people of humble origin as long-distance runners, wrestlers, tennis players, or fencers, both to exhibit their skills and compete against their neighbor's servants. These same athletes might then go on to earn their living as freelancers.

EARLY MODERN AND MODERN SPORT

Early modern physical contests thus displayed almost all of the distinctive features of modern sports, albeit sporadically and not evenly across all activities at all times. The most notable, generalized absences are the lack of any overriding bureaucracy that would administer and standardize rules and schedules, and consequently of any notion of championship. In short, the absence of what Huizinga called "technical organization and scientific thoroughness" and of what Georges Vigarello characterized as "le dispositif institutionnel et l'organisation sélective," institutionalized arrangements and organization based on selection.[55] For Huizinga these absences meant that early modern athletics still qualified as play, while for Vigarello it meant that they were not sports. But are these feature essential to the definition of a sport or are they simply non-signifying variants?

Modern sport had been described as the product of the Industrial Revolution and the technological mindset that both fostered it and developed out of it.[56] I would argue instead that the mindset toward technical organization and scientific thoroughness was already developing by the late fifteenth century, but the actual technology lagged behind. The impulse to see and compete against athletes from beyond the immediate vicinity was certainly present before the end of the fourteenth century and tournament leagues existed in Germany in the fifteenth, with regulations that applied on the national level by 1485.[57] Still, travel between cities was agonizingly slow. In Verona in 1786 the German poet Goethe watched a *pallone* match between a local team and one from Padua, about 80-km distant. By coach or on horseback it would have taken a minimum of ten hours to cover that distance, so intercity matches would at best be very infrequent.

The improvement of road surfaces in the early nineteenth century, followed by the establishment of rail lines, the telegraph, and later the telephone and air travel, expanded immeasurably the area of frequent feasible competition from regional to country-wide to inter-continental. And that in turn generated the organizational structures and bureaucracies that now govern and determine sport.

In short, and despite current scholarly opinion, early modern athletic contests exhibited the characteristics of sport as we know it in the twenty-first century, but in a more attenuated form. Such elements as were not present can be explained on technical grounds: the difficulties and uncertainties of travel made regular schedules impossible; on intellectual grounds: the culture was not yet scientifically based and hence concepts of quantity were not yet fully integrated; and on what we may loosely call socioethical grounds: even nation-states like England and France were regionally fragmented, lines of authority, though clear in theory, were not clear in practice; the notion of a supra-local sports bureaucracy would have been hard to grasp.[58] All of that meant that it was difficult to conceive of the multifarious forms of any creative endeavor as falling under the same lexical umbrella and consequently as being subject to the same critical criteria.

The use of words such as "theater" to encompass comedies, dramas, and tragedies, of "literature" to encompass poetry, novels, and short stories, of "art" to encompass painting, engraving, and sculpture, and of "sport" to encompass the full range of physical activities and contests is a phenomenon of the eighteenth and nineteenth centuries. And that does not mean that the forms of early modern athletics were not sport or that their practitioners would have refused to conform to the characteristics of sport as it now exists.

APPENDIX: SPORT AND WAR

Despite an understandable twentieth to twenty-first century repugnance to conceive of sport and war as being analogous—and concomitantly to reject any such analogy as superficial and purely metaphorical—the connections between the two run all the way from book 23 of Homer's *Iliad* and to the real, if symbolic, presence of the military at the Super Bowl.[59] Up to and including World War I (but with the exception of the Napoleonic wars), wars between nations were fought in order to win some specific and possibly quite tangible prize: the crown of France (100 Years' War) or of England (War of the Roses), the eradication of religious dissent (all the European wars between 1560 and 1648), the acquisition of territory (French and Indian War, Franco-Prussian War), the control of specific waterways (Trojan War, Crimean War), the untrammeled possession of African colonies (World War I). Until this last degenerated into futile trench warfare, wars between nations might last over several decades and would consist (like sports "seasons") of sporadic but repeated encounters, that is, battles, between national armies. At some point one of the two sides would no longer be able to "field a team," so to speak, and thus have to admit defeat, allowing the other to claim victory and the prize.

The battles themselves were often fought by agreement as to place and time, and were conducted—at least in the Middle Ages—according to rules derived out of feudal chivalry.[60] Their duration was usually very brief and their outcome undisputed (Antietam, 1862, claimed as a victory by both sides, was unusual in this respect). The goal of war and of battle was not death and destruction but the fragmentation of the enemy's fighting units, forcing him to withdraw from the field. Killing might be the means to that end but it was not the end itself. In all team sports, the deliberate injuring of an opponent—disallowed by the rules but practiced more or less openly—has a similar purpose: to weaken the opposing team's resolve and force them into a psychological retreat from the game.

The productive, economic developments generated by sport and war resemble each other and in both cases are at one or even two removes from the field of play. In terms of real, measurable effect, the actions performed by the athlete achieve nothing more than the expenditure of his/her energy; those performed by the soldier can be understood only as negatives, the annihilation of life and property. And yet in both sport and war those actions are deemed praiseworthy and since the Middle Ages have spawned industries whose only initial purpose was to produce implements that would facilitate those actions but that had no other function. However, once this industrial and technological capacity came into existence, it sought to maximize its utility by extending into other areas. Advances in metallurgy aimed at producing lightweight cannons that would not explode led on the one hand to the production of portable hand guns, fowling pieces, and lightweight swords—all of which were useless in war but had their role in civil life—and on the other to new uses for metal tubing, such as the four 20-meter high bronze columns that support the altar canopy in Saint Peter's in Rome. Caterpillar treads were first used for moving guns and tanks, but are now common on a variety of industrial vehicles. Football and military helmets were the models for protective headgear generally, and much of our leisure-wear clothing—T-shirts, sweatshirts, informal footwear—was originally produced for athletes.

As for the notion that sport is "war without weapons"—more accurately, "war without the shooting,"—it first appeared in George Orwell's ironically titled 1945 essay, "The Sporting Spirit." Though widely appropriated as defining sport as analogous to war, it was in fact a condemnatory extrapolation of fan behavior generally from what had happened during a supposedly friendly series of matches between teams from the United Kingdom and the Soviet Union immediately following the end of World War II.

NOTES

1. "Word Frequency Data," *Corpus of Contemporary American English,* http://www.wordfrequency.info/free.asp?s=y

2. See for example: *Le grand Robert,* https://www.lerobert.com/espace-numerique/enligne/le-grand-robert-de-la-langue-francaise-en-ligne-12-mois.html, *Das deutsches Wörterbuch* http://woerterbuchnetz.de/, the *Diccionario de la lengua española,* http://www.rae.es/ayuda/diccionario-de-la-lengua-espanola, and Nicola Zingarelli, *Il nuovo Zingarelli, vocabulario della lingua italiana* (Bologna: Zanichelli, 1987).

3. The chief proponents of sport as an exclusively modern phenomenon are Allen Guttmann, *From Ritual to Record. The Nature of Modern Sports* (New York: Columbia University Press, 1978), Norbert Elias and Eric Dunning *Quest for Excitement: Sport and Leisure in the Civilizing Process* (Oxford: Blackwell, 1986), Bruce Kidd, *The Struggle for Canadian Sport* (Toronto-Buffalo-London: University of Toronto Press, 1996), Georges Vigarello, *Passion Sport. Histoire d'une culture* (Paris: Textuel, 2000), and Georges Vigarello, *Histoire du corps I. De la Renaissance aux Lumières* (Paris: Le Seuil, 2005). However, the pseudo-antiquity of the modern Olympics obliges these scholars to accept the ancient Greek games as true sports.

4. Norman E. Gardiner, *Athletics of the Ancient World* (Oxford: Clarendon, 1930), vi, 3, and 105.

5. Johan Huizinga, *Homo Ludens* (Boston: Beacon Press, 1962).

6. Donald G. Kyle, "E. Norman Gardiner, Historian of Ancient Sport," *International Journal of the History of Sport* 8, no. 1 (1991): 28-55.

7. Garry Chick and John W. Loy, "Definitions," *The Encyclopedia of World Sport, Ancient Times to the Present*, eds. David Levinson and Karen Christensen (Santa Barbara-Denver-Oxford: ABC-Clio, 1996), 1.247–49.

8. Allen Guttmann, *Sports Spectators* (New York: Columbia University Press, 1986), 4.

9. Aristotle, *De interpretatione* 17b17–20a15; Aristotle, *Prior Analytics* 51b5–52b34.

10. A. J. Greimas, *Du sens. Essais sémiotiques* (Paris: Le Seuil, 1970).

11. What follows here is an abridged and altered version of material that appeared in John McClelland, "Sport," *Encyclopedia of Semiotics*, ed. Paul Bouissac (New York-Oxford: Oxford University Press, 1998), 593–96, and was expanded in John McClelland, *Body and Mind* (London-New York: Routledge, 2007), 12–18.

12. For more on the distinctions between work and play, see Chad Carlson "Three-Pointer: Revisiting Three Crucial Issues in the "Tricky Triad" of Play, Games, and Sport" in this volume.

13. This will be expanded in the Appendix below.

14. Roman Jakobson and Morris Halle *Fundamentals of Language* (The Hague: Mouton, 1956).

15. Contrary to that, of course, was the Anglo-American view in the late nineteenth to early twentieth century that honest participation ("how you played the game") was more important than winning.

16. On the emotional dimension of sport see Vigarello, *Passion Sport*.

17. If the players are indifferent to the outcome, then the activity is a pastime and not sport.

18. Some of the "sports" that figured in the 1896–1912 Olympics have now been downgraded to pastimes and others have ceased to exist.

19. Baseball and tennis have no time limit. Cricket's time is measured by the calendar, not the clock. Only soccer uses external time, but even there the referee may add some minutes if there has been a game delay.

20. John McClelland, "Sports Spectators and (the Lack of) Sports Arenas: From the Middle Ages to the End of the Eighteenth Century," *Grenzüberschreitung: Sport neu denken*, eds S. Scharenberg and Bernd Wedemeyer-Kolwe (Hoya: Niedersächsisches Institut für Sportgeschichte, 2009), 218–32.

21. In this connection it is worth noting that the costumes worn by serious athletes replicate the dress styles of pre-pubescent boys prior to about 1945: knee pants in baseball, North American football, golf (the "plus fours" that are now out of style); short pants in soccer, rugby, basketball, and ice hockey. Only in cricket and tennis have the athletes worn adult clothes, but these were the costume of the English gentleman on holiday: white pants and white shirts open at the neck.

22. Sports using small balls—baseball, tennis, cricket, golf—can be interrupted by rain but not necessarily by snow or cold temperatures. The Toronto Blue Jays home

opener (April 7, 1977) was played in a snow storm. The NHL Winter Classic and the NFL Super Bowl are played in outdoor stadiums in January, whatever the weather and the temperature.

23. David Young. *The Olympic Myth of Greek Amateur Athletics* (Chicago: Ares, 1985).

24. For example, the Duke of Gloucester in *King Lear* 1.1, speaking of his illegitimate son: "yet was his mother fair, there was good sport at his making."

25. Curiously, the fencing match that closes *Hamlet* is not referred to as "sport" but as "play." The equation of sport with hunting is a persistent one in English. W. A. Baillie-Grohman's *Sport in Art* (London: Ballantyne, 1913) consists almost exclusively of hunting scenes.

26. Elias and Dunningm *Quest for Excitement*, 110-111.

27. Many contemporary historians use the terms "modern sport" or "industrial sport" when discussing the emergence of new sporting forms in the late-eighteenth and nineteenth centuries. This common convention might avoid the concern raised here. Thank you to an anonymous reviewer for point this out.

28. Thomas Kyd, *The Works of Thomas Kyd*, ed. F. S. Boas (Oxford: Clarendon Press, 1901), 138, v. 134.

29. Edmund Spenser, *Poetical Works*, eds. J. C. Smith and E. de Selincourt (Oxford: Oxford University Press, 1970), 547;-48, vv. 73–84.

30. James I, "A Declaration Concerning Lawful Sports to Be Used," *Minor Prose Works*, eds. J. Craigie and A. Law (Edinburgh: Scottish Texts Society, 1982), 106.

31. Matthewe Walbancke, *Annalia dubrensia. Upon the yeerley celebration of Mr. Robert Dovers Olimpick Games upon Cotswold Hills* (London: Robert Raworth, 1636, facs. repr. Menston: Scolar Press, 1973), Joachim K. Rühl "Die 'Olympischen Spiele' Robert Dovers," *Annales Universitatis Saraviensis* 14 (Heidelberg: Carl Winter – Universitätsverlag, 1975), and Francis Burns "Robert Dover's Cotswold Olimpick Games: The Use of the Term 'Olimpick'," *Olympic Review* 210 (1985), 230–36.

32. Samuel Pepys, *Diary*, eds. R. Latham and W. Matthews, 11 vols. (Berkeley and Los Angeles: University of California Press, 1983).

33. John Dryden, *Vergil's Aeneid ... in the Dryden Translation*, ed. Howard Clarke (University Park and London: Pennsylvania State University Press, 1989).

34. Unless otherwise indicated, the written sources adduced in the remainder of this essay are set out in McClelland, *Mind and Body*, McClelland, "Ball Games," and John McClelland and Brain Merrilees S*port and Culture in Early Modern Europe* (Toronto: Centre for Reformation and Renaissance Studies, 2009). In addition, see Alessandro Arcangeli, *Recreation in the Renaissance* (New York: Palgrave Macmillan, 2003), Elisabeth Belmas, *Jouer Autrefois. Essais sur le jeu dans la France moderne (XVIe-XVIIIe siècle)* (Seyssel: Champ Vallon, 2006), and Alessandra Rizzi, *Statuta de ludo. Le leggi sul gioco nell'Italia di commune (secoli XIII-XVI)* (Treviso/Roma: Fondazione Benetton Studi Ricerche/Viella, 2012). The best pictorial sources are René d'Anjou, *Le livre des tournois du roi René*, eds. F. Avril et E. Pognon (Paris: Herscher, 1986), Alan Young, *Tudor and Jacobean Tournaments* (Dobbs Ferry, NY: Sheridan House, 1987), Richard Barber and Juliet Barker, *Tournaments: Jousts, Chivalry, and Pageants in the Middle Ages* (New York: Weidenfeld and Nicolson, 1989), Sydney Anglo, *The Martial Arts of Renaissance Europe* (New Haven, CT, and

London: Yale University Press, 2000), and Michael Flannery and Richard Leech, *Golf through the Ages: Six Hundred Years of Golfing Art* (Fairfield IA: Golf Links Press, 2004).

35. François Rabelais, *Gargantua*, 1534.

36. Pieter Bruegel, *Children's Games*, 1560, painting, Kunsthistorischesmuseum, Vienna.

37. For example, Bertrand During *Des jeux aux sports. Repères et documents en histoire des activités physiques* (Paris: Vigot, 1984).

38. McClelland, "Ball Games." In addition to the game contests there were also the non-contest sports: equestrian displays, horse vaulting, and acrobatics (the latter two were mostly performed by professional entertainers, but there is sporadic evidence of upper-class people also learning to do them).

39. Samuel Pepys reports that King Charles II lost as much as 4 ½ lbs. in afternoon of tennis. See Pepys, *Diary*, 8.419.

40. Sandra Schmidt . *Kopfübern und Luftspringen. Bewegung als Wissenschaft und Kunst in der Frühen Neuzeit* (Munich: Wilhelm Fink Verlag, 2008).

41. Dom Duarte, *Livro da ensinança de bem cavalgar toda sela* (1435).

42. In tennis, that is, *jeu de paume*, the game might be played with the hands alone or with a variety of paddles, bats, and racquets. Although in modern Italian *calcio* means soccer, in early modern times the word designated a distinctive game closer in style to rugby.

43. John McClelland, "Sport and Scientific Thinking in the Sixteenth Century: Ruling Out Playfulness," *Ludica, annali di storia e civiltà del gioco* 19–20 (2013–2014), 134–45.

44. On jousting injuries see Sébastien Nadot, *Le spectacle des joutes. Sport et courtoisie à la fin du Moyen Âge* (Rennes: Presses Universitaires de Rennes, 2012).

45. Jean-Michel Mehl *Les jeux au royaume de France du XIIIe au début du XVIe siècle* (Paris: Fayard, 1990).

46. *Pallone* was a precursor of volleyball.

47. Jean Froissart Œuvres*, ed. Kervyn de Lettenhove*, 25 vols. (Brussels: Victor Devaux, 1867-77), 14.253-69.

48. Jacques Ulmann has argued that morality is one of the defining elements of modern sport. See Jacques Ulmann, *De la gymnastique aux sports modernes* (Paris: Presses Universitaires de France, 1965).

49. Vigarello, *Passion Sport.*

50. Mehl, *Les jeux*; Belmas, *Jouer Autrefois.*

51. Pepys, *Diary*, 9.542.

52. Barber and Barker, *Tournaments*, 54.

53. Pepys, *Diary*, 6.3.

54. Flannery and Leech, *Golf through the Ages.*

55. Vigarello, *Histoire du corps*, 235.

56. Guttmann, *From Ritual to Record.*

57. Rühl, *Die "Olympischen Spiele" Robert Dovers.*

58. As Paul Dietschy has shown, it was still difficult to grasp in the late nineteenth century. See Paul Dietschy, *Histoire du football* (Paris: Perrin, 2010).

59. It is worth noting that the Department of Defense has used NFL games as recruitment venues. See Jared Dubin, "US Defense Department paid 14 NFL teams $5.4M to honor soldiers," *CBSSports.com*, last modified May 11, 2015, http://www.cbssports.com/nfl/eye-on-football/25181085/nfl-teams-received-54-million
  -from-defense-department-in-last-4-years.

60. Philippe Contamine, *War in the Middle Ages*, trans. Michael Jones (Oxford: Basil Blackwell, 1984), 254–55.

Chapter 6

The Impact of Mass Media on the Definition of Sport

Keith Strudler

In 1997, Rebecca Sealfon found herself a decorated championship figure on ESPN, at a point in the network's genesis that it already had requisite gravitas to make a sports star from what otherwise might be a mere mortal. Sealfon would, in later years, remain a well-known star, her victorious moments on the sports network replayed in perpetuity on the ubiquitous and asynchronous YouTube platform, where yesterday can truly be forever.[1]

This tale seems neither outstanding nor unfamiliar. In fact, it seems the now mundane process of creating athletic stars longitudinally is simply part of the circus that is "big time" sport, for lack of a clear delineation between professional and amateur. But Sealfon didn't play basketball, nor soccer, gymnastics, tennis, and certainly not the gender-stratified sport of football. The thirteen-year-old Sealfon spelled. More specifically, Sealfon won the 1997 Scripps Spelling Bee, which beginning in 1994 was broadcast on ESPN, a fairly rare departure at that point from the otherwise standard sporting fare of basketball, baseball, and assorted sports highlight programs.[2]

Sealfon's winning word was "euonym," which she spelled dramatically before jumping with elation. It was a celebration worthy of a World Series title, befitting of an event broadcast on the self-proclaimed worldwide leader of sports.

But was Sealfon a sports star? While nearly ridiculous in concept, today's spelling bee championship not only airs live in primetime on ESPN, but its climactic moments are featured prominently on the network's SportsCenter, likely in the notable "Top 10," where the day's star performers are recognized. Her victory, while excitable and tense, seemed to defy the key characteristic of all sporting definition—philosophical, sociological, or those borne in common sense. Yet, definitions and logic aside, for that particular moment in 1997, and in the ensuing years after, Seaflon would be a celebrated figure launched from a victorious moment on *the* American sports network. Scores of spellers—and video game players, Scrabble champions, and others on the edge of physicality, would find themselves on the inside of sports' great fishbowl—not as an outsider in a supporting role, like someone in the marching band—but as a featured star in the great drama known as sport.

This chapter will examine the meaning of sport from this very perspective. Specifically, how has the very meaning of this construct changed due to its symbiosis with mass media? While some may suggest that newspapers, radio, television, and their future incarnations simply covered sport, the vast industrial influence of this relationship may have done far more than amplify these leisurely pastimes. They may have changed their inherent meaning altogether, or at the very least created new interpretations of accepted definitions.

HISTORY OF SYMBIOSIS

While sport certainly outdates its mediated variant, the history of their partnership is long and robust. Newspapers and magazines began this symbiotic relationship, helping sports to become well known, quickly creating an industry of stars. As sport grew—in consort with industrialization, vibrant cities, and disposable time and income—so did its media coverage and capitalization. While sport used newspapers to promote its product, newspapers used sport to sell papers and advertising.[3] Sports such as baseball and college football catered to their journalistic peers in hope of growth and positive coverage. Newspapers understood the vast economic engine that could be sports reporting, as the constitution of their respective papers grew upward to 12 percent to 20 percent of all content devoted to sport by the 1920s[4]—a far cry from the highly politicized press of the 1800s, where journalistic muckraking, not hero building, was the worthy of print. Newspapers found a broadening middle-class readership—and even a working and lower class—through coverage of baseball, where the emergent profession of sports journalism fit well into newspaper's growth.[5]

Such turned some sporting properties into national phenomena with distinct brand properties. For example, college football was portrayed as tough and uniquely American, filled with American characters embellished by verbose and poetic sports journalists.[6] While the defining characteristics of the sports themselves may not have changed, their place in the social conscious did. Sport would become literally front page fare, or in the case of college football, the front porch of American universities.[7] The public would regard sport in a vastly different contextual regard, an evolution that changed sport, or at least certain sports, from activity to aspirational pursuit. Athletes would become not simply contestants, but rather essential figures in the hierarchy of American excellence.

This would only continue in greater earnest with the widespread development and proliferation of more immediate media. For example, radio literally brought sport and its players into homes while also creating a new economy around popular sporting fare. Such was clearly true for college football, where notable programs were rewarded handsomely for their broadcasts, while others languished in relative obscurity.[8] It would even help build the identity of entire programs, such as Notre Dame, which continued its quest toward America's Catholic University through widespread broadcast distribution of its football team's games.[9] Clearly, the development and wide distribution of television would solidify that relationship and help determine both the future and essence of major sport. Driven by football, but inevitably all major sports in the United States, sport largely could not exist in its current form without the support of television revenues.[10,11]

When professional football (the NFL and AFL) emerged as a televised sport in the 1960s, the symbiotic relationship between the leagues and networks allowed for concessions from sports leagues. This was true for virtually all televised sport, where game alterations included when games would be played, what types of surfaces they would be played upon, and many rule changes and accommodations to best suit the needs of a television audience.[12] Similar sporting adaptations have been made in other popular sports, such as the NBA with both its shot clock and three-point lines, both changes to the very nature of the sport to make it more exciting in the television age.[13] These developments continued further, when networks themselves "created" new sports, such as the X Games or ABC's Super Stars competition. Certainly, while these products seem to have the standard characteristics and defining qualities of sport, it's clear that they emanated from the needs of the media empires and the corporations that owned them. In other words, might they still be sport in the traditional sense? Perhaps. But clearly, the impact of media has changed the very nature of sport and often its genesis. Certainly, those impacts have important ramifications toward the essence, the meaning of sport itself, particularly for those with such symbiotic ties to the modern corporate media complex.

Further altering the nature of the relationship between sport and media was the widespread proliferation of cable sports television, most notably the 1979 launch of ESPN and its signature SportsCenter program, which used smart, edgy anchors to bring each day's sports highlights.[14] Among other things, the network (and later its family of networks, beginning with ESPN2) changed the way that the larger society viewed sports, bringing creativity and an emphasis on highlights (as opposed to longer form journalism and the games themselves) to the larger viewing public.[15] SportsCenter changed the way in which sport was consumed and understood—from whole parts and traditional highlights to exciting moments narrated by nearly comedic monologues. This shift certainly changed how fans viewed sports—and likely the amount and frequency of it as well. Such change in the American sports psyche over time would alter our perceptions of the games themselves, made clear by the frequency of press releases by colleges and high schools across the United States when one of their players was a part of SportsCenter's "Top 10" of the day.

While television has been and still remains an essential symbiotic economic partner in the vast sports enterprise, the digital landscape driven by Internet and mobile technology has further altered, increased, and individualized the world of sports media. Where sport was consumed in living rooms on increasingly flat screens, the infinite bandwidth and lowered barrier to broadcast has allowed for endless choice of sports consumption.[16] Networks—broadcast, cable, on-demand, broadband, and otherwise—broadcast to individual sports tastes, making each person's consumption habits vastly different than someone in their own house, much less across the country. Where networks often served as true agenda setters in determining what constituted sport (at least from a profitable corporate perspective), that determination is now left largely in the hands of an increasingly diverse and stratified viewing public. What sport is, for lack of better terminology, now is negotiated through the contours of a two-way flow of information. What once was football, basketball, and baseball, may now be far more.

This certainly doesn't even take into account the vast impact of user driven content platforms, such as YouTube, which both rebroadcasts, and some might say bastardizes the construct of sport itself as a viewable commodity. While much of YouTube's content comes directly from television itself, sports content is both selective and recontextualized through the editing process, altering its meaning and differentiating it from more standard media sports fare.[17] YouTube, even more than the typically frenetic sports television highlight programs, allows for sport to be reframed drastically, including the addition of sound and the selective choice of action. Additionally, it is inherently consumed asynchronously, allowing people to experience this individually at their leisure. YouTube sports clearly has relations to traditional sports media, but it is also distinct. Its version of sport is simply different than shown on television, and clearly different than what one would watch in person. It lacks the essence of sports, instead becoming simply a slice of athleticism set to sound. Such depiction brings to question the defining characteristics of sport itself, particularly as the use of YouTube (and other digital video platforms) continue to attract such large segments of the sports viewing populace.

SPORT AND GOALS

While it's clear that sport and media have become remarkably interwoven and that the influence of media has clear influence on particular sports and their rules, regulations, and norms, this doesn't inherently mean that the notion of sport itself has changed. What of Bernard Suits influential notion of the lusory attitude, accepting constitutive rules in order to maintain the notion and integrity of sport?[18] How might the influence of media alter or influence this essential concept? More importantly, has the influence of media changed the lusory attitude and lusory means toward goal achievement, altering the notion of what sport is?

Perhaps the answer to this lies deep in the inherent and evolving sense of goals and goal attainment manifest in the growth of sports media, where a massive entertainment complex has created an economy that has turned athletes, coaches, and sport administrators into millionaires and essential power brokers in and outside of the sports industry. For example, NBA mega star LeBron James was ranked second in the 2014 *Forbes* list of the world's most powerful celebrities.[19] The money professional athletes command off-the-court rival, and in many cases surpass what they can earn in the field of play. That would be particularly pronounced for Olympic athletes or those in that particular vein, as they can amass millions of dollars through a combination of winning, personality, and good fortune. An exemplar of this is history's most decorated Olympian Michael Phelps, who has earned approximately $55 million in endorsement revenue,[20] yet very little from swimming itself (the United States Olympic Committee pays a relatively nominal sum—in the thousands—for American gold medalists).[21] At some point, the attainment of revenue becomes far more appealing a goal than those seemingly inherent to the game itself. In fact, a potentially strong differentiator between amateur and professional sports is this particular goal, outcome, and assumed benefit from participation—the desire to make money, often as much as possible, as opposed to the more conventional goals of winning and fundamentally sound play.[22] Athletes in popular, mass-mediated and spectated sports play for different reasons to achieve different goals, even if those goals were never the genesis of the activity nor prescribed in the rule of the sport itself. Such would explain the veteran NFL player who sits out training camp, even an entire season, simply to generate a larger contract. One might expect, given a traditional reading of the goals, rules, and regulations of sport, that sitting on the sidelines would be counterintuitive to sport itself. Yet, in the context of professional sports, it is simply logical. The goals, and means of achieving them, have largely shifted. It is thus reasonable that, for those participating in well-funded professional sports, the pre-lusory goal of sport is fixated on financial gain, of which winning is simply a means to that achievement (or can be—as countless professional athletes have earned vast wealth despite never winning a professional championship of note). The lusory means, in this reading of sport, involve things that might otherwise seem grotesquely out of bounds, from sitting out games to choosing to play for an inferior team (with higher salary cap considerations). Defining sport becomes difficult when, dependent on the finances of its particular version (say, youth baseball vs. the Major Leagues), the means and goals are so vastly different and often distorted.

Of course, simply because athletes choose to maximize their salaries does not inherently change the meaning of sport itself. One might assume that the overall meaning of any individual sport (e.g. basketball) would be the same or relatively similar, whether rosters are complete with professional athletes or elementary school novices. Athletes participating in such fare must accept the requisite lusory means toward the pre-lusory goal, it would seem. However, the vast impact of mass media may have changed, or perhaps contextualized the very means toward goal attainment. Such might be best understood from the frame work of playoff NBA basketball, particularly a vital game filled with superstar athletes that drive ratings, advertising sales, and sponsorship revenues. In all regards, it is in the league and network's best fiscal interests to create meaningful entertainment fare that largely maintains and grows audience share, thus enhancing revenue potential, the most vital goal for continuation of the league.

To do this, certain "rules" might be negotiated, or situationally negotiated. For example, while basketball players and fans might fully accept and acknowledge the goal of trying to get the basketball into the basket without traveling with the ball. Yet in the NBA, it's widely accepted that athletes may in "travel" with the basketball, particularly such that it results in a sensational drive to the basket or helps increase scoring.[23] Further, it's possible that star players receive particularly favorable alterations of standard rules within the context of a particular game. It's been noted that in the NBA, star players are less likely to be assessed a foul than their non-star peers in a game in a loose ball situation, where both are scrambling for possession.[24] This dichotomy is particularly acute when a star player already has multiple fouls, meaning subsequent calls might result his ejection from the game (or at least predicating his spending additional time on the bench). Keeping star athletes in the game and able to play freely is accomplished by selectively and relatively altering lusory means, drastically altering the nature this particular sport. Referees are also likely to call fewer fouls toward the end of close games, not wanting to decide the outcome of the game.[25]

Due to the influence of corporate media, participants in sporting events may not inherently accept, nor need to accept particular rules in pursuit of goals, whatever those particular goals may be. Clearly, this changes any individual sport from its expected form. Televised, professional sport is different than other forms. But perhaps this changes the nature of sport itself. Perhaps it is not vital for all participants to accept lusory means, or at least not accept them all the time. Perhaps the influence of media has changed the very defining character of sport, such that lusory means are neither constant nor inherently proscribed, but rather a sociological artifact that alters with time, situation, and individual influence. Those adhering to Suits' definition may not agree with that malleable perspective on sport, but certainly the millions of sports fans who watch professional sports—virtually all of whom understand the changing nature of rules throughout the course of any game—would understand this quite simply.

INTERNALISM, EXTERNALISM, AND VALUES OF SPORT

Perhaps the reason many families promote sport to their children is because of the assumed positive values learned through participation.[26] For example, Stephen D. Keener, the president and chief executive of Little League International, noted that youth participants in baseball and softball can learn teamwork, shared goal attainment, leadership and sportsmanship, and how to handle both winning and losing.[27] These would be values that are essential not simply for sport itself, but rather ones that would be useful as children both progress through their adolescent development (school, relationship building, etc.) as well as their transition to productive adults. If one were to believe in these values, in many ways tenants of the functionalist sociological perspective of sport,[28] then dropout from organized youth sport—an increased problem as more children withdraw from traditional youth sports in current years than in past[29]—would be a detriment.

Similar arguments are made toward watching sports, particularly toward the worship of mass mediated sports heroes, positioned as one of the few spaces where the heroic archetype still exists.[30] This heroic figure has changed and transitioned due to the influences of media, but he (or to a lesser degree, she) has embodied important social values and cultural assumptions.[31] As politicians and other figures may have sunken from heroic consideration, American society in particular has continued its fascination with sports figures as heroes, those who can teach children means of functioning not simply in sport, but also in life. It is this thirst for perceived social values that has created legendary status for a handful of star athletes, including the recently retired baseball player Derek Jeter, who is widely regarded as a heroic figure that embodies important positive social values.[32] It's also likely why we feel betrayed when a heroic sports figure strays from this perceived value system, such as the case for New England Patriots Tom Brady for his suspected involvement in the so-called "Deflate-Gate" scandal allegedly involving improperly deflating footballs before an NFL playoff game.

This notion of relative rule structure, values, and ethics in the mediated sports landscape certainly create questions about sport, particularly mediated sport, and concepts of internalism and externalism. Those who promote the positive value system of sport might espouse internalism in sport, that sport can embody positive value systems unique to itself, perhaps values that can help spectators and participants create a moral system for dealing with ethical dilemmas in the real world.[33] This would stand in contrast to externalism, where sport simply reflects the value systems prevalent in society.[34] One can argue both for a variety of sports, and, dependent on particular value systems and the nature of the sport itself, both can be foundational for promoting positive ethical behaviors.

Yet what does the impact of mass media have on internalism and externalism in sport? Does it change the nature of sport and the ways in which values are part of sport itself? Perhaps it's worthwhile to consider the values of mediated sport against less publicized versions of the same sport. As discussed previously, financial gain is a primary goal and value of professional -mediated sport, as is individual fame and acknowledgment. These values aren't inherent to nor do they emanate specifically from the sport (say, basketball), but rather through sport's symbiotic tie to other corporate machines, including networks and corporate sponsors. The relationship between those entities has helped make the values of corporate society also the values of professional, mediated sport. Or, as members of the United States Olympic Basketball team showed in 1992 (also known as the Dream Team), the most important value in earning an Olympic gold medal was money, as Michael Jordan and several teammates ensured the medal ceremony didn't interfere with a longstanding profitable relationship with Nike.[35] Covering up a Reebok logo with an American flag that would be seen on global television would protect Jordan's (and others) financial interest, even if that largely defied the social norms of the Olympics.[36] In this regard, the influence of television seems to have ensured externalism in sport, where athletes simply amplify the prevailing value system at large, or as Olympic teammate Charles Barkley asserts (in a Nike commercial, no less), that he is in fact not a role model.[37]

Of course, externalism may not be the guiding truth for the game of basketball itself (nor other sports). One could argue that without television, without sponsors, and without the future promise of these, athletes like Jordan and Barkley would play a sport that embodies internalism. For example, take the convention of pick-up basketball. In that semiformal process where neither media nor corporate interests regulate behavior, players negotiate rules, fouls, and other standards to keep the game both fair and moving ahead.[38] In this regard, basketball, and sport has its own distinctive value system, one that could help both participants and observers to better ethically navigate the world around them. Where compromise, self-control, and accommodation may not fully be part of the larger value system of society, it very much is part of the working culture of pick-up basketball, a tenant of internalism in sport. Thus, it may not be the case that internalism nor externalism is true for sport. Instead, the influence of media and capitalism may change that very nature.

THE PLACE OF PHYSICAL EXERTION

Beyond the construct of values and capitalism, sports media has also potentially changed the very notion of sport and physical exertion. Loy,[39] Suits,[40] and many other philosophers, sociologists, and cultural critics have asserted the essence of physical activity as a key defining characteristic of sport. While it's certainly not the only quality of a sport, it is a vital one, keeping delineation between games and sport. Such defining characteristic is true for sociologists, a long list of whom historically have included physical exertion as part of the definition.[41] This would largely protect against items such as the aforementioned Spelling Bee or poker—two well-televised events on ESPN—from fitting into that definition.

Yet the continued influence of media, and potentially the fracturing of mediated viewership, seems to potentially alter that reality—or at least present a different version of it. ESPN created a bit of controversy when it recently began to regularly air video game tournaments on its ESPN2 television platform, even as the network's CEO declared it a competition, not a sport.[42] This comes in addition to their coverage of video games based on sports, such as the EA Sports's Madden video game. Controversy aside, ESPN (and other sports networks) have broadened their coverage beyond traditionally physical events, if they do embody other qualities of sport. Yes, they may not follow Suits' nor many other's definitions, but they appear on the world's most powerful sports television empire, often retain essential characteristics of philosophical and sociological definitions of sport, and command relatively large spectatorships, at least in the niche driven world of modern sports media.

In fact, understanding the role of physical exertion in the multimedia sports age may be futile, if not impossible. Years ago, ESPN decided on wide spread coverage of bass fishing tournaments, building on the success of televising NASCAR.[43] This agreement was built on the growing capitalization of outdoor activities—such as fishing—and their potential for advertising revenues.[44] Again, it's financial gain, not athletic ones, that seemingly determine sporting culture. Drawing hard lines around sport and its definition based on the amount of exertion and complexity of skill may be every so increasingly difficult. Checking the TV listing—and the day's SportsCenter Top 10—may be increasingly more consistent and genuine.

CONCLUSION

Sport is, by all regards, a socially constructed and defined construct. Despite the length of its existence, we have long negotiated its constitution, its rules, and certainly its participants. In fact, anyone watching the original Modern Olympic Games of 1896, much less the Ancient Games of thousands of years prior, would concede the notion of sport then was vastly different than that of today. Such is dictated by countless social institutions, ranging from demographic shifts to changing gender norms to medical technology. Yet nothing has impacted sport in that time period more than the vast enterprise of corporate media. Through its symbiotic growth, sport and its very defining character may have changed. At the very least, the definition seems far more open to relative interpretation, particularly for those sports at the forefront of fame and wealth.

Perhaps that has shifted the locust of control to a small group of very powerful individuals. Whereas sport was perhaps once overseen by school and local administrators, now the control has shifted toward those both overseeing vast media enterprises, professional league administrators, and even top professional athletes. In fact, of *Sports Illustrated*'s 2013 list of the most powerful people in sports, five of the top seven were either league commissioners or network president/CEOs.[45] While it may not be proscribed in their considerable contracts, certainly it is within the framework of their highly consolidated power to not only produce and broadcast sport, but also to somewhat dictate its very essence.

But what of Rebecca Sealfon, the thirteen-year-old who in 1997 won a spelling bee—the spelling bee—on ESPN? Was Sealfon an athlete, and is competitive spelling a sport? In a word, p-e-r-h-a-p-s.

NOTES

1. Heiten Samtani, "A Spelling Champ Whose E-U-O-N-Y-M Should Have Been 'Joy,'" *WNYC*, last modified March 23, 2015, http://www.wnyc.org/story/302349-a-spelling-champ-whose-e-u-o-n-y-m-should-have-been-joy/.

2. "History," *National Spelling Bee*, http://spellingbee.com/history.

3. Robert W. McChestney, "Media Made Sport: A History of Sports Coverage in the United States," in *Media, Sports, and Society*, ed. Lawrence A. Wenner (New York: SAGE Publications, Inc., 1989), 57.

4. Jennings Bryant and Andrea M. Holt, "A Historical Overview of Sports and Media in the United States," in *Handbook of Sports Media*, eds. Arthur A Raney and Jennings Bryant (Mahwah, NJ: Lawrence Erlbaum, 2006), 37.

5. Jon Enriquez, "Coverage of Sports," in *American Journalism: History, Principles, Practices*. ed. W. David Sloan and Lisa Mullikin Parcell (Jefferson, NC: McFarland, 2002), 199.

6. Michael Oriard, *King Football: Sport and Spectacle in the Golden Age of Radio and Newsreels, Movies and Magazines, the Weekly and the Daily Press* (Chapel Hill: University of North Carolina Press, 2001), 28.

7. "College Sports 101," *The Knight Commission on Intercollegiate Athletics,* 2009 http://www.knightcommission.org/collegesports101/table-of-contents.

8. Ronald A. Smith, *Play-by-Play: Radio, Television, and Big Time College Sport* (Baltimore, MD: Johns Hopkins Press, 2001), 30.

9. Ibid., 35–36.

10. Robert V. Bellamy, Jr., "Professional Sports Organizations: Media Strategies," in *Media, Sports, and Society,* ed. Lawrence A. Wenner (Newbury Park, CA: Sage, 1989), 120.

11. John A. Fortunato, "The NBA Strategy of Broadcast Television Exposure: A Legal Application," *Fordham Intellectual Property, Media and Entertainment Law Journal* 12, no. 1 (2001): 135.

12. David B. Sullivan, "Broadcast Television and the Game of Packaging Sports," in *Handbook of Sports Media,* eds. Arthur A Raney and Jennings Bryant (Mahwah, NJ: Lawrence Erlbaum, 2006), 137.

13. Justin Kubatko, "Keeping Score: The Story Arc of the 3-Point Shot," Off the Dribble Blog, last modified February 10, 2011, http://offthedribble.blogs.nytimes.com/2011/02/10/keeping-score-the-story-arc-of-the-3-point-shot/.

14. Bryant and Holt, "A Historical Overview of Sports and Media in the United States," 37.

15. Rudy Martzke and Reid Cherner, "After 25 Years, ESPN Still Channels How to View Sports," *USA Today,* last modified August 17, 2004, http://usatoday30.usatoday.com/sports/2004-08-17-espn-25-years_x.htm.

16. Jeff MacGregor, "Everything Everywhere All at Once," *ESPN,* last modified May 24, 2003, http://espn.go.com/espn/story/_/id/9308052/never-easier-follow-niche-sports.

17. Markus Staff, "Sports on YouTube," in *The YouTube Reader,* eds. P. Snickars and P. Vonderau (Stockholm: National Library of Sweden, 2009).

18. Bernard Suits, "The Elements of Sport," in *The Philosophy of Sport: A Collection of Original Essays,* ed. Robert G. Osterhoudt. (Springfield, IL: Charles C Thomas, 1973), 50. Suits' definition of sport is widely influential and has spurred a large literature that expands, criticizes, and responds to Suits' definition. See Chad Carlson, "A Three-Pointer: Revisiting Three Crucial Issues in the "Tricky Triad" of Play, Games, and Sport" in this volume.

19. Kurt Badenhausen, "LeBron James Tops World's Most Powerful Athlete 2014," *Forbes,* last modified June 30, 2014, http://www.forbes.com/sites/kurtbadenhausen/2014/06/30/lebron-james-tops-worlds-most-powerful-athletes-2014/.

20. Justin Moyer, "Why Michael Phelps Can't Be the Man We Want Him to Be," *Washington Post,* last modified October 1, 201, http://www.washingtonpost.com/news/morning-mix/wp/2014/10/01/why-michael-phelps-cant-be-the-man-we-want-him-to-be/.

21. Chris Smith, "U.S. Athletes Already Owed $240,000 In Olympic Medal Bonuses," *Forbes,* last modified February 6, 2014, http://www.forbes.com/sites/chrissmith/2014/02/16/u-s-athletes-already-owed-240000-in-olympic-medal-bonuses.

22. Anthony Laker, *Sociology of Sport and Physical Education: An Introductory Reader* (New York: Routledge, 2001), 5.

23. "NBA to Alter Traveling Rules," *ESPN*, last modified October 16, 2009, http://sports.espn.go.com/nba/news/story?id=4563546.

24. Tobias Moskowitz and L. Jon Wertheim, *Scorecasting: The Hidden Influences Behind How Sports Are Played and Games Are Won* (New York: Crown Publishing, 2011), 21.

25. Ibid., 25.

26. Mark H. Anshel, *Sport Psychology: From Theory to Practice* (San Francisco: Benjamin Cummings, 2003), 349.

27. Steven D. Keener, "Sports Teach Kids Valuable Lessons," *New York Times*, last modified October 10, 2013, http://www.nytimes.com/roomfordebate/2013/10/10/childrens-sportslife-balance/sports-teach-kids-valuable-lessons.

28. Laker, *The Sociology of Sports and Physical Education*, 9–10.

29. Steven J. Overman, *The Youth Sports Crisis: Out-of-Control Adults, Helpless Kids* (Santa Barbara,CA: ABC-CLIO, 2014), 149.

30. Daniel Boorstin, *The Image: A Guide to Pseudo-Events in America* (New York: Atheneum, 1978).

31. Leah R. Vande Berg, "The Sports Hero Meets Mediated Celebrityhood," in *MediaSport*, ed. Lawrence A. Wenner (New York: Routledge, 1998), 153.

32. Paul White, "Why Derek Jeter Remains Admired after So Many Years," *USA Today*, last modified September 10, 2014, http://www.usatoday.com/story/sports/mlb/2014/09/09/derek-jeter-appreciation/15354565/.

33. Robert L. Simon, *Fair Play: The Ethics of Sport, 3rd Edition* (Boulder, CO: Westview Press, 2010), 46. There is a large literature in the philosophy of sport on the nature of internalism and externalism. See Francisco Javier López Frías, "Broad Internalism and Interpretation: A Plurality of Interpretivist Approaches" in this volume.

34. Ibid, 46.

35. Mike Littewin, "Jordan Hid Allegiance under Flag, Cover-up Discloses Nike Won Shoe War," *Baltimore Sun*, last modified August 9, 1992, http://articles.baltimoresun.com/1992-08-09/sports/1992222100_1_reebok-nike-jordan-put.

36. See Heather L. Reid, "Defining Olympic Sport" in this volume.

37. Newsweek Staff, "I'm Not a Role Model," *Newsweek*, last modified June 27, 1993, http://www.newsweek.com/im-not-role-model-193808.

38. Thomas McLaughlin, *Give and Go: Basketball as a Cultural Practice* (Albany: State University of New York Press, 2008), 200–201.

39. John W. Loy, "The Nature of Sport: A Definitional Effort," *Quest* 10, no. 1 (1968): 6.

40. Suits, "The Elements of Sports."

41. Tim Delaney and Tim Madigan, *The Sociology of Sports: An Introduction* (Jefferson, North Carolina: McFarland & Company, 2009), 12.

42. Nick Schwartz, "ESPN People Are Freaking Out Because ESPN Televised eSports," *USA Today*, last modified April 26, 2015, http://ftw.usatoday.com/2015/04/espn-esports-heroes-of-the-dorm-reaction. See also Joey Gawrysiak, "Video Games as Sport" in this volume.

43. Bill Sargent, "ESPN Bets Bass Fishing Is TV Hit," *Florida Today*, October 30, 2005.

44. Sally Beatty, "ESPN Buys Assets of Bass Fishing Organization," *Wall Street Journal*, April 5, 2001.

45. "SI's 50 Most Powerful People in Sports," *Sports Illustrated*, last modified March 6, 2013, http://www.si.com/more-sports/photos/2013/03/06/50-most-powerful -people-sports.

Part 2

BORDERLINE CASES

Chapter 7

Borderline Cases

CrossFit, Tough Mudder, and Spartan Race

Pam R. Sailors, Sarah Teetzel, and Charlene Weaving

In this chapter, we analyze the new emerging popular "fitness" trends of CrossFit, Tough Mudder, and Spartan Race to determine whether these borderline cases ought to be classified as sports. All three activities involve an extensive militaristic rhetoric and are practiced by "weekend warriors" and some elite athletes alike. The events are popular in North America, Europe, and Australia. In examining the three activities, we analyze them in conjunction with Bernard Suits' argument that sports are games plus the addition of four additional characteristics: (1) the involvement of skills; (2) the skills must be physical; (3) a wide following of the game must exist around the world; and (4) the following is persistent and stable rather than a fad.[1] To do so, we evaluate the rules set by each event's organizing body to determine whether the events should be categorized as sports.

The roots of many current fitness trends can arguably be found in the invention of parkour by Georges Hebert at the turn of the twentieth century. Hebert sought to develop obstacle course training for the French military,[2] and his influence can be found not only in current forms of parkour but in several other similar events that have sprung up through the years. For example, pitched more as a comedic spectacle for a television audience, "WipeOut," billing itself as the "world's largest obstacle course," began in 2008, and features average people taking spectacular falls on oversize playground-like obstacles.[3] "American Ninja Warrior" debuted in 2009, and may be described as the athletic version of "WipeOut," featuring an obstacle course so daunting that only very few people in the world have ever successfully completed.[4] What these events have in common is the integration of skills that push the boundaries of traditional sports or stem from obstacle course training. In this paper, we focus our attention on three specific events: (1) CrossFit, (2) Tough Mudder, and (3) Spartan Race.

CROSSFIT: BEING WEAK IS A CHOICE

CrossFit was developed in the 1990s by Greg Glassman and is promoted as a physical exercise philosophy *and* as a competitive sport. The exercises generally involve high intensity interval training, plyometrics, and strongmen-like tasks, or "constantly varied functional movement, executed at high intensity, across broad time and modal domains."[5] The idea is to switch up or *cross* exercises. According to the CrossFit website:

> CrossFit begins with a belief in fitness. The aim of CrossFit is to forge a broad, general and inclusive fitness. We have sought to build a program that will best prepare trainees for any physical contingency—not only for the unknown, but for the unknowable . . . We have a worldwide network of more than 5,500 affiliated gyms and more than 35,000 accredited CrossFit Level 1 trainers. And, we have created the Sport of Fitness, known as the CrossFit Games, where we crown the Fittest Man and Woman on Earth.[6]

CrossFit involves group exercises, in classes, where the workout in and of itself is a type of competition. Specifically, participants engage in time trials trying to complete the "Workout of the Day" (W.O.D.s) faster than their other competitors. Due to the extreme nature of the CrossFit movement, it has faced considerable criticism.

Journalist Cliff Weathers describes the CrossFit "sports-fitness" brand as a cult and likens it to a Navy SEAL physical training exercise.[7] Heather Havrilesky, a writer for the *New York Times,* rhetorically questioned why a group of CrossFit participants swinging sledgehammers over their shoulders wouldn't join a roofing crew for the day instead.[8] Havrilesky argues that CrossFit represents an extreme form of exercise:

> Extreme this, extreme that. Another attempt to void inner emptiness and numbness brought on by a vapid culture—another way to live in anything but the now. . . . The whole notion of pushing your physical limits—popularized by early Nike ads, Navy SEAL mythos and Lance Armstrong's cult of personality—has attained a religiosity that's as passionate as it is pervasive. . . . And as with most of sports culture, there is no gray area. You win or you lose. You leave it all on the floor or you shamefully skulk off the floor with extra gas in your tank.[9]

A blogger for the *New York Times*, Christie Aschwanden, notes that the W.O.D.s intensity and lack of rest in between activities fit with "CrossFit's unofficial mascot, Pukey the Clown."[10] Ashwanden describes CrossFit as a cultural identity embraced by its participants, whose view of themselves is changed by their immersion into the rituals of CrossFit. In reviewing

J.C. Hertz's book, *Learning to Breathe Fire: The Rise of CrossFit and the Primal Future of Fitness*, which includes stories of participants whose lives have been completely reshaped (both literally and figuratively) since joining CrossFit, Ashwanden adds a cautionary note. As she explains, the only references for the impressive claims of dramatic results Herz describes are articles from the organization's own publication, the *CrossFit Journal*.[11]

Outside of the informal competition between participants in daily W.O.D.s, the CrossFit Games occur yearly. The CrossFit Games website proclaims, "They are world-renowned as a grueling test for the world's toughest athletes and a thrilling experience for spectators."[12] Since its inception in 2007, the CrossFit Games have become "one of the fastest growing sports in America," according to *Forbes*.[13] The website further states that the Games were created to fill a void because no other test of physical fitness exists: "From Ironman triathlons to the NFL, all other athletic events neglected to accurately test fitness. Even decathlons, while testing a relatively wide range of abilities, missed vital components of physical fitness."[14] Finally, the website boasts that they have surpassed 10,000 affiliates, more gyms than the number of Little Caesar's pizzerias in America.[15] In 2013, over 138,000 people registered for the CrossFit Games, which was a 100 percent increase from 2012.[16] Participants are required to follow specific rules to compete at the CrossFit Games, which ESPN2 broadcasts, including abiding by an anti-doping policy. The drug testing process is clearly laid out and a list of prohibited and banned substances is provided to participants.[17]

The actual competition events change yearly. According to 2014 female champion, Camille Leblanc-Bazinet,

> The person who wins is the person who does statistically best overall. So, for example, this year our first event was 1,000 yards of swimming in the ocean with huge waves and then kettlebell squats with burpees. Then you have another event, you need to do squats with a bar overhead with the most amount of weight. Another event is running and then you have to do pull-up. They really try to test everything.[18]

Interestingly, when asked if she thought CrossFit was changing how individuals view women's fitness, Leblanc-Bazinet noted that women are proud of being strong, a view that aligns with the marketing trend "strong is the new skinny."[19] Consequently, there are opportunities for women to experience empowerment in CrossFit that they may not find in other traditional activities like aerobic fitness classes.[20]

W.O.D.s are given creative names such as "Bad Karma," "Jonesworthy," "Nasty Girls," "Tabata This," and "Filthy Fifty." In 2005, Glassman began naming W.O.D.s after fallen military and police service members who were killed in the line of duty.[21] Expanding on this in a 2013 article, Eric Lemay argues that CrossFit perfectly reflects the current environment of American militarism:

> As long as there's been political philosophy, there have been ideas about how to train for war. Socrates sounds something like a CrossFitter in Plato's *Republic* when he discusses the needs of soldiers, making a distinction between "warrior athletes" and "ordinary athletes." The problem, he claims, is that ordinary athletes are crippled by their monotonous training routines. . . . Ordinary athletes can't deviate, can't adapt. And that's exactly what soldiers need to do. For Socrates, warrior athletes should be "like wakeful dogs," ready.[22]

Through its inclusion of military rhetoric and metaphors, CrossFit appeals to a wide range of individuals, from "weekend warriors" to "hard-core" athletes, their tastes and beliefs shaped by a view of the world as an unsafe war zone. Nevertheless, the relationship between CrossFit and the military doesn't sit well with everyone:

> One piece of the brand identity that never sat well with me was Crossfit's identification with the military. The central website regularly features photos of military personnel; in discussing "types" of Crossfitters "tactical athlete"— denoting military or police personnel—is commonly listed alongside "sports athletes," "casual athletes" and so on; uniformed service personnel—including police and fire—receive discounted memberships; and the hardest workouts are "Hero WODs" named for deceased military personnel who were Crossfitters.[23]

We mention the military rhetoric that surrounds CrossFit because it helps contextualize the movement's wide following and popularity. Sport and militarism have a long intertwined history, and CrossFit, despite emerging only in the 1990s, has a significant military influence similar to other traditional mainstream sports like rugby.

TOUGH MUDDER: A QUICK AND MUDDY HISTORY

The beginning of the obstacle racing trend dates back to January 1987, when William Wilson, often known as Mr. Mouse, organized the inaugural Tough Guy race in England. The race, which billed itself as "The Safest Most Dangerous Event in the World," began as a cross-country race with a few obstacles and has grown each year. Harvard Business School student Will Dean visited Wilson in 2008 and pitched the idea of expanding Tough Guy internationally. Soon after, in May 2010, Dean directed his first obstacle race in the United States, the Tough Mudder. Realizing that the race was remarkably similar to Tough Guy, Wilson sued Dean, claiming that Dean had appropriated the format and design of Tough Guy. After a long and ugly court battle, Wilson agreed to accept a $725,000 settlement from Dean.[24]

Dean adamantly emphasizes that Tough Mudder is *not* a race; there is no timing and there are no results. If a participant fails to complete an obstacle, or chooses to skip one altogether, there is no penalty. This is very different from other obstacle races where the goal is to finish the event first, either individually or as part of a team. Dean's Tough Mudder describes itself as "probably the toughest event on the planet."[25] The courses are typically ten to twelve miles of military-inspired obstacles, originally designed by the British Special Forces, which are run in mud. Events now take place in Canada, the United States, the United Kingdom, Australia, and New Zealand. Tough Mudder's website describes marathons as "boring," adding: "Road-running may give you a healthy set of lungs, but will leave you with as much upper body strength as Keira Knightley."[26] It is considered a fast growing athletic activity and is marketed, as noted, as a challenge and team-building event rather than as a race. In 2013, "more than seven hundred thousand people paid around a hundred and fifty dollars each for the privilege of suffering through a Tough Mudder," resulting in over $115 million of revenue for the company. [27]

Tough Mudder perpetuates the need and desire to be tough. For example, the website notes that participants deserve to drink beer, but first they must earn it. Tough Mudder also highlights the importance of training entrenched with this ideal, "Before you sign up for another BS juice cleanse or Squats & Milk, set yourself a real goal. It'll be hard to sit around in your sweatpants eating cereal and watching 'something that definitely isn't porn', when you're preparing for ten miles and twenty obstacles."[28] Moreover, before each race, the national anthem is played and Mudders take the Mudder Pledge:

> I understand that Tough Mudder is not a race but a challenge.
> I put teamwork and camaraderie before my course time.
> I do not whine—kids whine.
> I help my fellow mudders complete the course.
> I overcome all fears.[29]

The appeal of this culture is not limited to men. Lizzie Widdicombe, a journalist for the *New Yorker*, describes her first experience in a Tough Mudder race, noting:

> Things were good. Trail running isn't so bad! I thought, for the first time in my athletic career. Then, at a bend in the path, I heard whoops, and blood-curdling screams. It sounded like a village being attacked by marauding barbarians. In a clearing in the woods were two metal dumpsters, each eight feet wide and thirty feet long, filled with nine thousand gallons of melting ice, mixed with mud, to create a near-freezing slush. Ladders were propped up against the sides of them, and young people were lining up to jump in, as spectators cheered.[30]

Tough Mudder has cleverly crafted names for each obstacle, like the Fire Walker—a run through burning firewood, and Electroshock Therapy—where people dash through dangling wires that deliver ten-thousand-volt electric shocks. With respect to the longevity of the Tough Mudder, Widdicombe suspects that as long as there is a need for males to be macho and prove their manliness, the Tough Mudder will continue.[31]

SPARTAN RACE: NO HOLDING HANDS HERE

Since 2010, Tough Mudder's main competitor has been the Spartan Race. Originally designed by the United States military as obstacle courses, Spartan Races vary in length from the Spartan Sprint (3-plus miles, 20-plus obstacles) to the Spartan Beast (13-plus miles, 30-plus obstacles), and the Spartan Beast and Ultra Beast (26-plus miles, 60-plus obstacles), which ESPN describes as a "true test of will."[32] Spartan Race presents itself as the toughest of the obstacle races. The company emphasizes that you will be "ranked, timed, and judged."[33] Joe De Sena, Spartan's founder, a former Wall Street trader, contrasts his event with Tough Mudder's form of "instant gratification," which he attributed to "the softening of America, to every-child-gets-a-trophy, to noncompetitive events, where there's no timing and it's just about holding hands."[34]

Unlike the Tough Mudder, which does not feature an overall winner, since 2011 a World Championship Spartan Race has taken place. The fall 2015 World Championship was contested in Lake Tahoe. It featured two days of competition with 10,000 participants and was filmed by NBC Sports.[35] De Sena notes he would like to see the Spartan Race become an Olympic event by 2020, or at least by 2024.[36] Obstacle course activities and names in the Spartan races echo historical mythological athletic prowess such as a fire jump, a Herculean foist, spear throw, and a Tyrolean traverse. However, as with the Tough Mudder and CrossFit fitness pursuits, it is not clear that competitions of this nature should be considered sports. Now that these three borderline cases of activities have been described, the next step toward assessing whether they are sports is to engage in some conceptual clarification to determine the category to which each belongs. To do so, we will examine definitions of sport found in the philosophy of sport literature.

DEFINING SPORT

In examining each of the above activities, we have focused on some of the key rules and eligibility criteria associated with each one. A central tenet of sport is the participants' agreement to accept the rules to allow the contest to occur. As philosopher Graham McFee contends, "one feature of modern sports, marking them out from folk games, was the use (or presence) of a codified system of rules."[37] The rules of many sports emerged in eighteenth-century England when the standardization of rules transformed spontaneous play into games, and the subsequent growth of competition encouraged the formation of standardized rules.[38] Simple athletic events and blood sports, such as cockfighting, required rules to govern the competition after the popularity of events grew to the point where social conventions required specification. According to historian Wray Vamplew: "Claims that 'my horse or messenger is faster than yours,' 'my bodyguard is tougher than yours' or simply 'I'm better at this game than you' inevitably led to stake-money challenges. Once this occurred, then rules had to be formalized to determine how the contest would be organized and decided."[39] With higher stakes involved, a demand grew to establish standardized rules for events to prevent cheating.[40] While gambling influenced the development of systems of rules, other social, economic, and political factors also contributed to rule development in sport.

Contributing factors included participants' and organizers' expectations of fair play and their desire to ensure their opponents followed the rules. The development of technologies also helped develop systems of rules because competitors needed to know whether new innovations were permissible or banned.[41] By the 1820s, governing bodies for several modern sports had been formed.[42] The distribution of rulebooks to different geographical areas allowed the same version of sports to be played in national and international competitions. Shared understanding of what the event involves and how winners and losers are decided is an essential component of an activity fitting into the category of sport. The importance of rules in sport is highlighted in philosopher Jim Parry's explanation that, "the first task of an international federation, for example, is to clarify rules and harmonize understandings so as to facilitate the universal practices of its sport."[43]

Attempts to define sports often start with Bernard Suits' widely influential definition of games, which includes four necessary and sufficient conditions.[44] According to Suits:

> To play a game is to engage in activity directed toward bringing about a specific states of affairs, using only means permitted by specific rules, where the means permitted by rules are more limited in scope than they would be in the absence of rules, and where the sole reason for accepting such limitation is to make possible such activity.[45]

Four elements of games are found in Suits' definition: (1) the goal, (2) the means one can use to achieve the goal, (3) the rules of the game, and (4) the attitude players must adopt, which is known as a lusory attitude.[46]

Philosophers of sport have given considerable attention to distinguishing games and sport with the debate centering on whether all sports are games. Stemming from his conception of games, Suits posited sports involve the same four elements of games with the addition of four additional requirements: (1) the involvement of skills; (2) the skills must be physical; (3) a wide following of the game must exist around the world; and (4) the following is persistent and stable rather than a fad.[47] While subsequent critics have contended that definitions of sport based on Suits' criteria may be too vague or too ambiguous, too narrow or too broad, and may lack internal consistency,[48] definitions of sports and games stipulated by Suits are accepted by the majority of sport philosophers worldwide and what we will use in our analysis of fitness trends moving forward. To begin analyzing whether emerging fitness activities should be viewed as sports, an examination of the rules of these activities is necessary. Emphasis is placed on clarifying rules because rules "define particular sporting activities, and collectively contribute much to saying what sport in general is."[49] To introduce a new sport to a population, the rules in force should be clear and just, and not discriminate against participants. Rule-based definitions of sport often divide rules into the subcategories of constitutive rules, regulative rules, and auxiliary rules.[50]

Briefly, constitutive rules, which define a game and distinguish a particular game from other games, enable a game or sport to occur. This type of rule provides the conceptual framework to make sense of the sport or game and explains how competitors win.[51] Philosopher Warren Fraleigh points out, "constitutive rules specify in advance the special area of the sports contest, its duration, the specific state of affairs to be achieved by contestants or the prelusory goal, and the means used to achieve that goal, or lusory means."[52] The rules that specify the penalties that participants face as a consequence of violating a constitutive rule are known as the regulative rules, which regulate advantages that athletes may seek to obtain by directly or indirectly violating constitutive rules.[53] For example, in the Spartan Race, participants must do burpees if they fail to complete an obstacle before they can proceed.[54]

A third category of rules, known as auxiliary rules, set limits on who can participate and under what conditions, thereby imposing eligibility standards and pre- and post-event requirements.[55] These rules "specify a number of extra-lusory requirements that reveal certain aspects of the institution governing the game or the milieu in which the game takes place."[56] Examples of auxiliary rules include rules related to: safety concerns; exposure to physical stress; empirical classifications such as age, sex, and weight; arbitrary restrictions implemented for social and political reasons; deliberate exclusions of groups or nations; limits on numbers of participants; uniform regulations; professional or amateur status; training hours or techniques; and, banned substances and methods.[57] Rules of this nature can be considered "the law of the sports associations"[58] because they are set by each governing body to match its values and preferences. This category of rules often has direct implications for equity and inclusion as it focuses on eligibility, so it is of particular importance in our analysis of emerging fitness trends.

To function optimally, rules must apply to all competitors equitably and impartially, and the codification of a sport's constitutive, regulative, and eligibility rules contribute to creating universality and impartiality. For this reason alone, the rules of recent fitness activities require scrutiny. According to Vamplew, "There is nothing in the nature of sport itself that determines who can and cannot play. In the purest form of sport only self-exclusion should apply. . . . Exclusion is a cultural creation specific to sports in a certain domain at a particular time."[59] When sports were developing, and systems of rules were being put in place, most rule makers and participants were white, male members of the aristocracy who practiced sports in private, members-only clubs. The majority of sport-governing organizations that emerged were far from inclusive and democratic, and membership was often contingent upon the athlete being a member of the 'appropriate' gender, race, and social class.[60] An ethos-based approach to sport acknowledges the conventions and norms associated with the playing of the game in a specific area.[61] While the letter of the rule expresses in an explicit manner the substance of the rule, the spirit of the rule, on which an ethos approach is based, "is the reason why the rule makers made that particular rule a constitutive rule."[62] The spirit of a rule incorporates the principles that motivate the rule.[63] A danger of an ethos-based approach to sport is the possibility of a society condoning activities that permit, for example, racism, sexism, homophobia, or harm to participants. Having laid out approaches and associated dangers, we now apply the framework to our three borderline cases: CrossFit, Tough Mudder, and Spartan Race.

SPORTING APPLICATION

Suits' work on games and sport provides a framework by which the borderline cases described earlier may be evaluated. First, the four elements of games must be present: there must be a goal, acceptable means to achieve the goal, rules, and a lusory attitude held by the players. The lusory attitude entails a spirit of competition, which Suits makes explicit in defining sports as "competitive events involving a variety of physical (usually in combination with other) human skills, where the superior participant is judged to have exhibited those skills in a superior way."[64] This connection of competitiveness to the lusory attitude is clear if we imagine a case in which an athlete fails to put forth his or her best effort in an attempt to win. In such a case, the athlete would be condemned for having the wrong attitude. The wrongness of the attitude is that it is non-lusory.[65] Further, sports must involve physical skills and there must be a persistent and stable following of the game around the world. If we apply these criteria to the cases under consideration, we see that none fares very well. We begin with the case that should least likely be considered a sport, and end with the case that has elements that more closely resemble the necessary and sufficient conditions of sport.

Tough Mudder has a goal: participants seek to travel from point A to point B, encountering obstacles along the way. There are specified means by which to achieve that goal: on foot, with assistance as needed from others. However, the participants lack the lusory attitude—since Tough Mudder is noncompetitive—and, arguably, the activity lacks regulative rules, since there are no penalties for failing to complete obstacles. As Herz explains, "Finish time is completely beside the point. What's important is the dramatic intensity and social bonding of the event, the laugh-about-it-later, we're-in-it-togetherness of the suck."[66] The event requires skills that are physical, so it passes on that account, and it boasts a wide following—people participate in it, at least, even though they don't follow results (since there aren't any) or show up to buy tickets to spectate. Given these limitations, we can conclude that Tough Mudder is *not* a sport.

Similarly, Spartan Race has a goal (travel from point A to B, completing obstacles along the way), means (on foot, without assistance), rules (participants have to do burpees as a penalty for failing to complete obstacles), and the appropriate lusory attitude (as Spartan Race is a competitive event that produces a winner). It involves physical skills and currently has the same sort of following as Tough Mudder. However, Spartan Race's aspirations to Olympic status, following in the model of triathlon, distinguish it from Tough Mudder, which has no such stated aspiration. In fact, Spartan Race has already taken steps toward that goal, creating the United States Obstacle Course Racing organization (USOCR) in 2014 to sanction and insure races now and provide ranking services in the future. In the same year, the International Obstacle Course Racing Federation was founded with the mission of promoting obstacle course racing and work toward making it an Olympic sport.[67] Thus, while Spartan Race does not meet the criteria for a sport at present, because it fails on the institutional requirement, it is moving in that direction and would seem likely to attain that status in the not-too-distant future.

Finally, CrossFit, at least in its usual incarnation, has two of Suits' goals, the noncompetitive goal of completing the day's W.O.D. and specified means to accomplish it, distinguishing between doing the W.O.D. "as prescribed" or "scaled" (modified for those who cannot manage it as prescribed). But there are no rules in the sense that CrossFitters will not be removed from the workout if they fail to follow the W.O.D. specifications exactly, and the lusory attitude is decidedly absent, since CrossFit emphasizes its supportive, rather than competitive, environment. Even when Pukey the Clown is in the gym, so to speak, it's because participants push themselves to better their own previous performances, not to best their fellow CrossFitters. Participants need not engage in competitors with anyone but themselves. It certainly involves physical skills, and enjoys wide participation, but it does not yet have a stable following and the continued duration of its popularity remains in question. Much of this changes, however, if the focus switches from everyday CrossFit to the annual CrossFit Games, which have goals, specified means, rules, and the appropriate competitive attitude. Also, the Games involve physical skills and enjoy a wide following, although as the first rendition did not take place until 2007 there is not enough history to be able to judge the persistence and stability of that following.

To the contrary, in discussing CrossFit and injuries, Herz argues that CrossFit is a sport, but she bases this conclusion on a dubious distinction between fitness and sport. For Herz, sports offer "the experience of team play, the development of coordination, and the acquisition of strength and skill," while fitness is about "trying to forestall or reverse physical decline. The benefits, aside from reduced pant or dress size, are mostly invisible: a decrease in the likelihood of diabetes, osteoporosis, Alzheimer's, depression, and a host of other ailments."[68] A distinction based on the visibility of benefits is weak at best; even if we accept it for the sake of argument; we counter that there's not so very much difference between a decrease in physical ailments and an increase in coordination and strength.

The best way to characterize CrossFit is as a training method for, or precursor to, a sport, in provision of the element of physical skills. As Beresini puts it: "CrossFitters didn't know what they were training for until obstacle racing came along. But it's not a one-way relationship: the obstacle racing phenomenon could not have happened without CrossFit."[69] Through participation in CrossFit, people gain the physical skills necessary to participate successfully in activities like Tough Mudder or Spartan Race. Of course, those skills are seen at their most useful in the CrossFit Games since the events tested are designed to showcase the skills practiced in CrossFit workouts. Thus, we would categorize CrossFit as a fitness activity and the CrossFit Games as a nascent sport, lacking only evidence of a persistent and stable following.[70]

CONCLUSION

After describing the new emerging popular "fitness" trends of CrossFit, Tough Mudder, and Spartan Race, we explained Bernard Suits' argument that sports are games plus the addition of four additional characteristics: (1) the involvement of skills; (2) the skills must be physical; (3) a wide following of the game must exist around the world; and (4) the following is persistent and stable rather than a fad. Using the criteria adopted from Suits, we then examined the rules set by each event's organizing body to determine whether the events should be categorized as sports to reach the following conclusions. Tough Mudder is a fitness activity, but not a sport. Spartan Race is not yet a sport, but is moving toward becoming one. The workouts practiced in Cross-Fit are a means for attaining the physical skills necessary to sports, but Cross-Fit as usually practiced in gyms across the world is not a sport. However, the CrossFit Games share the same category as Spartan Race, not yet a sport, but on the way to meeting the criteria of sport.

NOTES

1. Bernard Suits, *The Grasshopper: Games, Life and Utopia* (Toronto: University of Toronto Press, 1978).

2. See http://www.methodenaturelle.de/en/methode-naturelle/history/.

3. *WipeOut* official site, http://abc.go.com/shows/wipeout/about-the-show.

4. A few competitors have completed early stages, but even fewer have made it through the final challenge course. See Sonia Saraiya, "Mission Impossible: How 'American Ninja Warrior' Masters the Art of Losing," *Salon*, last modified February 5, 2012, http://www.salon.com/2015/02/05/mission_impossible_how_american _ninja_warrior_masters_the_art_of_losing/.

5. J.C. Herz, *Learning to Breathe Fire: The Rise of CrossFit and the Primal Future of Fitness* (New York: Crown Archetype, 2014), 4.

6. "CrossFit: Forging Elite Fitness," *Crossfit.com*, accessed December 16, 2014, http://www.crossfit.com/cf-info/what-is-crossfit.html

7. Cliff Weathers, "CrossFit is a Cult: Why So Many of its Defenders are So Defensive," *Salon*, October 22, 2014, http://www.salon.com/2014/10/22/ crossfit_is_a_cult_why_so_many_of_its_defenders_are_so_defensive_partner/

8. Heather Havrilesky, "Why Are Americans So Fascinated With Extreme Fit-ness?" *New York Times*, October 14, 2014, http://www.nytimes.com/2014/10/19/ magazine/why-are-americans-so-fascinated-with-extreme-fitness.html

9. Ibid.

10. Christie Ashwanden, "An Insider's Guide to CrossFit," *New York Times* (blog), August 18, 2014, http://well.blogs.nytimes.com/2014/08/18/crossfit-book-breathe-fire/

11. Ibid.

12. "Reebok CrossFit Games," Crossfit.com, accessed December 16, 2014, http:// games.crossfit.com/.

13. Ibid.

14. Ibid.

15. Eric Lemay, "CrossFit Mirrors American Militarism: The Fitness Craze Reflects the Country's Ongoing Transformation From a Culture of Sports to a

Culture of War," *Salon*, September 7, 2013, http://www.salon.com/2013/09/08/crossfit_nation_partner/.

16. "Reebok CrossFit Games."

17. "CrossFit Games Drug Testing Program," *Crossfit.com*, accessed December 16, 2014, http://media.crossfit.com/games/pdf/2014CrossFitGames_DrugTestingProgram_140104.pdf.

18. Katrina Clarke, "Quebec Student Camille Leblanc-Bazinet Crowned 'Fittest Woman on Earth' at 2014 Reebok CrossFit Games," *The National Post*, July 28, 2014, http://news.nationalpost.com/2014/07/28/quebec-student-camille-leblanc-bazinet-crowned-fittest-woman-on-earth-at-2014-reebok-crossfit-games/.

19. Ibid.

20. Although not central to the overall borderline cases classification, we think it is relevant to note that one could interpret some of the names for W.O.D.s as involving traditional sexist framing. One example is a sequence of exercises performed at high intensity known as "Fran." CrossFit founder, Glassman, explains why he named the workout Fran noting: "I thought anything that left you flat on our back, looking up at the sky, asking, 'What the fuck happened to me?' deserved a female name. Fran is a workout that hits you like a femme fatale or force of nature." Glassman's remarks can be interpreted in a positive light, in honoring the strength and toughness of women, but one can also question why unnecessary gender distinctions were introduced to the W.O.D. vocabulary. This analysis needs to be developed further. See "Ode to Fran," *Youtube.com*, accessed December 16, 2014, https://www.youtube.com/watch?v=KVxzDOYv85k.

21. Erin Beresini, *Off Course: Inside the Mad, Muddy World of Obstacle Course Racing* (New York: Houghton Mifflin Harcourt, 2014), 79.

22. Lemay, "CrossFit Mirrors American Militarism."

23. Samir Chopra, "Crossfit and the Military: A Way Forward," last modified August 17, 2013, http://samirchopra.com/2013/08/17/crossfit-and-the-military-a-way-forward/

24. Scott Keneally, "Playing Dirty," *Outside Magazine*, November 2012, http://www.outsideonline.com/outdoor-adventure/multisport/Playing-Dirty-November-2012.html

25. See https://toughmudder.com/

26. "Tough Mudder," accessed December 16, 2014, https://toughmudder.com/events/what-is-tough-mudder.

27. Lizzie Widdicombe, "In Cold Mud: The Obstacle-Racing Craze gets Serious," *The New Yorker*, January 27, 2014, http://www.newyorker.com/magazine/2014/01/27/in-cold-mud

28. "Tough Mudder."

29. Ibid.

30. Widdicombe, "In Cold Mud."

31. Ibid.

32. "Spartan Race," *Spartan.com,* accessed December 16, 2014, http://www.spartan.com/#

33. Ibid.

34. Widdicombe, "In Cold Mud."

35. "2015 Reebok Spartan Race World Championship Crowns Champions in Lake Tahoe," *Spartan.com*, October 5, 2015, accessed June 22, 2016, http://www.spartan.com/en/race/detail/843/overview.

36. Dan England, "Mud, Sweat and a Whole Lot of Tears," *SBnation.com*, May 20, 2014, http://www.sbnation.com/longform/2014/5/20/5220672/amelia-boone-spartan-world-champion-profile-obstacle-racing.

37. Graham McFee, *Sport, Rules and Values: Philosophical Investigations into the Nature of Sport* (London: Routledge, 2004): 1.

38. Allen Guttmann, "Rules of the Game," in *The Sport Studies Reader*, ed. Alan Tomlinson (London: Routledge, 2007), 24.

39. Wray Vamplew, "Playing with the Rules: Influences on the Development of Regulation in Sport," *International Journal of the History of Sport* 24 (2007): 856.

40. Vamplew, "Playing," 846, 857.

41. Vamplew, "Playing," 860–63.

42. Sports that had developed a "recognized central organization" by the 1820s included sailing, archery, and prizefighting. See, for example, Vamplew, "Playing," 845, 848.

43. Jim Parry, "Sport and Olympism: Universals and Multiculturalism," *Journal of the Philosophy of Sport* 33 (2006): 200.

44. Suits, *The Grasshopper*.

45. Bernard Suits, "What is a Game?" *Philosophy of Science* 34 (1967): 156.

46. Suits, *The Grasshopper,* 36.

47. Bernard Suits, "The Elements of Sport," in *The Philosophy of Sport: A Collection of Essays*, ed. Robert Osterhoundt (Springfield, IL: Charles Thomas Publisher, 1973), 52–60. Objections from fellow philosophers of sport about whether performance sports, such as diving, met his criteria for games led Suits to revise his position on sports in 1988 and declare not all sports are members of the category games. See Bernard Suits, "Tricky Triad: Games, Play, and Sport," *Journal of the Philosophy of Sport* 15 (1988): 1–9. Klaus Meier responded rejecting the revision proposed by Suits, arguing that all sports are in fact games that involve physical skill, but a wide and stable following is not necessary for a game to be a sport. See Klaus V. Meier "Triad Trickery: Playing with Sport and Games," *Journal of the Philosophy of Sport*, 15 (1988): 11–30. See also Chad Carlson, "A Three-Pointer: Revisiting Three Crucial Issues in the "Tricky Triad" of Play, Games, and Sport" in this volume.

48. See, for example, Frank McBride, "A Critique of Mr. Suits' Definition of Game Playing," *Journal of the Philosophy of Sport* 6 (1979): 49–52.

49. Robert G. Osterhoundt, "The Term Sport—Some Thoughts on a Proper Name," *International Journal of Physical Education* 14 (1977): 13.

50. Klaus V. Meier, "Restless Sport," *Journal of the Philosophy of Sport* 12 (1985): 64–77.

51. See Meier, *Restless Sport*, and Sigmund Loland, *Fair Play in Sport: A Moral Norm System* (New York: Routledge, 2002), 15. See also Randolph Feezell, "On the Wrongness of Cheating and Why Cheaters Can't Play the Game," *Journal of the Philosophy of Sport* 15 (1988): 59 and Debra Shogan, "Rules, Penalties, and Officials: Sports and the Legality-Morality Distinction," *Canadian Association for Health, Physical Education, Recreation and Dance Journal* 54 (1988): 6–11.

52. Warren Fraleigh, *Right Actions in Sport: Ethics for Contestants* (Champaign, IL: Human Kinetics Publishers, 1984), 68. See also R. Scott Kretchmar, "Philosophy of Ethics," *Quest* 45 (1993): 7–8. In sport, the application of formalistic thinking leads to the view that "a game is only a game if it is played in accordance with the formal rules of that particular game." Heather Sheridan, "Conceptualizing 'Fair Play': A Review of the Literature," *European Physical Education Review* 9 (2003): 163–184. If an athlete does not adhere to the rules of the game, then he or she is not participating in a valid game and therefore cannot win the game.

53. McFee, *Sport,* 43.

54. The distinction between constitutive and regulative rules in sports stems from Kant's discussions of constitutive and regulative principles and Searle's work on Speech Acts. See Meier, "Restless Sport," 68–69. See also John R. Searle, *Speech Acts: An Essay in the Philosophy of Language* (Cambridge: Cambridge University Press, 1969), 41. In response to Searle's discussion of constitutive and regulative rules, philosopher Gordon Reddiford adds, "certain commitments, for example to win, and certain values and satisfaction—all very intimately related to games play—are not, and could not be, constitutive rules of a game." See Gordon Reddiford, "Constitutions, Institutions and Games," *Journal of the Philosophy of Sport* 12 (1985): 41.

55. Meier, "Restless Sport."

56. Cesar R. Torres, "What Counts as Part of a Game? A Look at Skills," *Journal of the Philosophy of Sport* 27 (2000): 84.

57. Meier, "Restless Sport," 71, and Meier, "Triad Trickery," 18.

58. Christoph Lumer, "Rules and Moral Norms in Sports," *International Review for Sociology of Sport* 30 (1995): 268.

59. Vamplew, "Playing," 851–852.

60. Vamplew, "Playing," 855.

61. Fred D'Agostino, "The Ethos of Games," *Journal of the Philosophy of Sport* 8 (1981): 7.

62. Fraleigh, *Right Actions,* 70.

63. Graham McFee, "Spoiling: An Indirect Reflection of Sport's Moral Imperative," in *Values in Sport: Elitism, nationalism, gender equality and the scientific manufacture of winners,* ed. Torbjörn Tännsjö and Claudio Tamburrini (London: E&FN Spon, 2000).

64. Suits, "Tricky Triad," 2."

65. For an in-depth examination of what is problematic in cases where athletes fail to try their best, see Pam R. Sailors, Sarah Teetzel and Charlene Weaving, "*Lentius, Inferius, Debilius*: The Ethics of 'Not Trying' on the Olympic Stage," *Sport in Society* 18 (2015): 17–27.

66. Herz, *Learning to Breathe Fire,* 182.

67. "Home," *International Obstacle Racing Federation,* http://www.obstaclesports.org/.

68. Herz, *Learning to Breathe Fire,* 126.

69. Beresini, *Off Course,* 77.

70. And that lack would not be taken as a disqualifier by anyone who follows Meier in arguing that a game can be a sport *without* a wide and persistent following.

Chapter 8

Evolution of the Action Sports Setting

Chrysostomos Giannoulakis

and Lindsay Pursglove

In recent years *action*, *lifestyle*, *alternative,* or *extreme* sports have attracted the attention of both academia and the industry. The action sports industry started to grow in the early 1990s, but it was not until recently marketers and practitioners realized the immense power words like *action, extreme*, and *alternative* hold for youth markets. A focus on individual characteristics and athlete skills, in addition to the social and cultural aspects, led to initial and continued participation in action sports.[1] Wheaton argued that upon their emergence in the 1960s, lifestyle sports have experienced "unprecedented growth both in participation and in their increased visibility across public and private space."[2] Currently this segment of the sport industry is regarded as high growth from a participation (demand) and delivery (supply) standpoint.[3] Due to lack of formal structures, the action sports industry has faced a relatively chaotic expansion in reference to mainstream sports, but still organic and unprecedented. To this extent, action sports continue to reach a global young audience, particularly a lucrative affluent and white male demographic, whereas established worldwide organizations (e.g., the International Olympic Committee), as well as professional sports in North America (e.g., football, basketball, and baseball) steadily suffer a lack of interest and participation from youth audiences. Despite their proven popularity and growth, the critical inquiry is to what extent action sports will continue to grow, and how the sector will maintain its risky, free, individualistic, and non-conformist character that separates them from mainstream activities.[4] To this end, it is also important to critically examine and analyze how these sports have evolved from a social, political, and commercial standpoint. Therefore, the purpose of this chapter is to (a) provide information on the current status of action sports, including their definition and utilization of additional terms such as *lifestyle*; (b) illustrate the sociocultural evolution of board sports (i.e., surfing, snowboarding, and skateboarding) and Bicycle Motocross (BMX) as representative and popular ambassadors of the sector; and (c) to discuss the future of the action sports.

WHAT ARE ACTION SPORTS?

The popularity of action sports has captured the interest of the academic community and has stimulated the emergence of new theoretical developments and productive avenues of enquiry.[5] A plethora of academics and practitioners alike have attempted to conceptualize and develop operational definitions of this specific segment of the sport and leisure industry. For instance, Bennett and Lachowetz suggested action sports are "an eclectic collection of risky, individualistic, and alternative sports such as skateboarding, BMX biking, surfing, street luge, wakeboarding, and motocross."[6] Wheaton utilized the term *lifestyle sports* in her studies as an expression adopted by members of the cultures themselves, since it reflects both the characteristics of these activities and their wider sociocultural significance.[7] From a sociological perspective, Rinehart described action sports as activities that provide alternatives to mainstream sports and mainstream values.[8] Indeed, providing an all-encompassing definition may constitute a challenge, due to the fact that each sport is unique from each other. In addition, different sports encompass variant characteristics based on their *alternative, lifestyle, extreme,* or *hazardous* status. Thus, different academic perspectives on the study of these sports have resulted in the adoption of various terms used to describe specialized sports that incorporate risk, lifestyle, technicality, and a distinct social identity of participants. A constant debate still exists among academics and practitioners over the proper use of operational terms, a fact that warrants the need for constant and continued analytical revision of what defines alternative activities in comparison to more *traditional, dominant,* or *mainstream* activities. Among parallel expressions observed in the academic literature, such as *extreme, alternative, lifestyle, whiz, action sports, panic sport, postmodern, post-industrial,* and *new sports,* the term *action sports* is adopted throughout this chapter, a term coined predominantly within the North American sport industry.

Overall, action sports may be categorized as noninstitutionalized informal sport activities. Common elements that characterize them include (a) the element of risk and danger inherent in the activity, (b) emphasis of participants on their creative, artistic, and aesthetic expression, (c) the individualistic attitude toward the activity, and (d) a nonconformist mentality to practicing the activity beyond formal structures and regulations. In particular, the element of risk is what creates excitement around action sports and media promote this sense of heroism through *extreme* acts. Wheaton also purported one of the defining characteristics of these sports is their sponta-neity, where individuals practice the activity in primarily informal settings, which are unsupervised and lack external regulation or institutionalization.[9] In a recent case study with key stakeholders in Australia, Kellett and Russell identified the following characteristics of the skateboarding sector: (a) lack of formal structures, (b) largely unregulated, (c) overlapping roles of suppliers, participants, and program developers, (d) not highly dependent on government funding for survival, (e) very attractive to entrepreneurs, and (f) lifestyle products such as video games, clothing, and music are integral to the industry.[10] Nonetheless, action sports such as snowboarding, kite surfing, and BMX have experienced a continuous *sportization* process both at the elite level (e.g., Olympic Games, X Games, etc.) and the amateur level. This progression involves a shift toward competitive and regularized forms of participation and governance.[11] Furthermore, the increased commoditized elements embedded in action sports, in addition to the parallel influx of mainstream athletic companies, have created pressures from the commercial and leisure sector to professionalize, institutionalize, and regulate alternative activities.[12]

Interestingly, there are conflicting dynamics between alternative sport participants who want to preserve and control their sports as they become commoditized, and the corporate world that gradually takes ownership and wants to present these sports as mainstream.[13] To this end, consumer capital-ism has invaded action sports subcultures in a complicated and contradictory manner.[14] Skateboarding is a representative case of this paradox. Events such as the X Games and the Mountain Dew Action Sports Tour provide a plat-form for sponsorship opportunities, media exposure, and a celebrity status to athletes. As a result of new role models, younger skateboarders demonstrate a more professional approach to the sport and perceive it as an opportunity for a money-making career. Beal and Wilson found that crucial components of the skateboarding culture included the nonmainstream aspects of creativity/artis-tic sensibility, a commitment to the actual process, and an individualistic atti-tude.[15] However, the authors suggested commercialization has undermined skateboarding's core values and the sport has impacted the mainstream itself. On one side, skateboarders are not totally opposed to the increasingly com-moditized status of the sport, since it supports the popularity and provides funding for athletes, skateparks, and grassroots opportunities. On the other hand, there are rising concerns regarding commercial aspects affecting the ethos of skateboarding from a subcultural perspective. For instance, in action sports terms, sponsored athletes are termed *ambassadors* of the brand, and their role has become rather sophisticated. It used to be the case that athletes were just photographed wearing apparel, demonstrating the products used in advertisements, and placing stickers on their equipment. Nowadays action sports brands raise the value of their professional teams beyond marketing by bringing endorsers deep into the design process and creating athlete-driven products. The increased team involvement in formulating the brand identity is another sign of the continuing transition of the action sports industry to a mainstream character, since it imitates the sponsored athlete model conventional athletic companies utilize with media training, product knowledge, and the entire "make-up" process. Overall, action sports participants' identity has changed in relation to mainstream and their own assessment of the commercialization process. As the action sport segment is gaining the attention of mainstream culture and commercializing, the gap between action sports and traditional sports is getting smaller.[16] Paradoxically, whereas action sports participants (e.g., snowboarders, skateboarders, surfers, etc.) used to be marginalized and even banned from practicing their activities in public spaces (e.g., ski resorts, parks, beaches, etc.), the gradual appeal on younger audiences and their parents have placed action sports on the forefront of the global sport economy.

STATUS OF ACTION SPORTS

In the late 1990s, television and corporate sponsors recognized the huge potential of action sports as a means to attract a young male audience. In 2007 there were more than three hundred action sports competitions around the world, generating $100 million in media investment.[17] The LG Action Sports World Tour is one of the largest action sports events and production companies. The group develops more than two hundred events annually, half of which are televised.[18] Doug Frisbee, Marketing Manager of the automobile company Toyota, commented on the Action Sports World Tour:

> One of the primary advantages is that those tours allow for endemic brands and brands like Toyota that are outside of the industry to co-exist and work together in the same environment. It helps maintain authenticity of the sports and the culture, but helps it grow with new sponsors and new money.[19]

Companies in North America spent approximately $138 million to sponsor board sports and freestyle motocross in 2007.[20] The popularity of board sports is also reflected in consumer spending; they are worth $9.9 billion per annum, with roughly 80 percent of this amount coming from sales of related apparel, shoes, and accessories. Broken down by sport, the industry consists of $5.5 billion for skateboarding goods, $3 billion for snowboarding, and $3 billion for surfing.[21] This is an indication that action sports have been subjected to the major forces of the commercialization process.[22]

There are approximately over 150 million individuals participating in action sports worldwide, of which 20 million are surfers, 40 million skateboarders, and 18.5 million snowboarders.[23] In addition, skateboarding, snowboarding, and motocross are considered to be the three fastest growing sports in the United States in recent years among action sports.[24] The rapid and often unregulated growth of action sports is based on the increasing popularity and the growing interest among Generation Y (i.e., born between 1977 and 1994) and Generation Z (i.e., born after 1994) consumers and their parents in activities that represent an antiestablishment and unconventional character. Members of the Generation Y cohort encompass approximately 25 percent of the U.S. population and yield an estimated $250 billion dollars in buying power.[25] Generation Y members have been identified to consume action sports more than any preceding generation, leading some to label action sports as "Gen-Y sports."[26] A survey study conducted by Turnkey Sports Poll with four hundred senior-level industry executives spanning professional and college sports, indicated extreme sports have done the best job of activating the 12–17 demographic (63.08 percent followed by the National Basketball Association, 10.75 percent).[27] It is estimated action sports boast over 58 million consumers between ages 10 and 24.[28]

The boosted media coverage of action sports through outlets such as NBC (i.e., Mountain Dew Action Sports Tour) and ESPN (i.e., Summer and Winter X Games) have also contributed to the immense growth of alternative activities. The increasing popularity of action sports and the continuous growth of the industry has created competitive dynamics between mainstream athletic companies and core lifestyle entities. The lucrative status of the industry, which is founded upon the extended number of potential participants from the Generation Y and Z markets, has attracted the attention of dominant sport brands like Nike and Adidas. Nike has managed to establish its strong presence through the Nike Skateboarding (SB) shoe line by signing well-known professional skateboarders to endorse its products and sponsoring grassroots skateboarding events on a local and national level. Nike's Action Sports category, which includes Nike 6.0 and Nike SB, is considered the fastest growing category within the Nike brand, as it yields $390 million in business with prospects of doubling this figure by the end of 2015.[29]

EVOLUTION OF ACTION SPORTS—THE CASE OF BOARD SPORTS AND BMX

Thorpe noted "good sociology is historically informed and contextually grounded."[30] Thus, it is important to consider the evolution and sociocultural nature of action sports when investigating the phenomenon. Furthermore, it is essential to implement a systematic contextualization when examining the contemporary alternative sports setting; namely, facilitate an all-encompassing contextualization of cultural phenomena relative to the historical evolution of action sports.[31] Current trends in academic research illustrate a merge between sport sociology, sport management, and sport consumer behavior fields in order to further examine and understand action sports both from a subcultural and commercialization perspective. Scholars and marketing professionals need to approach each sport of the action sports family individually; not merely and exclusively as a whole. Finally, researchers should examine the broader social and historical context of action sports, while taking into account dimensions of cultural change and development.[32] Evidently, every discipline of the action sports family has developed socially and politically in a different social context compared not only to modern organized sports, but to other action sports as well. Donnelly suggested, "In the 1960s and 1970s the new leisure movement embodied the philosophy of the counterculture by rejecting the overly modernized, technologized, and bureaucratized world of traditional sport, and embracing free, fun, cooperative, and individualistic activities."[33] For the purpose of this chapter, we also illustrate the historical evolution and social context of two popular segments of action sports, board sports and BMX.

Surfing

The three board sports (i.e., surfing, skateboarding, and snowboarding) have been characterized as a "love triangle" due to similarities in attitude, motion, and dress. From a historical context, surfing is considered the *godfather* of board sports. Although surfing originated in Hawaii, modern surfing began in California and diffused to Australia.[34] Specifically, surfing developed as an autonomous sport in California. The technical contributions of Californians and the impact of Hollywood surf movies on the sport have been well documented. Two other fundamental conditions have received less attention: mass consumer capitalism and county authorities.[35] Consumer capitalism created the social space in which surfing developed as an acceptable hedonistic pastime in California. The commercialization of the bourgeois culture and the spread of consumer capitalism in the 1920s and 1930s helped liberate the revealed body. Consumer capitalism introduced a new culture of pleasure and a new tolerance of the revealed body essential to surfing's acceptance; it "required a new lifestyle embodied in the ethic of a calculating hedonism, and a new personality type, the narcissistic person."[36]

In the 1960s, traditional surf lifesaving evoked images of hegemonic masculinity. In contrast to traditional surf lifesavers, recreational surfers had a more harmonious and hedonistic image. Surfing was seen as a freeing experience, rather than something done in *healthy leisure time*.[37] In the early

1970s, the "surfie" element was considered not only to be an object of discipline in Australia, but youths as a social category made themselves known as potentially irresponsible at a time of growing employment.[38] Two riding styles emerged in the mid-1960s: (a) Hawaiian surfers danced with waves, flowing in smooth rhythm with their natural direction; and (b) Australian surfers danced on waves, *conquering, attacking*, and reducing them to stages on which to perform.[39] During the 1950s, the media labeled surfers undisciplined, indulgent, and decadent; they were rotten, long-haired, unwashed drug addicts.[40] Booth noted surfers' lifestyles manifest in distinctive tastes, aesthetic and ethical dispositions, argot, dress, and humor, all of which separate surfers from non-surfers.[41] The author added these lifestyles also reflect cultural and temporal variations. According to a subcultural study on perceived *aestheticization* in surfing cultures, "surfing involves an experience of self-transcendence that is shared via the interaction of local participants and mediated through the global dissemination of images of the sublime."[42]

As surfing competitions started to expand within the sport, it was difficult for competitive surfing and the anticompetition ethic of the counterculture to co-exist.[43] Interestingly, amateurism was never an obstacle in the development of surfing. Early surfers endorsed and advertised products, wrote newspaper and magazine columns, and made their living from associated industries.[44] Competitions in the early 1960s that offered prizes and money became widely available in the United States. After nearly three decades of intense lobbying, professional surfers finally secured an international umbrella sponsor; in 1993, Coca-Cola announced a three-year sponsorship of a grand prix surfing circuit. Surfing joined international soccer and the Olympic Games as Coca-Cola's third global sport.[45] At this period of time surfing was legitimatized and professionalism ensured surfing's respectability. However, professional surfers have remained the principal source of tension within the movement. Booth suggested:

> Many devotees consider the strict codes of conduct, manufactured hype and gloss, and bureaucracy of professionalism the antithesis of surfing's hedonistic ideals. It is no coincidence that criticisms of surfers finally evaporated after the creation of institutional structures with an explicit disciplinary content.[46]

Overall, surfing has continually embraced capitalist culture via professionalization of surfers, with surfing competitions being a pivotal component of the global surf culture.[47]

Skateboarding[48]

Skateboarding, along with surfing, became popular in the 1960s. However, skateboarding went underground in the late 1970s and early 1980s. Since the medical fraternity condemned skateboarders as dangerous, skateparks could not secure the appropriate insurance policy and protection, and city authorities banned boards from their streets.[49] Furthermore, the evolution of the punk movement within the skateboarding community had a negative impact on the public perception of the activity.[50] Punks embraced *do-it-yourself* philosophies and methods as a rejection of mass culture, a form of political protest, and celebration of uncompromised self-expression.[51] Becky Beal performed a plethora of subcultural studies with skateboarders and found contemporary skateboarders were consciously rejecting some of the meanings and forms of mainstream sports. Specifically, skaters reveled in an informal physical activity in which they could express themselves in risk-taking and artistic ways. On a regular basis they challenged adult authority and expressed disdain for extrinsic rewards and standards. As a result, the anticompetitive status of skateboarders remained an integral element of the skateboarding subculture. Additional elements that characterize the skateboarding culture include focus on individuality, self-direction, and lack of formal rules and infrastructure.[52]

Skateboarders use what is conventionally considered *front-region public settings,* such as parks and city streets, to display their backstage style and values. Beal and Weidman suggested authenticity for skateboarders is not determined by a successful front-region performance.[53] Rather, authenticity "is proven in the back region through an internalization and public display of the norms and values of the skateboard culture" such as creativity, self-expression, nonconformity, and individualism.[54] Despite the nonconformist character of skateboarding, various commercial interests have tried to capitalize on the activity by promoting it as part of the dominant sport culture, more like a mainstream and legitimate sport that promotes competition, win-at-all-costs attitude, and extrinsic rewards.[55] Interestingly, skaters have a keen appreciation for the skateboarding history, since they honor legendary skaters from the past and admire longevity in the industry. Finally, a deep and long-term commitment to the sport and lifestyle is another form of authenticity.[56]

Currently, skateboarding continues to grow at remarkable rates; as of 2007, there were approximately 2,200 skateparks and more than 13 million skateboarders in the United States, which corresponded to almost 6,000 skateboarders per park.[57] Skaters for Public Skateparks have collaborated with the Tony Hawk Foundation and the International Association of Skateboard Companies to create the Public Skatepark Development Guide, which provides recommendations and concrete guidelines to entities interested in campaigning for a skateboard park in their community.[58] Such an initiative would have been inconceivable 10–15 years ago, when skateboarding was still forbidden in the majority of urban areas in the United States. Howell found that the relationship between skateboarding and urban cities started to change in the late 1990s, while skateboarding was utilized as a tool for urban development and skateboarders were involved in the decision-making and design phase.[59] This was attributed to (a) the commercial power of the sport, and (b) the visibility of skateboarding through media that resulted in parents supporting and motivating their children to practice the sport. Skateboarding has been widely publicized to mainstream markets via media outlets such as Skate TV and Fuel TV, two channels wholly dedicated to action sports. Extensive exposure through skateboarding reality series such as *The Life of Ryan* and *Rob and Big* featured on MTV provide mainstream advertisers with back door access to the most cherished and fickle demographic—the teens to twenties.[60]

Snowboarding

Snowboarding originated in the United States in the late 1960s. It reached its highest peak in terms of popularity in the mid-1980s. Along with it came an early *bad boy* image, based largely on the fact that adolescent males comprised the majority of snowboarders at the time. A rebel reputation was established and is still prevalent today, despite snowboarding's vast appeal to men and women of all ages. It should be noted that surfers and skateboarders, who in the early 1960s formed part of the same subculture, had a major influence in the development of snowboarding. Snowboard was created by borrowing heavily from the existing practices and cultures of surfing and skateboarding.[61] Mainstream society recognized snowboarding as a variant of surfing.[62] In the late 1960s and early 1970s snowboarders symbolized *snow surfers*.[63] Surf, skate, and snowboard cultures were initially perceived as *wasteful, selfish,* and *irresponsible* and condemned devotees as *itinerants* and *louts*.[64] Furthermore, the public perception characterized those board sports as undisciplined, hedonistic activities and lifestyles.[65] In the late 1960s, snowboarding was considered as a rebellious activity against the established skiers. There was a perception that snowboards ruined the slopes and made the terrain unsuitable for skiing. As of 2003, there were only three ski resorts in the United States that did not allow snowboarding. The sport's limited popularity ensured the activity remained "unspoilt and helped consolidate a unique identity and culture, as participation demanded true commitment."[66] Snowboarding remained *nonmainstream* until the sport was exposed to the commercial world during the mid-1980s.

Despite the fact that intense commercialism appeared as a threat to snowboarding's traditional values and philosophies, the sport maintained its authentic character and status, in contrast to surfing. This was achieved by imitating skateboarding's model of professionalism, which is based primarily on professional athletes' image.[67] Within snowboard and skateboard, success is not a necessary component to becoming a professional athlete. A plethora of athletes have their own brand and promote their own products just by riding the mountain or the skatepark. Thus, the traditional modernized sport competitive spirit is absent from these two board sports, and this had a major effect on maintaining their authentic character. It is an oxymoron that in the early 1990s many snowboarding companies attempted to commodify snowboarding's perceived irresponsible and uncontrolled image.[68] Humphreys noted:

> The majority of snowboarders, like participants in related activities, such as tow-in surfing and skateboarding, and in music-based subcultures such as punk, reject widespread commercial co-optation. The basis of this rejection resides in an artistic philosophy that values freedom and self-expression, but which, ironically, is responsible for increasing the popularity of snowboarding.[69]

In 1994 snowboarding was officially declared as an Olympic sport, an avenue that accelerated snowboarding's transition to a more mainstream and socially acceptable sport. The 1998 Winter Olympic Games in Nagano was the first time snowboarding was performed as an Olympic sport.[70] Apparently, the marriage between the Olympic movement and snowboarding continues to produce tensions and compromises by both constituents.[71] Despite this tenuous relationship, snowboarding has evolved into one of the most popular winter sports and is now well-established as a competitive sport. Nevertheless, it has been suggested that snowboarding's increased popularity, institutionalization, and mediatization has influenced its alternative status and nature.[72]

BMX

The inception of BMX began in the 1960s to early 1970s in parking lots and empty fields of Southern California. Children on modified 20-inch bicycles would ride around jumping objects on an obstacle course to show their cycling skills that mimicked the techniques and format of Motocross.[73] These bicycle skills were first captured by the movie industry. In fact, mainstream movies such as *Rad* and *BMX Bandits* popularized the sport and can be credited as the initial exposure for youth in the 1980s.[74] In his extensive research on the relationship between the BMX subculture, subcultural media, and the industry itself, Nelson argues that the history of BMX freestyle is inseparable from the history of the activity's mediatization.[75]

In 1974, while BMX was booming all over the country, George Esser founded the National Bicycle League (NBL), as part of the National Motorcycle League. Over the years the NBL emerged as its own independent non-profit organization governing BMX nationwide. In 1977, a similar BMX sanctioning body called American Bicycle Association (ABA) was created.[76] For over thirty years, the two national governing bodies competed for tracks, riders, and races. In 2011, the ABA bought out and absorbed the NBL, gaining their tracks and rider memberships and creating a single governing body known as USA BMX. Since 2011, USA BMX has controlled BMX racing at all local, state, regional, and national levels.

The establishment of national governing bodies shortly after the inception of the sport in parking lots has laid the path for what the sport has become today. Unlike other action sports that are unstructured, BMX racing needs the structure of an organization to provide tracks for participation, membership, and event scheduling. When a sport uses modes of organization, it is creating an identity for its communities.[77] This organization creates a network of participants through membership and activities that drive the community identity. Thus, individuals become members and the sport is legitimatized.[78] Montgomery and Oliver provided a networking model that supports the importance of a network and its activities as an essential part of a process in establishing new social entities.[79] It is these social entities within sport communities that maintain one's identity and participation in the forefront in order to establish one's place within the community. Participants' identity and personal expression are defining elements associated with the term *lifestyle sport*.[80] Through its governing body, USA BMX has created a network and structure that mimics the community concept in action sports. What follows is an illustration of how BMX racing fosters the evolution of the sport and cultivates membership structure and fan base.

The BMX sport culture is intertwined with competition and noncompetition elements. While the format of a race is the most important aspect of the culture, the manner in which riders identify themselves is significant as well. To be considered an *authentic* lifestyle sport participant, being part of the subculture is essential. Authentic membership of lifestyle sport subcultures is determined by attitude, style, and world-view, and participants' identities are formed by embracing a certain lifestyle and commitment in time and money.[81] BMX racers identify themselves in two manners: (a) classification based on age and expertise; and (b) number plates on the handlebars of the bicycles that may be personalized via shape, size, colors, and stickers. BMXers utilize their own terminology, and they have a unique understanding of techniques and track structures. These factors, in addition to the competition and structure of the sport, drive the sport culture.

BMX racing culture is present on and off the track. Individuality, creativity, and inclusivity are three core values that attract and retain participants.[82] The inclusivity culture promotes commonalities as a group within the governing league; yet, individuality and creativity are needed so participants feel distinctive and unique. Riders are encouraged to be creative and put a personal brand on specific tactics and tricks, bike specifications, and uniform style. Supporting the community atmosphere of BMX, it is common for racers, their families, and fans to schedule their lives around practices and races. BMX fans and participants schedule BMX race weekends as others would vacation time as tourists, potentially increasing sport tourism for host cities. The time these individuals spend traveling together creates bonds that are an integral and lasting part of the BMX community, a unique aspect for such an individualized sport. Whether a racer is participating locally or internationally, the BMX racing culture remains consistent. Interestingly, while action sports have been associated with and predominantly known to serve the Generation Y consumer, BMX racing serves a much wider demographic. In 2010, there were approximately 1.8 million BMX participants in the United States.[83] Classifications for male and female racers start as young as two and three years old on their Strider (pedal-less push bicycles), all the way up to 60 years of age and over. Typical participant characteristics in BMX racing events are comprised of a wide range of age, proficiency, and skills.

Although BMX began as a racing formatted sport, the sport continues to evolve. Beginning with the creation of sanctioning bodies to govern the sport nationwide and with its increased spectator popularity, an additional element of the sport has emerged: BMX Freestyle. The sport is known as the trick part of BMX and became popular via the ESPN X Games in the mid-1990s. BMX Freestyle encompasses multiple disciplines of BMX such as street, park, vert, trails, and flatland. Due to the popularity of the X Games and other similar tour stop competitions, BMX Freestyle is now what is associated and thought of by mainstream audiences as BMX. Freestyle is an obvious assimilation of BMX due to media exposure. For instance, when BMX racing lost its television coverage with ESPN, its popularity and participation rates experienced a significant decline.

Another pivotal change for the sport of BMX racing happened in 2008. During the 2008 Beijing Summer Olympic Games, BMX racing made its Olympic debut with elite men and women racers under the cycling discipline. BMX racing as an Olympic sport has infiltrated its program development from grassroots level through all levels of the sport.[84] The sport's national governing body has incorporated programming such as the Olympic Day to capitalize and gain interest in BMX racing through Olympic-themed initiatives. For example, the United States Olympic Committee (USOC) and USA Cycling partner on a yearly basis and "offer a free day of BMX racing at participating BMX tracks around the United States . . . the goal of Olympic Day is to promote the Olympic values and participation in the sport across the globe regardless of age, gender, or athletic ability."[85]

The sport's Olympic debut in 2008 transformed formal BMX racing and will continue to drive change in the future. This was evident when USA Cycling and the USOC built amateur and elite tracks at the Olympic Training Center in Chula Vista, California. The Olympic track has since created a need for specialized tracks and racers outside of the Olympic Training Center. Part of that change to keep BMX racing viable is making BMX tracks more challenging. Many of the tracks now create bigger/taller jumps, steeper starting hills, and longer tracks to make each race more action packed. This has allowed a path for riders to grow and progress within the sport as they advance in skill status from amateur to elite and on to Olympic level. Such infrastructure transformations have resulted in the creation of the United Cycliste International (UCI) aspect of a BMX racing series internationally called UCI BMX Supercross.

Bicycle Motocross has experienced a plethora of transformations since its inception in the 1960–1970s. What was once just kids riding around empty lots has now turned into one of the founding members of the action sports movement. Yet, it is still grounded in the fact that anyone can participate at the amateur BMX racing level if one can ride a bicycle. The structure of BMX racing leads to participant identity and culture on and off the track. BMX's product cycle has changed and evolved through its history, culture, and the future of the sport will continue to be determined by action sport industry forces and trends, especially as related to the complex dynamics involved in the commercialization process of lifestyle sport cultures, the mass market, and the development of BMX.

FUTURE OF ACTION SPORTS

Action sports have evolved rapidly and are now recognized as a common mainstream sport segment, which will continue to incorporate business practices and characteristics of traditional modern sports. Associations of traditional sport characteristics include "corporate sponsorship, larger prize monies, rationalized systems of rules and governance, hierarchical and individualistic star system with athletes, and win-at-all cost value system."[86] Notably, the core infrastructure of action sports is not founded upon government funding; most facilities, such as skateparks, rely primarily on grassroots and community initiatives. With a few exceptions of action sports that have been labeled Olympic sports (e.g., snowboarding, BMX racing), the alternative sport setting is predominantly unregulated, and participants are not engaged in formal coaching or training patterns. For instance, the official coaching of parents in skateboarding is antithetical to core values, but often parents feel more comfortable supporting their children in supervised settings.[87]

A central element to comprehending the immense popularity and expansion of action sports is the impact of corporate forces.[88] The action sports segment has been defined based on the needs and wants of Generation Y and Z consumers. The purchasing power behind these generations is leading the growth of action sports. However, as Generation Y ages and Generation Z becomes the dominant consumption generation, action sports will have to adapt and reform to remain current and popular. Generation Z individuals, as the newest generation, were born after 1994 and they are in their formative years, which implies this generation is yet to be defined.[89] It would be certainly interesting to examine how action sports organizations will market and engage Generation Y consumers as they get older, and yet embrace the new up and coming Generation Z youth audience. The evolution of Generation Y and Z participants also has an impact on boarding subcultures. Beal and Wilson discussed concerns of long-term skateboarders regarding the influx of young children in the sport.[90] They thought younger participants approached skateboarding as a cool trend and were doing it because it was popular, as opposed to developing a lifestyle. Inevitably, action sports have an increased potential for additional growth, as they continue to be widely promoted via mainstream media outlets. Marketing experts within the sport industry have noted that if action sports are to be accepted as legitimate sports, they need to be aired on a more consistent basis.[91] Some of the major action sports events as the X Games are only aired once per year. Wade Martin, the Mountain Dew Action Sports Tour General Manager, suggested:

> The biggest thing we can do is to provide exposure to the sports and bring them to a bigger audience. In the case of the Dew Tour we bring it to people on a constant basis over the course of five months. Last year [2005] in our first year, we had more than 41 million people watch the shows. That's 41 million people who weren't watching the tour before it began. Certainly our hope is that it translates into a trickle-down effect to the industry-more people participating and more people buying.[92]

If action sports are to become accepted by mainstream, their image will have to extend beyond the framework of amateur, unregulated, and sporadic events. Industry trends indicate that in order to reach the mass audience, action sports must become more than just a spectacle; current and potential consumers need to develop a genuine rooting interest.

The main challenge concerning the future of action sports is to maintain their authenticity and legitimacy, as well as their lifestyle or alternative character. Giannoulakis introduced the concept of "authenticitude" in action sports, a combination of the words authenticity and attitude, as he discussed the new management paradigm in the industry.[93] The authenticitude battle between mainstream and core organizations has resulted in an authenticity game, where brands either fake or actually render authenticity to establish their presence in the market. Simultaneously, the influx of larger mainstream companies, like Nike and Adidas, has forced core brands to expand to the masses in order to survive in a highly competitive business environment. The authenticity notion in the action sports setting is more prevalent than ever, as lifestyle sport participants are in the process of finding a balance between maintaining the subcultural elements of their activities and the business world that is commoditizing these activities in the name of profit and media coverage. Interestingly, the majority of action sports, such as boarding cultures, emerged from the new leisure movement imbued with an individualistic and anticompetitive ethos.[94] Thus, the emerging marketing trend to expand action sports to the masses by utilizing mainstream media outlets may jeopardize their authenticity, integrity, and originality.

NOTES

1. Holly Thorpe, "Understanding 'Alternative' Sport Experiences: A Contextual Approach for Sport Psychology," *International Journal of Sport and Exercise Psychology* 7 (2009).

2. Belinda Wheaton, *The Cultural Politics of Lifestyle Sports* (New York and London: Routledge, 2013), 2.

3. See Gregg Bennett, Robin K. Henson, and James J. Zhang, "Generation Y's Perception of the Action Sports Industry Segment." *Journal of Sport Management* 17 (2013); and Pamm Kellett and Roslyn Russell, "A Comparison between Mainstream and Action Sport Industries in Australia: A Case Study of the Skateboarding Cluster." *Sport Management Review* 12 (2009).

4. Kellett and Russell, "A Comparison between Mainstream and Action Sport Industries in Australia."

5. Wheaton, *The Cultural Politics of Lifestyle Sports.*

6. Gregg Bennett and Tony Lachowetz, "Marketing to Lifestyles: Actions Sports and Generation Y," *Sport Marketing Quarterly* 13 (2004): 239.

7. Belinda Wheaton, "Mapping the Lifestyle Sport-Scape," in *Understanding Lifestyle Sport: Consumption, Identity and Difference*, ed. Belinda Wheaton (New York and London: Routledge, 2004).

8. Robert Rinehart "Emerging Arriving Sport: Alternatives to Formal Sport," in *Handbook of Sport Studies*, eds. Jay Coakley and Eric Dunning (London: Sage, 2000).

9. Wheaton, *The Cultural Politics of Lifestyle Sports.*

10. Kellett and Russell, "A Comparison between Mainstream and Action Sport Industries in Australia."

11. Maarten van Bottenburg and Johan Heilbron, "De-Sportization of Fighting Contests: The Origins and Dynamics of No Holds Barrred Events and the Theory of Sportization," *International Review for the Sociology of Sport* 41 (2006).

12. Wheaton, *The Cultural Politics of Lifestyle Sports.*

13. Joy C. Honea "Youth Cultures and Consumerism: Alternative Sport and Possibilities for Resistance." (Presentation, annual meeting of the American Sociological Association 2004).

14. Maureen P. Donnelly "Studying Extreme Sports; Beyond Core Participants" *Journal of Sport and Social Issues* 30 (2006).

15. Becky Beal and Charlene Wilson, "'Chicks Dig Scars': Commercialization and the Transformations of Skateboarders' Identities," in *Understanding Lifestyle Sport: Consumption, Identity and Difference*, ed. Belinda Wheaton (New York and London: Routledge, 2004).

16. Lotte Salome and Maarten van Bottneberg, "Are They All Daredevils? Introducing a Participation Typology for the Consumption of Lifestyle Sports in Different Settings." *European Sport Management Quarterly* 21 (2012).

17. "The Action Sports Market," *Active Marketing Group*, 2007, http://www.activenetworkrewards.com/Assets/AMG+2009/Action+Sports.pdf

18. Cullen Poythress "Major Action-Sports Tours and Their Effect on the Core Industry." *Transworld Business*, December 2006.

19. Ibid., 24.

20. "Spending on Action and Adventure Sports," *IEG Sponsorship Report.* Last accessed September 6, 2013. http:/www.sponsorship.com/iegsr/subonly/topic_article.asp?id=2563

21. Matt Higgins, "In Board Sports, Insider Status Makes Gear Sell," *The New York Times*, last modified November 24, 2006. http://www.nytimes.com/2006/11/24/sports/othersports/24brands.html?pagewanted=all&_r=0

22. Holly Thorpe, "Beyond 'Decorative Sociology': Contextualizing Female Surf, Skate, and Snowboarding," *Sociology of Sport Journal* 23 (2006).

23. Ibid.

24. Beal and Wilson, "'Chicks Dig Scars.'"

25. Beth A. Cianforne and James J. Zhang, "Differential Effects of Television Commercials, Athlete Endorsements, and Venue Signage during a Televised Action Sports Event," *Journal of Sport Management* 20 (2006).

26. See Bennett and Lachowetz, "Marketing to Lifestyles;" Bennett, Henson, and Zhang, "Generation Y's Perception;" and Cianfrone and Zhang "Differential Effects."

27. Turnkey Sports Poll, "Sports Business Journal In-Depth," *Sports Business Journal* 7 (2006).

28. Bennett and Lachowetz "Marketing to Lifestyles."

29. Brandon Gomez "How did Nike get the Swoosh into Skateboarding? A Study of Authenticity and Nike SB," (master's thesis, Syracuse University, 2012).

30. Thorpe "Beyond 'Decorative Sociology,'" 208.

31. Ibid.

32. Ibid.

33. Peter Donnelly, "Sport as a Site for 'Popular' Resistance," in *Popular Cultures and Political Practices*, ed. Richard S. Gruneau (Toronto: Garamond Press, 1988), 74.

34. Douglas Booth, "Surfing 60s: A Case Study in the History of Pleasure and Discipline," *Australian Historical Studies* 26 (1994).

35. Douglas Booth "Expressions Sessions: Surfing, Style, and Prestige," in *To the Extreme: Alternative Sports Inside and Out*, eds. Robert E. Rinehart and Synthia Sydnor (Albany: State University of New York Press, 2003).

36. Douglas Booth "Ambiguities in Pleasure and Discipline: The Development of Competitive Surfing," *Journal of Sport History* 22 (1995), 192.

37. Alan Law, "Surfing the Safety Net: Dole Bludging, 'Surfies' and Governmentality in Australia" *International Review for the Sociology of* Sport 36 (2001).

38. Ibid.

39. Booth, "Ambiguities in Pleasure and Discipline."

40. Ibid.

41. Booth," Expressions Sessions."

42. Mark Stranger, "The Aesthetics of Risk: A Study of Surfing," *International Review for the Sociology of Sport* 34 (1999), 273.

43. Douglas Booth, "Surfing: From One (Cultural) Extreme to the Other," in *Understanding Lifestyle Sport: Consumption, Identity and Difference*, ed. Belinda Wheaton (New York and London: Routledge, 2004).

44. Booth," Expressions Sessions."

45. Booth, "Ambiguities in Pleasure and Discipline."

46. Ibid., 206.

47. Wheaton, *The Cultural Politics of Lifestyle Sports*.

48. See also Brian Glenney, "Skateboarding, Sport, and Spontaneity: Towards a Subversive Definition of Sport" in this volume.

49. Wheaton, "Mapping the Lifestyle Sport-Scape."

50. Duncan Humphreys, "Shredheads Go Mainstream? Snowboarding and Alternative Youth," *International Review for the Sociology of Sport* 32 (1997).

51. Thorpe "Beyond 'Decorative Sociology.'"

52. Wheaton, *The Cultural Politics of Lifestyle Sports*.

53. Becky Beal and Lisa Weidman, "Authenticity in the Skateboarding World," in *To the Extreme: Alternative Sports Inside and Out*, eds. Robert E. Rinehart and Synthia Sydnor (Albany: State University of New York Press, 2003).

54. Ibid., 351.

55. Becky Beal "Disqualifying the Official: An Exploration of Resistance through the Subculture of Skateboarding," *Sociology of Sport Journal* 12 (1995).

56. Beal and Weidman, "Authenticity in the Skateboarding World."

57. Jennifer Sherowski, "Skatepark Advancement 101," *Transworld Business*, May 2007.

58. Ibid.

59. Ocean Howell, "Skateparks as Neoliberal Ground." *Space and Culture* 11 (2008).

60. Sean Mortimer, "Skate TV: Reaching Millions More than Endemic Media, Skateboard TV Shows are Impacting and Dividing the Industry," *Transworld Business*, February 2008.

61. Donnelly, "Studying Extreme Sports."

62. Humphreys, "Shredheads Go Mainstream?"

63. Duncan Humphreys, "Selling Out Snowboarding: The Alternative Response to Commercial Co-Optation," in *To the Extreme: Alternative Sports Inside and Out*, ed. Robert E. Rinehart and Synthia Sydnor (Albany: State University of New York Press, 2003).

64. Douglas Booth, "Surfing 60s: A Case Study in the History of Pleasure and Discipline," *Australian Historical Studies* 26 (1994).

65. Ibid.

66. Humphreys, "Shredheads Go Mainstream?" 149.

67. Ibid.

68. Ibid.

69. Humphreys, "Selling Out Snowboarding," 407.

70. Ibid.

71. Wheaton, *The Cultural Politics of Lifestyle Sports*.

72. See Belinda Wheaton, "Introducing the consumption and representation of lifestyle sports," *Sport in Society* 13 (2010).

73. "The History of BMX Racing," *USA BMX: The American Bicycle Association*, last accessed January 17, 2015, http://usabmx.com/site/sections/7.

74. Joy C. Honea, "Beyond the Alternative vs. Mainstream Dichotomy: Olympic BMX and the Future of Action Sports," *Journal of Popular Culture* 46 (2013).

75. Wade Nelson, "The Historical Mediatization of BMX Freestyle Cycling," *Sport in Society* 13 (2010).

76. See "The History of BMX Racing"; and Honea "Beyond the Alternative vs. Mainstream Dichotomy."

77. Kari Steen-Johnsen, "Networks and the Organization of Identity: The Case of Norwegian Snowboarding," *European Sport Management Quarterly* 8 (2008).

78. Ibid.

79. Kathleen Montgomery and Amalya Oliver, "A Fresh Look on how Professions Take Shape," *Organization Studies* 28 (2007).

80. Steen-Johnsen, "Networks and the Organization of Identity."

81. Salome and van Bottenburg, "Are They All Daredevils?"

82. Lindsay Pursglove "Bicycle Motocross (BMX): Transformation from Niche to Mainstream," (master's thesis, Barry University, 2009).

83. "Bicycling (BMX) Participation Report 2010," *Sports and Fitness Industry Association,* accessed November 10, 2014, http://www.sgma.com/reports/24_Bicycling-%28BMX%29- Participation-Report-2010.

84. Steven J. Bullough "A New Look at the Latent Demand for Sport and its Potential to Deliver a Positive Legacy for London 2012," *International Journal of Sport Policy and Politics* 4 (2012).

85. "Olympic Day." *USA BMX: The American Bicycle Association*, accessed January 17, 2015, https://www.usabmx.com/site/bmx_races?series_race_type=Olympic+Dayandsection_id=64andyear=2014.

86. Thorpe "Understanding 'Alternative' Sport Experiences," 372.

87. Beal and Wilson, "'Chicks Dig Scars.'"

88. Wheaton, "Introducing the consumption and representation of lifestyle sports."

89. Kaylene C. Williams, Robert A. Page, Alfred R. Petrosky, and Edward H. Hernandez, "Multi-Generational Marketing: Descriptions, Characteristics, Lifestyles, and Attitudes," *The Journal of Applied Business and Economics* 11 (2010).

90. Beal and Wilson, "'Chicks Dig Scars.'"

91. Poythress, "Major Action-Sports Tours and Their Effect on the Core Industry."

92. Ibid., 24.

93. Chrysostomos Giannoulakis, "The 'Authenticitude' Battle in Action Sports: A Case-Based Industry Perspective," *Sport Management Review* (in press).

94. Donnelly, "Studying Extreme Sports."

Chapter 9

Skateboarding, Sport, and Spontaneity

Toward a Subversive Definition of Sport

Brian Glenney

Just as great writing upends rules of grammar, or great scientific discoveries exceed the bounds of scientific methodology, so too is great sport made when the rules by which it is defined are disrupted.[1] From Maradona's "Hand of God,"[2] Nelson's "Hack-a-Shaq,"[3] and Perry's "Spitball,"[4] to most recent moments: Kam Chancellor's leap over the offensive line to block a field-goal and John Wall's "yo-yo" or "extended" dribble, there are numerous sport "moments" or "cases" that exemplify sport at its best by disruption or subverting normal rules of play.[5] By subversion, I mean the manner in which a participant undermines established game-play in a way that demonstrates the limits of rule for controlling play.[6] The claim defended here is that the subversion of rules is not just the basis of making great sport, but is intrinsic to the play of sport itself and should be counted part of sport's definition.

I motivate this argument with the example of subversion in the fringe sport skateboarding, which provides a window into self-critical aspects of sport as a rule-governed activity. I then contrast this sport as subversion claim with traditional "formalist" theories of sport, which define sport by its constitutive rules—rules without which the sport would not exist.[7] Though I am not the first to discuss a subversive definition of sport,[8] this paper is unique in that it presents subversion as a kind mutualism—where sport is a mutual quest for human excellence.[9] I conclude by applying this "subversive" definition of sport to standard theoretical problems in the philosophy of sport: What makes sport unique? Why is there significant interest in being sport participators and spectators? What makes sport a valuable human activity?

SKATEBOARDING AND SPORT

Skateboarding is not a "mainstream" sport, but an "alternative" or "extreme" sport.[10] By this definition then, skateboarding is less established and its participants and fans represent a subculture, but one that is emerging in the commercial market competing with other mainstream sports. Skateboarding has undergone commercialization and commodification by mainstream markets such as ESPN[11] and other major sports brands like Nike and Red Bull,[12] further suggesting that its "sports" status must be at least a part of its current description.

Skateboarding competitions are both common and popular. Like other sporting events, they include timed "runs," where competitors used standardized equipment to test their abilities against others on standardized obstacles such as ramps and rails for awards. Many skateboarding competitions, such as The Battle at the Berrics or ESPN's X Games have rules, such as a prohibition on the body touching the ground when performing a trick (even though there are a large variety of tricks, such as the no-comply, lay-back grind, etc. which include feet and hands touching the ground when performed). Such contests become sources for ranking skateboarders by both the public and skateboarders themselves.[13] There even exist impromptu pseudo-contests in parks and on the street like "SKATE"—a game akin to the basketball shooting game called 'HORSE' but played with skateboard tricks.

Skateboarding's status as a sport is often in question because it is also perceived as a lifestyle involved in symbolic and embodied performances of subversion or resistance to mainstream rules and norms. The practice of skateboarding itself involves, "bodily expression and performance to subvert—at least symbolically—this mainstream discipline and control."[14] Skateboard tricks are often identified as a form of "free expression," a "temporary escape or sense of empowerment through movement,"[15] Hence, the practice and conception of skateboarding is antithetical to the very competitions in which skateboarders often participate—skateboarding is a paradox.[16]

In a previous paper on skateboarding and sport, my coauthor Steve Mull and I argue that skateboarding's paradoxical nature provides an environment for emergent or "re-wilding" forms of interactive play that emerges from the tension of skateboarding as rule-bound and rule-subversive, "a specific kind of integrative interaction, one where the skateboarder is influenced by his environmental conditions (similar to sport) and at the same time subverts the intended use of the environmental conditions."[17] This double use of architecture is "symmetrical"; like skateboarding's predecessor 'surfing' it is an activity at once controlled by its natural wave-form architecture while also subverting the wave-form by "riding" the wave and engaging in trick play: turning, flipping, spinning, and so on.

The uniqueness of skateboarding's "interaction" is made more visible by contrasting it to normal play in mainstream athletic sports. Normal sport play can be described as having an "asymmetrical" relation, or merely active relation with its architecture—sport activity is (largely) controlled by the architecture and the associated rule-bound activities. Even in "performance" forms of sport that are defined as "dangerous,"[18] such as ski jumping and ice skating, qualitative elements of artistic display similar to skateboarding are exhibited,[19] but tricks are standardized with specific "point totals" that emphasize standardization of architecture and rules. Consider even the new performance-oriented winter Olympic sport of ice dancing; ice skaters cannot engage in tricks that involve the walls surrounding the ice rink or that include skaters using their hands to move across the ice. Such possibilities are expected in skateboarding, even in contest conditions.

In skateboarding, those with the most creative and expansive uses of architecture are granted the most social capital for their efforts.[20] Competitive skateboarding landscapes, while standardized to a degree,[21] are present for maximizing their manipulation in most skateboarding competitions. Why? Skateboarding is different in that normal skateboarding play "re-wilds" its environment—the skateboarder is influenced by his environmental conditions (similar to sport) and at the same time subverts the intended use of the environmental conditions.

What relation might the skateboarding paradox have to sport?[22] Might important aspects of sport also be a "re-wilding" form of interactive play? I argue for a parallel form of paradox and occasional "re-wilding" interactivity in sport. I follow Malaby who, after presenting famous examples of rule subversion (or re-wilding interactivity): Julius Erving's "dunk," Cousy's "dribble out," and Brady's "tuck," states: "The rules that defined the game were correctly applied, but the particular outcome in a particular case showed up the limits of the rules for encompassing the game as the participants (and spectators) saw it."[23] In other words, sport has the potential for moments of re-wilding interactive play where rules are shown to be limited in controlling play—where rules are subverted.

MUTUALLY EXCLUSIVE GOALS IN SPORT

The history of sports is witness to progressive change.[24] But one element is traditionally viewed as static: constitutive rules, rules that "create or define new forms of behavior."[25] Constitutive rules cannot change as they define the nature of a sport, providing operational criteria for sports activity—how to win and how to lose. For instance, in soccer the winning team moves the ball by dribbling, passing, and shooting into the opposing team's goal the most. Other rules regulate this play, sometimes penalizing participants that undermine constitutive rules, such as a penalty kick for making hand contact with the ball. Some have gone so far as to argue that if a constitutive rule is broken when playing a sport, that sport is no longer being played.[26] Such is the view of traditional "formalist" schools of thought.[27]

Antiformalist thinkers, like conventionalist D'Agostino,[28] point out that not only are constitutive rules broken in the practice of sport, breaking them becomes part of playing a sport.[29] Dunks, dribbling out time (prior to shot clock rules), and contact fouls to slow game-play are all cases in basketball where the rules of play are thwarted as a norm for competitive advantage. Breaking these rules in basketball is so common as to be a standard strategy of game-play.[30]

The formalist/antiformalist debate is significant, not for its disagreement but for what it suggests about the nature of sport: that sport has an internal conflict between formal and antiformal play. Much like the paradox found in skateboarding, there is a tendency for sport participants to subvert the very rules by which a sport is defined—there seems to exist mutually exclusive goals in sport itself. The dilemma can be stated as follows:

Mutually Exclusive Goals in Sport (MEGS)

1. Either sport is defined by rules or (exclusive) subversion of rules.
2. If defined by rules, the most salient goal of sport activity is to achieve rule-bound competitive success.
3. If defined by subversion of rules, the most salient goal of sport activity is to disrupt rule-bound competitive success.
4. In practice, sport activity is both achievement and disruption of rule-bound competitive success.
5. Activities that enjoy mutually exclusive goals are paradoxical.
6. Thus, in practice sport activity is paradoxical.

Much has been written supporting premise (2), particularly by formalists. Premise (1) requires an "all or nothing" assumption about rules in sport. While not all will believe this assumption is warranted with respect to sport itself, 'all or nothing' seems to characterize much of the scholarly literature cited above on rule following in sport. We can find further insight on this "all or nothing" description in premise (1) by considering the nature of subversion in sport in premise (3), to which I now turn.

SPORT AS SUBVERSION

Malaby anticipates the idea of subversion as sport when considering the nature of games as "processional."[31] (Malaby views sport as a subset of games.) Games like *Monopoly*, football, and *Pac-Man* have a, "semibounded and socially legitimate domain of contrived contingency that generates interpretable outcomes."[32] In other words, games are fundamentally "becoming" or in transition. There is no essential feature of gaming that makes it unique, except that it exists in a process of becoming. For Malaby, games are:

> [N]ot reducible to their rules. This is because any given singular moment in any given game may generate new practices or new meanings, which may in turn transform the way the game is played, either formally or practically (through a change in rules or conventions).[33]

Malaby's processional definition of games illuminates the spontaneity and consequent upending of rules in sport play as a part of its nature, while recognizing that rules are required for this spontaneity to exist, "Games are distinctive in their achievement of a generative balance between the open-endedness of contingencies and the reproducibility of conditions for action."[34]

Malaby's processional theory of games provides a context for my claim of sport as subversion accounting for how and why sport is an act of becoming and process: sport exists in tension between rule following and rule disruption. Hence, sport as subversion explains how sport maintains an active procession. In addition, the public conception of skateboarding as a subversive lifestyle provides an ideal for sport as processional as it exemplifies a constant overcoming of itself—in a constant state of innovative activity. What it means to skateboard is in a constant state of re-definition and flux. But why might sport exist as a process of becoming? A further piece of defining sport might shore up this more existentially charged question: why sport?

Mutualism provides a basis for why sport exists: competition in sports is meant to bring out behavior that transcends human limits and thereby brings achievement beyond what could be anticipated.[35] Why do we do sport? To be better at being who we are. Who are we? Beings limited by our embodiment, an embodiment that can be transcended by great people at great moments. The opening quote of this chapter by David Foster Wallace, for instance, conveys a kind of mutualism in sport, writing about great tennis play as a demonstration of transcending limits of the body's activity.[36] Simon et al. note a similar insight from Dellattre with specific regard to sport "moments":[37]

> Such moments are what make the game worth the candle. [I]t is the moments where no letup is possible, when there is virtually no tolerance for error, which make up the game. The best and most satisfying contests maximize these moments and minimize respite from pressure.[38]

These moments, like Maradona's "Hand of God,"[39] Princeton's 1895 defeat of Yale,[40] Federer's fourth-round play against Agassi in the 2005 U.S. Open,[41] suggest that sport provides a context for human excellence, where the pressure from two competing groups or individuals generate unpredictable and spontaneous outcomes.

Mutualism alone cannot define sport as providing conditions for great sport moments. These seem to be dependent on another feature of sport: when participants engage in activity that transcends the normal adherence to sport rules. In fact, the insight of mutualism is not so much that competition elicits excellence, but rather that mutualism identifies such moments as the basis of great sport.

SPORT MOMENTS

What is a moment? What are the conditions for a moment? And finally, why is a moment of significant interest to participants and spectators of sport? What seems to be the common feature in the example above is that a moment requires some form of surprising feat—a spontaneous achievement—that advances beyond normal rule-bound play. This is not to say that a moment is always obvious when it occurs, but rather it is something that generates a need for re-assessing a sport. When a moment occurs, self-critical questions arise: How do we make more moments like that one? Do we need to add or remove regulative rules to control or free sport play? Is it still the same or a different sport?

An insightful parallel comes from epistemology: when thought generates a new belief, other beliefs need to change in order to cohere and this causes a problem of knowing which beliefs are affected by the new belief—the "frame problem."[42] Sport moments seem to invite a similar kind of "frame problem," where the relevance of an event or case for defining the nature of a sport becomes confused. Let me briefly explain this allusion to the frame problem.

Daniel Dennett pointed out a dilemma in the coherence theory of truth: that when one adds a new belief, other beliefs must be updated, but it is not obvious which beliefs require revision without inspecting all of the beliefs to see if they are in fact relevant, and it is just not possible to inspect all beliefs for relevance.[43] Moments in sport seem to trigger a frame problem, where it is not clear which rules in a system of play need to be updated when a 'moment' occurs. For instance, the U.S. women's team won the World Cup in 1999 on a common 'rule-breaking' tactic by the goalie Briana Scurry of taking steps prior to the kick, creating a sense of confusion as to why this tactic was so often used when it was in fact contrary to the rules of the game.[44] Or the Reddy Mack's 1887 play where he interfered with the catcher after he had crossed home plate, ceasing to be a 'base runner.'[45] These plays are moments in sport because they produce confusion, which lead to a questioning as to whether or not rules need to be updated.

A problem for defining a sport follows this idea of "moments." If we read moments as events that generate frame problems and, more generally, if sport moments support the notion that sport involves subversion and consequently is a processional activity rather than one having an "essence" or "kind," then how is it that individual sports remain the same over time? And how is it that sport itself is a recognizable human activity if in fact it is always in process? I turn now to try and specify this problem as one of re-identification of a sport over time and then gesture at an initial response.

A RE-IDENTIFICATION PROBLEM

There are problems with grounding the nature of sport on subversive moments alone, such as Nozick's point that sport moments require comparisons with the performance of others—that a necessary condition for a 'moment' is a context that includes a class of the achievements by fellow competitors.[46] More problematic still is the formalist contention that one cannot upend the constitutive rules of sport without changing the sport itself. To my mind, the formalist claim is a kind of re-identification problem—can a participant or observer of sport recognize it after a significant amount of time has passed? The claim that I would like to test is whether these moments that upend the rules of sport change the sport. Is basketball a different game now that contact fouls are a normal strategic maneuver for slowing down the time clock? What constitutes "difference" in sport?

One clue to "difference" in sport may be the ability to re-identify a sport over many changes. Consider this scenario:

> Imagine a person who was an expert participant in sport X, but due to some strange incident becomes comatose for forty years. During her brief recovery (she awakens with no memory loss or damage to her brain of any kind), she watches two television channels that feature sports X and Y respectively. Both sports are quite similar in appearance, having similar equipment, architecture, and officiating. Given that no one provides her a way to identify which sport is which—no one names the sport or provides a clue as to whether it is the sport that she once played—would she identify sport X?[47]

Let's consider the possibility that she did in fact re-identify her sport, even though sport X evolved and changed over time and sport Y appeared to be very proximate to sport X in its identifiable characteristics. Re-identification may be possible even if they may not be able to know which exact features make the sport identifiable and even if the sport is itself immature and in a period of significant transition, so much so that it is not clear if it even is a sport. In sum, it seems possible that re-identification can be had against many odds.

Skateboarding appears to be a good test case for such a scenario, being itself barely fifty years old, with the bulk of scholars declaring that it is not a sport, and with numerous 'imitator' sports that have either branched off from skateboarding or currently share in a number of its culture and practices: longboarding, snowboarding, wakeboarding, etc. Consider, for example, that the coma patient is Patti—a champion skateboarding competitor in 1975 turned post-comotose skateboarding observer in 2015. Say that she recognized skateboarding in 2015 even if the competing channel showed competitions from skateboarding's latest branch-off sport, longboarding.

How might have Patti re-identified her sport after it has undergone forty years of change? The equipment used could only be identifiable in the broadest sense—wheels supporting a board—and is certainly not a distinguishing feature from the comparative sport, longboarding. The competitive architecture of skateboarding has changed dramatically, now including ramps, rails, steps, etc. The tricks are forehead-smacking amazing compared to the turns, tic-tacs, and handstands of her past. The rules that are said to define a skateboarding competition are minimal at best: a time constraint of the run and the judging the skater's performance on diversity, quantity, technicality, style, and risk of the tricks landed. So how might Pattie have done it?

We can begin to answer this question when we recognize that Patti's ability is not unlike the ability of other re-identifications of other human activities. Take, for instance, someone, let's call him Tom, who can identify over 2,000 years of the human activity known as science while ironically claiming that everything about science has changed or undergone "paradigm shifts" of incommensurable research agendas. The techniques, methods, results, etc. have all undergone unsettling change and yet they are all recognized as part of a historical thread of what we identify as science.

Like Tom, Patti's recognition may not be dependent on some specific set of rules of skateboarding, but rather an understanding that for a thing to be, it must change, rules and all, but that the activity should change around a specific gravitational center: an object of inquiry as it were, perhaps even an interactive "re-wilding" form of play.[48] This is not so much to answer the question in terms of how Patti reidentifies sport, but rather that Tom and Patti's re-identification is not something that is particularly surprising, opposing the formalists who seem to think that some permanent structures, viz. rules, are requisite for re-identification or identity over time.

The insight of Patti, by way of Tom, is that human activities, by their very nature, are in constant evolution that sometimes results in paradigmatic shifts in equipment, architecture, and rules. In the context of Patti's possible re-identification, subversion of sport seems obvious: if defined by disruption of rules, the goal of sport activity is to disrupt rule-bound competitive success, to transcend limits whether they be laws of nature or laws of society, including sport rules. It is simply not the case that rules somehow maintain the identity of human activity, whether intellectual pursuits like science, athletic pursuits like skateboarding, or game pursuits like chess.[49]

CONCLUSION

Highlighting the processional nature of sport provides a lens for insight into the what, how, and why of sport. What makes sport unique? The value of sport emerges from the definition of sport as subversion: sport lends itself to moments of transcending constraints of human forms both human embodiment and rule-grounded domains of activity. Why is there significant interest in being sport participators and spectators? Humans are in a process of becoming and sport provides a mirror that allows us to observe and record our constant over-body-achieving. This observation and recording of human transcendence through sport activity makes participation and observation incredibly popular, something of intrinsic interest to all human cultures and subcultures. How is sport a valuable human activity? The specific kind of transcendence of one's embodiment provided by sport makes it unique to spiritual, aesthetic, and intellectual human activities. Sport subverts the preconceived conditions of embodiment just as great writing upends pre conceived rules of grammar and scientific discoveries undermine paradigmatic views of the physical world.

These answers based on the "subversive moment" open up a concluding worry. It is difficult to praise all of the subversive sport moments discussed here. While they are all important moments—they are all game changers—it is difficult to simply praise this behavior and furthermore educate others to do likewise. There is something unethical in some of these subversive practices, largely because the manner in which they subverted the rules was scandalous—it was not so much a subversion of the rules but a cheating of the rules. Had the officials observed the breaking of the rules, such as Maradona's "Hand of God," a penalty would have been called and the rules would have ruled. So, there is reason to believe that in some sport moments, no real subversion occurred.

I'm not suggesting that the difference between subversion and cheating is obvious, but examples of praiseworthy subversion of the rules might help clarify the difference. Take John Wall's "yo-yo" dribble that looks like a pass to another player but which yo-yos back into the hands of the dribbler. Rather than going unobserved it is observed, and still fakes the defense. There is something momentous about such novel actions and suggests that real moments of sport subversion exist that are not bogged down by cheating concerns. Real subversion can cheat cheating.

NOTES

1. Special thanks to Andy Dicker, director of Element Skate Camp, for allowing me to conduct research on the nature of skateboarding as a volunteer at Element Skate Camp, Summers 2014 and 2015. Also, thanks to the directors of Elemental Awareness Foundation and my crew The Worble for conversations and continued insight into the re-wilding of skateboarding and life. Many thanks to former Los Angeles Laker Mike Penberthy for many talks about the craft of sport and encouraging the ideas in this essay. Finally, thanks to Shawn E. Klein and Lequez Spearman for reading and commenting on previous drafts of this chapter.

2. Claudio M. Tamburrini, *The 'Hand of God'?: Essays in the Philosophy of Sports* (Goteborg: Acta Universitatis Gothoburgensis, 2000).

3. Brian Skinner, "Scoring Strategies for the Underdog: A General, Quantitative Method for Determining Optimal Sports Strategies," *Journal of Quantitative Analysis in Sports* 7, no. 4 (2011).

4. Craig K. Lehman, "Can Cheaters Play the Game?" *Journal of the Philosophy of Sport* 8, no. 1 (1981).

5. I use the term "subversion" to indicate the interventionist strategies used in sport that, while maintaining the "letter" of the law, disrupt normal play. To "subvert" a rule is not to belligerently disregard it—to commit a foul or cheat—but rather to do something more radical; to use a rule in a way that generates a novel form of play. Though subversion often has political meaning. (See Paul W. Blackstock, *The Strategy of Subversion: Manipulating the Politics of Other Nations* (Chicago: Quadrangle Books, 1964), it is used here most generally to indicate the manner in which participants upend, intervene, or undermine an established system.)

6. The term "obversion," literally disruption by going over or against, may be a more accurate term for what I argue here, though it's common use in formal logic prevents this literal usage.

7. Bernard Suits, *The Grasshopper: Games, Life, and Utopia* (Toronto: University of Toronto Press, 1978).

8. Thomas Malaby, "Beyond Play: A New Approach to Games," *Games and Culture* 2, no. 2 (2007).

9. Robert L. Simon, Cesar R. Torres, Peter F. Hager, *Fair Play: The Ethics of Sport, 4th Edition* (Boulder, CO: Westview Press, 2015): 47.

10. Robert Rinehart, "Inside of the Outside: Pecking Orders Within Alternative Sport at ESPN's 1995 'The eXtreme Games'," *Journal of Sport and Social Issues* 22, no. 4 (1998).

11. Ibid.

12. Wez Lundry, "Subvert the Dominant Paradigm," *Thrasher*, October 1, 2002.

13. Rinehart, "Inside of the Outside."

14. Belinda Wheaton, "After Sport Culture: Rethinking Sport and Post-Subcultural Theory" *Journal of Sport and Social Issues* 31 (2007): 288.

15. Michael Atkinson and Brian Wilson, "Bodies, subcultures and sport," in *Theory, Sport and Society*, ed. Joseph Maguire and Kevin Young (Bingley, UK: Emerald Group, 2002): 386.

16. Vivoni also identifies this paradox, writing: "Purpose-built spaces such as public skate parks both marginalize skateboarders from city centers and serve as training grounds for appropriating urban spaces. While in the streets, skateboarders are both criminalized for defacement of property and commodified as urban guerrilla performance artistry. These contradictions disable straightforward claims founded on mutually exclusive processes of contestation and cooptation." Francisco Vivoni, "Spots of Spatial Desire: Skateparks, Skateplazas, and Urban Politics," *Journal of Sport and Social Issues* 33 (2009): 145.

17. Brian Glenney and Steve Mull, "Skateboarding and the Re-Wilding of Urban Space," *Journal of Sport and Social Issues* (Forthcoming).

18. J.S. Russell, "The Value of Dangerous Sport," *Journal of the Philosophy of Sport* 32, no. 1 (2005).

19. Jim Parry, "Sport, Art and the Aesthetic," *Sport Science Review* 12 (1989).

20. *Dogtown and Z-Boys*, directed by Stacy Peralta (Sony Pictures Classics, 2001), documentary.

21. Many skateboarding competitions, such as The Battle at the Berrics or ESPN's X Games, do prohibit any part of the body from touching the ground during a trick. But this emphasizes how fluid of an idea a "trick" is in skateboarding, as many tricks involve feet, hands, and other parts of the body making contact with the ground, making it difficult to distinguish a successful trick from a failed trick.

22. In asking this question, I do not mean to claim that skateboarding is a sport. In Glenney and Mull, "Skateboarding and the Re-Wilding of Urban Space," we argue that skateboarding is only part sport, unique in its symmetrical inter-activity with its architecture.

23. Malaby, "Beyond Play," 103.

24. Some of this change is due to safety of the athletes, such as regulative rule change of the NHL's 2011 prohibition of body checking with or to the head of the player in hockey See Laura Donaldson, Mark Asbridge, and Michael D. Cusimano, "Bodychecking Rules and Concussion In Elite Hockey," *Plos ONE* 8.7 (2013): 1. Some regulative rule change is due to ease of officiating the rules, such as the NCAA's 1953 requirement that the torso crossing the plane of the finish line rather than the entire body defined a race's finish. See Eric D. Zemper, "The Evolution of Track and Field Rules during the Last Century." (Presentation, USA Olympic Team Trials for Track and Field, Eugene, Oregon – July 4, 2008, 16.) Change in sporting and safety equipment follows the progress of technological achievement; racquets, clubs, bats, balls, boards, helmets, pads, etc. have all undergone radical change. Even the architecture on which sport occurs—fields, pitches, ramps, and so on—have evolved with technology over time.

25. John R. Searle, *Speech Acts: An Essay in the Philosophy of Language* (New York: Cambridge University Press, 1969): 33.

26. William J. Morgan, "The Logical Incompatibility Thesis and Rules: A Reconsideration of Formalism as an Account of Games," *Journal of the Philosophy of Sport* 14 (1987).

27. Suits, *The Grasshopper.*

28. Fred D'Agostino, "The Ethos of Games," *Journal of the Philosophy of Sport,* 8 (1981).

29. It might be thought that H. L. A. Hart's suggestion of "rules of change," principled procedures that determine change in rules to do things like safety concerns, provide a formalist account of rule change, but it is not the procedures themselves which initiate this change but rather something in the sport itself and hence cannot account for the transitory nature of sport alone. See H.L.A. Hart, *The Concept of Law* (Oxford: Clarendon Press, 1984).

30. Skinner, "Scoring Strategies for the Underdog."

31. Malaby, "Beyond Play."

32. Ibid., 96.

33. Ibid., 103.

34. Ibid., 106.

35. Simon et al., *Fair Play.*

36. David Foster Wallace, "Federer Both Flesh and Not."

37. Simon et al., *Fair Play.*

38. Edward J. Delattre, "Some Reflections on Success and Failure in Competitive Athletics," *Journal of the Philosophy of Sport* 2, no. 1 (1975): 134.

39. Tamburrini, *The 'Hand of God'?*

40. Delattre "Some Reflections on Success and Failure in Competitive Athletics."

41. Wallace, "Federer Both Flesh and Not."

42. Daniel Dennett, *Brainstorms* (MIT Press, 1978).

43. Ibid., 125.

44. Simon et al., *Fair Play,* 21.

45. Ibid., 33.

46. Robert Nozick, *Anarchy, State, and Utopia* (New York: Basic Books, 1974): 240.

47. The seventeenth-century problem known as Molyneux's question is another example of a re-identification problem.

48. Glenney and Mull, "Skateboarding and the Re-Wilding of Urban Space."

49. David Shenk, *The Immortal Game: A History of Chess* (New York: Doubleday, 2006).

Chapter 10

Bullfighting

The Mirror and Reflection of Spanish Society

Teresa González Aja

One of the spectacles which causes the most controversy in Spanish society is 'bullfighting,' an activity which is difficult to define and which has been considered to be an art, a game, a spectacle, a rite, a sport, and even all of them combined. This chapter aims to show that bullfighting possesses of all these aspects, and especially to determine which components of sport are visible in "bullfights," either from the point of view of the spectacle itself, or from that of the figure of the bullfighter as a possible sportsperson. To help in this endeavor I will describe how the most important authors have analyzed bullfighting, with special reference to its origin and evolution, as in both cases there is a certain amount of confusion. This chapter will classify and clarify the different modalities of bullfighting which have existed in the past or which still exist today. The different interpretations which have been given to bullfighting will be considered in an attempt to elucidate what truth can be found in each of them, to conclude with what most interests us here: What sporting elements does it possess? The initial hypothesis is that the evolution of bullfighting is a similar case to that of the birth and evolution of sport, in its strictest meaning, that is, contemporary sport, with its English origin, born in the middle of the eighteenth century. Thus, if one of the characteristics of contemporary sport is that it has been transformed from heterogeneous popular games, with neither norms nor defined rules, into an activity with universally recognized rules, then the same has happened to bullfighting which has evolved, practically during the same time period, from an unregulated activity to an activity with perfectly defined rules which are universally accepted. Similarly it can be seen how the different social classes have become involved in different sports activities or bullfighting modalities; the case of rugby and soccer are emblematic in the field of sport, and bullfighting on horseback ["rejoneo"] and bullfighting on foot in their respective ambit. Both rugby and soccer have been transformed into a great spectacle which can be associated with a series of problems which Mason has defined in the case of sport but which can also be applied to bullfighting:[1]

- Money: the objectives of sport or bullfighting do not always coincide with commercial interests;
- Sexism: both activities have basically been identified with Caucasian men;
- Drugs: understood in their widest context, as I am not referring to the fact that bullfighters consume substances, but that measures are taken which limit the physical possibilities of the bull;
- Violence: not only on the sports field or in the ring, but also among the spectators, in the present case among the so-called *"aficionados,"* arguing about the supremacy of one bullfighter or another.

But before tackling all these questions, there is an aspect which should be clarified and which will be analyzed below: the death of the bull. Its death may be one of the factors which have been referred to in order to exclude it from being considered a sport; however, this is a factor which appears in hunting. But while in hunting the death of the animal can be considered a priority, in the case of the bullfight it is not *necessary*, the death constitutes an *event*.

The bull may leave the ring alive, in this case either as a hero or as a coward. The first case is stipulated in article 83 of the regulations which refer to the pardoning of the bull "for its courage and excellent behavior in all the phases of the fight (so that) the bull will be returned to the stables to be healed."[2] This pardon also means that it will never be fought again, as its purpose will be "its use as a stud to preserve the maximum purity and quality of the bulls."[3] But the bull can be rejected and leave the ring alive because of its cowardice, as if it refuses to fight, then the spectacle is impossible.

This controversial question, which will be analyzed in depth given its enormous importance, is just touched on here in order to emphasize that I consider that it cannot be used as a conditioning factor when deciding whether bullfighting can be included or not in the category of sports activities.

Bullfighting is thus an activity, as mentioned initially, which defies definition but one which undoubtedly moves the spectator, a human endeavor which arouses the passions. From political leaders to the general public, not to mention philosophers, novelists, psychologists, farmers, and so on, everyone has had (and has) an opinion about the so-called "National Fiesta"[4] and it is usually a passionate opinion, radically for or radically against, but in any case never indifferent. The spectator takes a stand on it because bullfighting demands that we define ourselves in the face of the spectacle, converting it, in the words of Tierno Galván into an "event," as "social events oscillate between facts and acts. . . . They appear as constituting social reality with a peculiar demanding characteristic: they demand not that we adhere to them, but that we define ourselves before them."[5] And the Spanish people *define themselves* before it, rejecting it mercilessly or defending it to the death, *but without defining it.* Bullfighting is the mirror and reflection of Spanish society. I think it is important to underline that interest in bullfighting is not just limited to Spain, and many researchers from other countries have been drawn to the phenomenon and have established their own theories on the origins and significance of bullfighting. In painting, sculpture, music, the cinema, literature, in all the arts in fact, the artists have been interested in this activity and have been joined by those who could be called the theorists: anthropologists, sociologists, and historians.

The literature on the topic is consequently abundant and historical interest has increased producing a series of excellent studies. Impossible to include them all, there are some which must be mentioned, like the one by José María de Cossío,[6] probably the most important work written on the subject, which constitutes an authentic encyclopedia with a multitude of graphic, historical, literary, and other documents of all kinds making it a fundamental work from which to begin any research endeavor. In the eighteenth, nineteenth, and the beginning of the twentieth centuries, the bases were established for many of the theories which are currently put forward, both on the origin of bullfighting and its significance. In the mid-eighteenth century a study on the origins of bullfighting written by Nicolás Fernández de Moratín met with great success which lasted until way into the following century.[7] Other works worthy of mention are those by the Count of Las Navas,[8] who collected together for the first time the oldest information referring to bullfighting, and that of the Marquis of San Juan de Piedras Altas who, conceiving it as an ever-changing process, established its structure in phases, the first considering *Bull hunters*, the second *Matadors*, the third *Knightly bullfighting*, and the fourth and last *Professional bullfighting.*

As regards the bullfighting technique, there are many texts by the bullfighters themselves on how to perform, and among the authors of treatises on bullfighting [*Tauromaquias*] the following are worthy of mention: *Tauromaquia o el arte de torear* by Pepe Hillo,[9] not the only bullfighter who has tried to give us his view of the spectacle, and Paquiro who gave us his *Tauromaquia completa.*[10] Texts by bullfighters are not however limited to Spain, for example the French essayist Claude Popelin,[11] wrote an excellent work entitled *Le taureau et son combat.*

Other writings which are worthy of particular attention are those of Álvarez de Miranda, on the religious aspects and, in a more recent era, those by Bennasar, Amorós, Guillaume-Alonso, or the in-depth study carried out by Wolff,[12] just to mention a few of the most important ones.

ORIGIN

With regard to the origins of bullfighting the link to Spain is commonly accepted. The bull, in its magical facet "appears more or less everywhere, in the ancient world, but its transformation in the bullfights is characteristic of the Iberian Peninsula and the Minoan culture."[13] This linking of bulls and Spain is considered as something which has "always" existed, and to prove it, archeologists and historians have based their conclusions both on remains like Spanish Neolithic cave paintings and texts by Diodorus which confirm the sacred character of the bull in the peninsula. [14] However the problem is still evident with regard to the so-called *National Fiesta*, that is, the bullfight. Moratín, mentioned above, does not accept the thesis that links bullfighting to the activities in the Roman circus, maintaining that they are autochthonous and were practiced first by the Arabs and then by the Spaniards.[15] He is the first to defend the thesis of an Arab origin which was generally accepted and widespread due to the fact that it was shared by his friend Goya, who created a series of prints, entitled *La Tauromaquia*, directly inspired by Moratín's text. This thesis was followed by many historians like López Pelegrín,[16] Bedoya,[17] or Sicilia de Arenzana,[18] although it does not possess a solid or documented basis. Equally lacking in documentary strength is the thesis maintained during the sixteenth and seventeenth centuries on the origin of Spanish bullfights in the Roman circus, defended by Pérez de Guzmán[19] and Isidoro Gómez de Quintana.[20]

This lack of solid documentation has meant that, currently, almost no historian maintains either of the two origins. After the work by the Count of Las Navas, much better documented than the former writings, and in which he defends bullfighting as a phenomenon which is exclusive to Spain, the origins of which go back to prehistoric times and to the need to control wild bulls; research followed a new direction which speaks of bullfights as a phenomenon linked to religious matters.[21]

In any case we should accept that the presence and representation of bulls have been a constant element in Spanish culture, both in its iconography and its literature, from prehistoric caves, through the Canticles of Alphonse X the Wise, up to Picasso himself.

EVOLUTION

In order to clarify the evolution of bullfighting it is necessary to give a brief history up to the present day. Reliable documentation exists from the sixteenth century on which permits us to follow its development. Bullfighting should be divided into two major areas on the basis of a fundamental aspect:

whether or not the final aim is the death of the bull. The first case encompasses *bullfighting on horseback* and *on foot* and the second what could be called *traditional games involving bulls.*

Bullfighting on Horseback and on Foot

The nobility, whose fighting mode was traditionally on horseback, spent its leisure time practicing different equestrian exercises among which the struggle with a bull held pride of place. It was excellent for developing military skills as well as (once transformed into a spectacle) winning the admiration of the ladies as well as the rest of the noblemen and serving as an example for the people. During the sixteenth and seventeenth centuries, an era of great splendor, there appeared a whole series of riding manuals which included a description of the "suertes" [modalities],[22] the lance [lanza] and the spear [rejón], in which the aim was to kill the bull from horseback with the lance, the second of which would evolve into the current bullfighting on horseback [*rejoneo*], in which the aim was only to slightly injure the bull in order to stimulate its fighting instinct.

Bullfighting on horseback therefore was part of the equestrian activities carried out by the noblemen with the object of training for war, but at the same time as a demonstration of social prestige. When firearms changed the way of fighting and the knights lost their defensive function, it was necessary to demonstrate their preeminence by other means. In this way the spectacle, which could be called 'sporting' pardoning the anachronism (because as stated initially, sport is being considered as a contemporary phenomenon which does not include what went before), would become the place where they could manifest physical strength which would be identified with moral strength. Thus the following equestrian games would become extremely important like cane games,[23] jousting and, of course, bullfights which would be held to commemorate different important events in the life of the nobility. An example is the reception for King Don Carlos in Burgos in 1520 where the program indicates that "there are bulls and canes for today and jousting for tomorrow"[24] or the festivities held in Toledo in 1533 on the occasion of the disembarkment of the emperor Charles V in Barcelona in which "those from the silk workers guild came out, more than seven hundred people richly dressed in silk of all colors . . . and the next day the same guild held a bullfight with six bulls in Saint Mark's square and played canes."[25] Bullfighting accompanied the nobles' festivals on innumerable occasions, whether royal or otherwise. The fact is that "at the end of the sixteenth century and especially all through the seventeenth century, the spectacle took the form of a great political and social parade which brooked no restrictions."[26] But not only the nobles accompanied their important events with bullfights, the church

did likewise for religious festivals like those celebrated for the canonization
in 1622, of Saint Isidor The Farm Laborer (patron saint of the present day
Madrid "feria"), Saint Ignatius of Loyola, Saint Francis Xavier, and Saint
Teresa of Avila.[27]

The eighteenth century would bring an important change, the noblemen
would no longer take part in the combat, but would restrict themselves to
being the patrons of the gentlemen who would fight on horseback and whose
names the chronicles did not think worthy of mention, naming only their
patrons, indicating that those who were fighting the bulls were evidently not
from the upper classes. Bullfighting from horseback began to decline and
fighting on foot started to develop.

Bullfighting on foot, that for Guillaume-Alonso was omnipresent,[28]
although in its beginnings, in the bull spectacles of the sixteenth and seventeenth centuries and even before, had already appeared in numerous chronicles of foreign travelers during the second half of the eighteenth century. In
this context the description written by Jean François Peyron is emblematic
when he admits that when he saw the first bull killed he was shocked, but
that after the second one his desire to see more grew and he thus devotes a
whole chapter to this festival[29] in which he mentions some of the bullfighters
who fought on foot at that time like Costillares, Romero, or Pepe Hilllo.[30]
Townsend also mentioned the latter,[31] and assumed that bullfighting was a
professional activity to the extent that he looked into the finances; that is,
how much each one was paid, from the alguazils, to the banderilleros, and
of course the matadors, whom he divides into two categories, with those he
calls 'matadors in chief' evidently being paid more.[32] Pepe Hillo would be the
one to establish the bases of bullfighting in his aforementioned *Tauromaquia*,
where he would state:

> We can reduce all knowledge about the art of bullfighting to two points which
> are: the offensive and defensive actions used by the bulls: whose different
> movements should be well studied, in order to counter them with their respec-
> tive techniques using intelligence, as it is impossible for the Bull to gore the
> "Matador"[33] if he uses them in the correct manner.[34]

Pepe Hillo conceived bullfighting as a struggle, as a combat between the
bull and the bullfighter. In fact, to fight the bull is to deceive an animal with
a piece of cloth in order to avoid being gored. Both, bull and bullfighter, fight
for their lives. The *fight* [*lidia*] would consist of the canons of combat against
the bull which would be developed in the nineteenth century with the creation
of the first official bullfighting regulations in 1852 based on the aforementioned text by Paquiro.[35]

The bullfight consists of a series of perfectly structured obsessively ritualized phases. The whole spectacle is regulated by threes.

The First Third or Third of the Lances

The matador uses the cape and the bull receives a series of stabs in the mound of muscle between the neck and the back of the bull [morrillo] from the picador, but

> More than wounding the bull, it is the test of its courage and the charge of the bull must always provoke the stabbing. Thus the picador must stay on the edge of the ring and wait, at the regulated distance (three meters) for the bull to charge, as a brave bull attacks if it feels threatened (. . .) The bull should charge leaving its own natural "terrain" and attack the picador's horse, not to try to free itself from it, but to knock it down, so that the more the bull 'wants' to fight the more it is hurt, but at all times it must be able to escape from the lance if it 'prefers' flight to fight.[36]

This section "represents the brutal (or titanic) form of combat."[37]

The Second Third or Third of the Banderillas

Banderillas, some adornments in the form of wooden sticks with colored paper frills and a barb on the end, are stuck into the bull's back. The purpose is to stimulate the bull with their movement. The man who 'plants' them defies the animal unarmed and escapes from its horns only by dodging or ducking, the pace should be quick and joyful, "man and bull—are face to face, totally unarmed (there is no cape or hypocritically padded horse) as if the only thing that was important was that they take the measure of each other before the final episode ...)."[38]

The Third Third or Third of Death

The matador faces the bull with the small red cape [muleta] and kills it with the sword:

> From the brute violence which was the beginning (...) we have moved on to a really cursed state in the work with the cape where everything is essentially based on a perverse seduction of the bull using the caress of the material, the temptation of the bullfighter who comes closer and closer to falling—a type of flowering of evil in acute and covert applause, in the full light of day of Satanic beauty.[3]

The importance of the spectacle would grow during the nineteenth century, the bullrings, with their stands divided into three sections (shade, sun, and sun and shade) and the three concentric parts of the ring, multiply; and the bullfighters, three for each bullfight, become semi-gods, in any case authentic idols. They would be the idols of the cosmos which is the ring, of this circular area where everything revolves around the bullfighter who provokes, directs, and brings everything to an end.

The public would choose a bullfighter to become their hero, with violent episodes erupting between the fans about who was the best. This happened, for example, in the cases of *Cúchares* and *El Chiclanero,* whose fans did not hesitate to confront each other both with insults and with blows and sticks, something which would be repeated among the *fans* in the case of Antonio Sánchez *El Tato* and Antonio Carmona *Gordito,*[40] when there were even knife fights. However, I feel it is important to underline that this rivalry between bullfighters which degenerated into violence among the spectators, had a great deal to do with the attitude of the bullfighters themselves. For example, in the case of José Gómez *Joselito* and Juan Belmonte, whose rivalry in the ring was evident; feelings did not degenerate into violence among the spectators due to the fact that each of the bullfighters esteemed and admired the other, and were friends. In fact a bullfighting club was formed called *Those of José and Juan,* as it was considered that to understand the essence of the bullfight it was necessary to count on both men.[41] These names along with those of Lagartijo, Frascuelo, Mazzantini, Machaquito, Guerrita, Bombita, el Gallo, Marcial Lalanda, Domingo Ortega, and so many others, would give rise to a Golden Age of bullfighting. One of these bullfighters, Juan Belmonte, would have a decisive influence on its development, because if the *fight* [*lidia*] is the work of the nineteenth century, the *art of bullfighting* [*toreo*] would be the great contribution of the twentieth century and this would come about thanks to him. Until the arrival of Belmonte, the technique of fighting was based on dodging and this demanded considerable physical qualities, and great agility in the legs. It wasn't a question of keeping the body immobile and even less of slowing down the charge. Belmonte lacked these physical qualities, so taking advantage of his long arms he became the master of the terrain, he substituted fighting with the legs with fighting with the arm, forcing the bull to do what he wanted, and thus the idea of *"tempering"* [*temple*] (using the cape to modify the charge making it slower or faster) was born, a search for balance between the rapid charge of the bull and the control and deceleration of the animal, in other words the long slow pass. Now the bullfighter *uses his art* [*torea*], he *incites* [*cita*] the bull and controls its rhythm, cadence, softness, and slowness. For Wolff "[a]ll the ambiguity (and strength) of the bullfight lies in this: in the fact that while facing the bull, the bullfighter models its charge and makes it his own work of art."[42] In this sense bullfighting has been defined as an art and the artist par excellence is Belmonte, whom intellectuals

like Valle Inclán, Pérez de Ayala, or Romero de Torres saw as the great inno-
vator who turned bullfighting into an authentic art.[43]

Traditional Games Involving Bulls

Less dangerous, and clearly differentiated because their purpose is not the
death of the bull, are the traditional games involving bulls which from the
thirteenth to the nineteenth century, and in some cases still today, are held
by the common people in a relatively unstructured manner. Here I could
mention the "running of the bulls" [encierros], which consist of chasing the
bulls through the center of the town following a preset route. Currently the
most famous ones are those held in Pamplona. Sometimes the bulls are run
at night, and in these cases the bull's horns are covered in resin which is set
on fire, as in the case of the Basque "fire bull." Sometimes the bulls were
tied with a rope and the aim was to pull then down to the ground, these are
"tied" [ensogados] or "roped" [enmaromados] bulls. There are other popular
types of games involving bulls, like those held during carnival or the "rocket"
[encohetados] bulls on which the frames for fireworks are placed, or the bulls
involved in the festivals of Moors and Christians.

Also highly popular are the informal amateur bullfights [capeas] where in
an enclosure, the bulls are challenged, using a piece of cloth, by young people
who at times perform acrobatics to show their agility and courage (nowadays in
some places this is done with a cow). Hemingway recommends the spectators
who want to learn about bullfighting to attend them because "the bulls do not
always go for the cloth because the bullfighters are learning before your eyes
the rules of combat . . . the spectator can see the mistakes of the bullfighters, and
the penalties that these mistakes carry,"[44] in short, they permit us to appreciate
the worth of a bullfight. For Hemingway the "capeas" are "a sport, a very sav-
age and primitive sport, and for the most part a truly amateur one" and he goes
on to state that the essential difference is the risk of death as "We, in games,
are not fascinated by death, its nearness and its avoidance. We are fascinated
by victory and we replace the avoidance of death by the avoidance of defeat."[4]

Death is therefore an essential component, it is omnipresent, even though
the end may not be the death of the bull, the danger to the bullfighter is constant, but although in the traditional games involving bulls the bull is kept
alive, in bullfighting the bull must die.

THE SIGNIFICANCE OF BULLFIGHTING

The death of the bull is undoubtedly the most sensitive topic with reference
to the National Fiesta. It seems that, nowadays, what is rejected is not so
much the fact that the bullfighter risks his life as the need for the bull to die

in almost all the fights, except in the cases that it is pardoned for its courage, or returned for its cowardice. Some authors like Álvarez de Miranda,[46] Pitt-Rivers, or Michel Leiris, justify this need on the basis of the 'sacrificialist' character of the bullfight. For Pitt-Rivers the sacrifice of the bull has a precise meaning: "Through the representation of an interchange of sex between the bullfighter and the bull and the immolation of the latter, which transmits its genesic potency to its conqueror, there is a transmission between Humanity and Nature: men sacrifice the bull and receive in exchange the power that it has."[47] Leiris states that:

> Every bullfight; like the sacrifice it is, tends towards its paroxysm: the causing of death, after which there can only be release, as after the possession of the object of desire, in love, or the death of the hero in a tragedy. In the case of the sacrifice, this paroxysm or point of maximum tension is the very moment of immolation. . . . Death which seemed, during the different passes, logically reserved for the bullfighter, passes through the sword to the bull. Thus, once the bull has been killed, order is restored and things are returned to their rightful place, what was on the left on the left, what was on the right on the right, the bad has been punished and the good rewarded.[48]

But for Francis Wolff, in his magnificent analysis on the need for the death of the bull, sharing in part the sacrificialist theory, as in any case the bull will be *killed*, it will always be the victim offered in a rite, although the lack of skill of the bullfighter may make him kill it in a clumsy and ineffective way giving rise to boos and being shamed. He goes further to say that:

> The man does not immolate, he triumphs. The animal does not die as a victim but rather it is the man who kills it like a hero. The means of execution by the sword should be "straight to the point" as the saying goes. Far from being the symbolic gesture of a priest, the blow with the sword is the true apotheosis of the brave. As the supreme technique that it is, it expresses more than any other, the sense and worth of the fight. It reclaims all the virtues of heroism: the indisputable value of physical endeavor, the firm resolution of the technical gesture, the frankness and loyalty of the confrontation, combined with the skill of deceit, because the right hand kills while the left hand deceives . . . *without blinding:* "deceiving without lying" . . . one more time.[49]

Bullfighting must therefore be much more than an animal sacrifice, and should be considered as a combat between man and an animal, for Wolff the matador should not be considered as a sacrificer, but rather as a gladiator who incarnates the values of the hero and (albeit remotely) the bullfight would be the heir of the knights' tournaments and related to hunting with dogs.[50] But bullfighting is profoundly different from these. While in the hunt the object is to capture the prey, as hunting is definitively "what one animal does to capture another, dead or alive, which belongs to a species which is vitally inferior it its own,"[51] in bullfighting the chase is reciprocal with identical intentions, to kill the other; and when this happens neither of the two have the least interest in the former mortal enemy. It is enough to see how the bull, once it has injured the bullfighter, leaves him alone if it thinks he is dead and on his side the bullfighter obviously does not take his prey home. But even more importantly, while in hunting it is necessary for the animal to have an escape route, that is the possibility of escaping, this is not so in bullfighting, where the situation has to be resolved in favor of one or the other, the bull or the bullfighter.[52]

> The bullfight is (therefore) the regulated combat between a man and an animal, or in other words, the representation of the struggle between two forms of life: serene power and intelligence—cunning—against the power of brute force, blind instinct . . . A man . . . declares himself capable of a heroic feat to win the admiration of all and attain glory.[53]

The words of old Peleus spring immediately to mind recommending "his son Achilles to always stand out and be superior to the rest."[54] The Greeks who always considered outstanding skill and strength to be the evident characteristic of all dominant positions, used the word 'aretē' to designate "in accordance with the way of thinking in ancient times, the strength and skill of the warriors or fighters, and above all heroic valor considered not in our sense of a moral action distinct from strength but intimately connected to it."[55] Existence is based on agōn (both struggle and contest) and it is in the agōn where aretē is measured, that is, the vigor and will to be "superior to the others."[56] I do not hesitate, therefore, to consider bullfighting as an 'agonistic' manifestation in the Greek sense of the term.[57]

An essential component of bullfighting is the fact that it is spectacle, and in this it is again different from hunting, as the latter is carried out far from the public eye and very often in total solitude. However, the bullfighter also enjoys relative solitude as it is him and the "rest," that is, it is a spectacle in which all the spectators are equal, the ring doesn't have the shape of a theater or a football stadium, it is formed of concentric circles and in the center are the bull and the bullfighter. "All of those who, without danger, watch the bullfighter risking his life are at that moment, from the Spanish point of view, inferior to him. And this inferiority makes them equal."[58]

But what does it mean to be a bullfighter? To quote Wolff: "The greatest honor for a bullfighter, i.e. someone who fights *bulls*, is to be called a bullfighter [torero]."[59] The cry that goes up from the bullring is that of Torero! Torero! When the bullfighter performs according to an ethic, a way of behaving, he then becomes *the torero*. It is an adjective which is applied, on special occasions in the Spanish culture, to a person who is not a bullfighter but whose behavior has nonetheless been moving and has provoked the necessary admiration to make them worthy of the title. The ethics of bullfighting are heroic and agonic ethics where will power is manifested exalting the victory of the man over nature and, as shown above, "assume relations among men in asymmetric positions as some are spectators of what others are doing."[60] The bullfighter constitutes an example of masculinity. Obviously without trying to say that appearance signifies identity, it is still true that if there is one figure in Spain which symbolizes masculine values, it is that of the bullfighter. He is therefore an archetype.[61] This concept of archetype can be extended to the bullfight itself, which is the archetype of spectacle as nothing is hidden, everything is visible,[62] following a scheme which is analogous with Greek tragedy, and presenting "the aspect of one of those revealing facts which illuminate certain dark parts of ourselves by provoking a type of fellow-feeling or similarity, and the emotional power of which is due to the fact that they are mirrors which reflect, objectified and already constructed, the very image of our emotion."[63] Hemingway would be the one to defend the bullfight as a tragedy in the strict sense of the word: "I believe that the tragedy of the bullfight is . . . ordered and . . . disciplined by ritual,"[64] and according to Galván "the bullfight recalls the play of the integrating elements of classical tragedy. The chorus with the unbearable threat of its elemental formulas, weaving fate between approval and laments: Dionysus, spectator. The characters of the action living the tragedy with lucidity; Apollo and Dionysus indestructibly united."[6]

We are faced then with a spectacle in which the hero fights to the death, a tragedy. Classical reminiscences are evident. Death is linked to the first sports manifestations of which we possess written descriptions; Homer tells us how agonistic competitions were held in the funeral rites in honor of Patroclus. Violence is something which is inherent in Greek agonism; the norms of the pankration,[66] or more accurately, the almost complete absence of them, confirm their different attitude in the face of death, in the face of violence. The Roman world made a display for centuries of its enjoyment of hand to hand combat in the figure of the gladiators.[67] During the Middle Ages and most of the Renaissance, the knights, from whom Coubertin would get his inspiration to establish his Olympic ethics,[68] traveled all over Europe fighting in tournaments and jousts, the great sports of the Middle Ages where death was omnipresent.[69] Spain would add to these activities, as has been seen, the canes and bulls. Bullfighting has its roots therefore in the same cultural events as modern sport. But if modern sport is the product of a particular society, the English one, bullfighting is the product of another society, the Spanish one, with its own values, in which "manliness" is one of the fundamentals. The similarities with regard to the developmental process are numerous, sport, initially the privilege of the upper social classes, would become part of the less privileged classes and be transformed.[70] The same can be said of bullfighting: bullfighting on horseback would give way to bullfighting on foot, in the lower classes. Furthermore, the same as sport, it would quickly become professionalized so that the inclusion of money would constitute one of its attractions with all the fame and admiration that goes with it.[71] This admiration for the sportsperson or the bullfighter, would lead the supporters to show their preferences in the form of violence in the stands, to congregate around the object of their admiration, although while in sport it is usually a team (at least in its most important manifestation, soccer) in bullfighting it is always a man, a "real man." Anyway in both cases it is a masculine universe, where the feminine presence is difficult to accept, more, logically, in bullfighting for obvious reasons, although there have been several women bullfighters.[72]

So, is bullfighting a sport? The bullfighter can be said to have physical qualities which include him in the group of what we call sportspersons, the bullfight clearly includes components we could call sporting, but bullfighting has this component of a fight to the death (not just symbolically, that is defeat), this necessary tragic character, which transforms it into more than a sport, into a tragic combat, into a rite, into a struggle for life or death, with the added aspect of an art, it is the immeasurability which moves us and makes us face an ethical dilemma before which we must define ourselves. We can feel horror or admiration, but we cannot remain indifferent, Spanish society continues with its incessant controversy, but the answer cannot possibly come from consensus, it has to be sought inside each one of us.

NOTES

1. Tony Mason, *El Deporte En Gran Bretaña* (Madrid: Civitas, 1994).
2. "Real Decreto 145/1996, de 2 de Febrero, Por el que se modifica y da nueva redacción al reglamento de espectáculos taurinos," in *Ministerio de Justicia e Interior* (Madrid: Official State Gazette, 1996), 8401 a 21.
3. Ibid.
4. In spite of being considered as such, an analysis of the geography of bullfighting reveals that the passion for this specatcle is not evenly felt all over the country, and we should recall that bullfights have recently been banned in Catalonia something which is provoking an important debate both at the public and polticial level. Furthermore, bullfighting is practiced outside of Spain, for example in France or Latin America.
5. Enrique Tierno Galván, *Desde el espectáculo a la trivialización* (Madrid: Tecnos, 1987), 47.
6. José María de Cossío, *Los Toros : tratado técnico e histórico* (Madrid: Espasa Calpe, 1943).

7. Nicolás Fernández de Moratín, *Carta histórica sobre el origen y progresos de las fiestas de toros en españa* (Madrid: Imprenta de Pantaleón Aznar, 1777).

8. Juan Gualberto López Valdemoro de Quesada Navas, conde de las, *El espectáculo más nacional* (Madrid: Sucesores de Rivadeneyra, 1899).

9. José Delgado Guerra (Pepe Hillo), *La tauromaquia o arte de torear* (Cadiz, 1796).

10. Fancisco Montes (Paquiro), *Tauromaquia completa o el arte de torear en plaza, tanto a pie como a caballo* (Madrid: Imprenta de D. José María Repullés, 1836).

11. Claude Popelin, *Le taureau et son combat* (Paris: Plon, 1952).

12. Citations to these works can be found Wolff, *Filosofía de las corridas de toros.*

13. Ángel Álvarez de Miranda, *Ritos y juegos del toro* (Madrid: Taurus, 1962), 15. Although some authors like Ortiz Cañavate, have linked both phenomena, they are a minority and in any case provide no evidence. Historians, including Arthur Evans, have not established historical connections between them. It cannot really be stated that bullfighting has a Cretian origin.

14. Diodorus Siculus, *Bibliotheca Historica,* IV, 18, 3.

15. This thesis only has solid documentation in the organization of bullfights in Seville from 1018 to 1021, when Abu-el Hassan became king of this city after breaking with the Caliphate of Cordoba.

16. S. López Pelegrín ("Abenámar"), *Filosofía de los toros* (Madrid, 1842).

17. Fernando G. de Bedoya, *Historia del toreo, y de las principales ganaderías de España* (Madrid, 1850).

18. F. Sicilia de Arenzana, *Las Corridas De Toros. Su Origen, Sus Progresos Y Sus Vicisitudes* (Madrid: Imp. y Lit, de N. González, 1873).

19. J. Pérez de Guzmán, *Origen E Historia De Las Fiestas De Toros* (s.d.).

20. Isidoro Gómez Quintana, *Apuntes históricos acerca de la fiesta de toros en España. Biografía De Los Más Célebres Lidiadores* (Cordoba: R. Molina, 1897).

21. Cf.: Álvarez de Miranda, *Ritos y juegos del toro.* The author presents an interesting study on the religious symbolism of bullfighting.

22. Argote de Molina, *Libro de la montería* (Seville, 1582). Pedro Fernández de Andrada, *Libro de la Gineta de España* (Seville, 1599). Bernardo de Vargas Machuca, *Libro de Exercicios de la Gineta* (Madrid, 1600). Gregorio Tapia y Salcedo, *Exercicios de la Gineta* (Madrid, 1643).

23. In the aristocratic bull festivals, also called "canes and bulls" the game of canes usually followed that of the bulls, in a type of second half.

24. Jenaro Alenda y Mira, *Relaciones de solemnidades y fiestas públicas de España* (Madrid 1903), 19.

25. Ibid., 31–32.

26. Bartolomé Bennassar, *Histoire de la Tauromachie. Une société du spectacle.* (Paris: Éditions Desjonquères, 1993), 21.

27. Ibid., 20.

28. Araceli Guillaume-Alonso, "Tauromaquia para un rey: fiesta de toros en la inauguración del Buen Retiro," (paper presented at the Fiestas de toros y sociedad, Seville, 2001), 284.

29. Jean François Peyron, "Des Fêtes, Combats ou Courses de Taureaux," *Nouveau voyage en espagne, fait en 1777 & 1778* (Londres—París 1782).

30. Ibid., 264.

31. Joseph Townsend, *A Journey though Spain in the Years 1786 and 1787* (London: C. Dilly, 1792), 346.

32. Ibid., 349–50.

33. Pepe Hillo died on May 11, 1801, gored by the bull *Barbudo*.

34. Hillo, *La tauromaquia o arte de torear*, 26.

35. Montes, *Tauromaquia completa o el arte de torear en plaza, tanto a pie como a caballo*.

36. Wolff, *Filosofía de las corridas de toros,* 79.

37. Michel Leiris, *Espejo de la tauromaquia* (Madrid: Arena Libros, 2014), 57.

38. Ibid., 58.

39. Ibid., 60.

40. Bennassar, *Histoire de la tauromachie. Une société du spectacle*, 61-62.

41. Ibid., 75.

42. Wolff, *Filosofía de las corridas de toros*, 180.

43. Bennassar, *Histoire de la tauromachie. Une société du spectacle*, 74.

44. Ernest Hemingway, *Death in the Afternoon* (USA: Charles Scribners Sons, 1932), 39.

45. Ibid., 37.

46. Álvarez de Miranda, *Ritos y juegos del toro*, 37.

47. Cited by Wolff, *Filosofía de las corridas de toros*, 86.

48. Leiris, *Espejo de la tauromaquia*, 56.

49. Wolff, *Filosofía de las corridas de toros*, 102–103.

50. Ibid., 98.

51. José Ortega y Gasset, "Sobre la caza," in *Veinte años de caza mayor del Conde de Yebes*, ed. El Viso (1943; reprint, 1983), 22.

52. On occasions the bull can be pardoned, when it has demonstrated physical qualities and above all exceptional moral qualities (particularly bravery), so that it can serve as a stud on the estate it came from (art. 83 of the Regulations of 1922).

53. Wolff, *Filosofía de las corridas de toros*, 99.

54. Homero, *Iliada-Odisea.*, trans. Luis Segalá, 1959 ed. (Barcelona: Vergara, 1969), 246.

55. Werner Jaeger, *Paideia*, 1957 ed. (Madrid: F.C.E., 1981), 22. For the development of the concept of "Aretē" see the chapter by this author, "Nobleza y Areté."

56. Teresa González Aja, "La educación heroica y agonal en el mundo homérico y su repercusión en las manifestaciones artísticas," *Historia de la Educación* 14–5 (1995–1996), 32.

57. This same term is used by Wolff when he talks of the "bullfight-combat." Wolff, *Filosofía de las corridas de toros*, 98.

58. Tierno Galván, *Desde el espectáculo a la trivialización*, 60.

59. Francis Wolff, "¡Torero!¡Torero!" La ética del torero y sus diez mandamientos" (paper presented at the Fiestas de toros y sociedad, 2001), 771.

60. Wolff has remarked on the characteristics of the ethics of bullfighting, from which I have taken a brief summary. Ibid., 777–80.

61. Compare, Teresa González Aja, "Trionfo e dominio nell'arena," *Lancilloto e Nausica* 26 (2003).

62. Wolff, *Filosofía de las corridas de toros,* 33.

63. Leiris, *Espejo de la tauromaquia,* 27.

64. Hemingway, *Death in the afternoon,* 9.

65. Tierno Galván, *Desde el espectáculo a la trivialización,* 62.

66. Teresa González Aja, *El deporte a través del arte : el mundo antiguo: del "agôn" al "ludus"* (Madrid: Dirección General de Deportes, Comunidad de Madrid, 2000), 71.

67. Ibid., 108 and following.

68. Pierre de Coubertin would base his Olympic idea on three pillars: Classical Greece, Sport as conceived by Thomas Arnold, and medieval chivalry. See in this regard "La restauración de los juegos olímpicos: Pierre de Coubertin y su época," in *In Corpore Sano. El deporte en la antigüedad y la creación del moderno olimpismo,* ed. Fernando García Romero and Berta Hernández García (Madrid: Sociedad de Estudios Clásicos, 2005).

69. J.J. Jusserand, *Les sports et jeux d'exercice dans l'ancienne France* (Paris 1901), 42. See also John McClelland, "Early Modern Athletic Contests: Sport or Not Sport?" in this volume.

70. In this sense the cases of rugby and soccer are paradigmatic.

71. Tony Mason, *El deporte en Gran Bretaña* (Madrid: Civitas, 1994), 91.

72. "Homenaje a las mujeres toreras En la muestra 'Una mirada femenina del toreo'," *Republica,* last modified May 6, 2011, http://www.republica.com/2011/05/06/homenaje-a-las-mujeres-toreras-en-la-muestra-una-mirada-femenina-del-toreo/.

Chapter 11

Why Some Animal Sports Are Not Sports

Joan Grassbaugh Forry

In 2014, the prestigious Westminster Kennel Club included a competition in agility, the fastest growing dog sport in the world, in its Westminster Dog Show festivities. In agility, dogs navigate a series of obstacles as directed by a human handler. The obstacles include several kinds of jumps, tunnels, a teeter-totter, an a-frame, a chute, and weave poles. There are criteria for executing each obstacle. The dog must execute each obstacle in order without making a mistake. The winner is the dog with the fastest time. At the 2014 Westminster Agility Championships, Soshana Dos and her three-and-half-year-old Border Collie, Glance, earned a chance to compete in the finals (which was called by former Olympic diver Greg Louganis). Halfway through their run, Glance went over a jump and was about to enter the weave pole obstacle when he stumbled and stopped. In agility lingo, this is called a "refusal." The dog may refuse or hesitate to engage an obstacle because of fear, injury, or confusion due to a breakdown in communication between handler and dog. Glance turned and looked at his owner-handler. Soshana picked up her dog and spoke to him softly as she walked out of the arena. Their run was over.

The moment only lasted a few seconds, but the look exchanged between dog and handler communicated something deeply meaningful. The dog did not want to continue. His owner-handler understood. She respected his decision and permitted him to stop. Greg Louganis speculated that perhaps Glance was injured or not feeling well. Louganis used the opportunity to point out that the dogs are the athletes in this sport and are subject to sports-related injuries just as human athletes.

This example is remarkable because it showcased exemplary communication and respect between human and animal. Additionally, Louganis' assertion that the dogs are the athletes brings an important consideration to the fore. Under what conditions can nonhuman animals be considered athletes? Ought we consider activities in which nonhuman animals are involved in the pursuit of winning athletic competitions, sports? Is dog agility the same kind of activity as, say, basketball? Under what conditions are animal sports morally justifiable, and, conversely, morally reprehensible?

In addressing these questions in this chapter, I appeal to a set of claims about the voluntary nature of play, games, and sport. Sport, insofar as it is rooted in an account of play, is voluntary. But, the actions and behaviors we volunteer are shaped by our experiences, contexts, and embodied characteristics. Human athletes engage in sport for myriad reasons, from sheer joy to lucrative financial gain. While the reasons a nonhuman animal might engage in sporting behaviors are more limited, it is not unreasonable to presume that an animal might be engaging in sporting behaviors for several reasons. As I will argue, the voluntary feature of animal engagement in sport is something we ought to consider more carefully. When the voluntary nature of play is compromised, I will argue, these animal sports fail to meet a basic tenet of a definition of sport. I will distinguish between activities with nonhuman animals that are not sports, animal sports that use bad practices, and ideal animal sports.

My two goals in this chapter are modest: (1) to raise questions about whether and what conditions human activities with nonhuman animals qualify as sport, and; (2) to offer a slightly more nuanced view of voluntariness in play, as it relates to sport and a subsequent ethical view regarding animals in sport. My hope is that this work will provide philosophers of sport with some new tools for analyzing human-animal interactions in sport. My view also attempts to argue against the view that any use of animals in sport is morally wrong, a view commonly advanced by strong animal rights positions.

ANIMAL ETHICS AND SPORT HISTORY

It is challenging, if not impossible, to summarize a field so broad and contentious as animal philosophy. Philosophical research on nonhuman animals has made tremendous gains in the recent past. Accounts of the human-animal relationship abound, drawing from diverse thinkers and traditions. Theoretical accounts in normative animal ethics have challenged ethical theories to include nonhuman animals as worthy of moral concern. Animal ethicists have also focused upon applied problems such as factory farming, zoos and circuses, fur production, hunting, and the treatment of wild animals. Most arguments in animal ethics conclude, though on very different grounds, that at least some kinds of harm to animals are morally objectionable and ethically unjustified.

However, the concept of harm is tricky, as are the grounds on which harms are deemed to be morally objectionable and ethically unjustified.

Animal ethicists commonly appeal to features of animal lives to establish that nonhuman animals (especially mammals) are the sorts of beings that can, indeed, experience harm. Consciousness, sentience, the ability to feel pain and pleasure, having preferences or interests, feeling emotions, having memories, and executing actions to pursue goals are all features of nonhuman animal lives that form the basis for various ethical views that claim that harming non-human animals is wrong. These features are, in many cases, empirically observable. Animal ethicists claim that these and other features of animal life are similar and comparable to features of human life. This is important because if these features are similar between species, then understanding what might constitute harm for nonhuman animals becomes easier. Like humans, nonhuman animals exhibit observable behaviors that indicate distress, fear, and pain, as well as eustress, pleasure, and joy. Like humans, nonhuman animal behaviors and emotional states correlate with physical changes such as elevated heart rates, increased cortisol levels, and increased respiration rates. Whether the ethical view regarding harm is based upon rights, virtue, or a utilitarian calculation, there is considerable agreement that *intentionally* causing nonhuman animals distress through fear or pain is morally wrong. One might object that there might be countervailing reasons for causing an animal fear or pain. In some cases, causing an animal fear or pain so is not only unavoidable, but justifiable. For example, when I take my dog to the veterinarian for vaccinations, he experiences distress and pain, but such distress and pain is ultimately for his own well-being and the public health of other beings he might encounter. Certainly, there are situations like this one that may justify causing pain and distress to nonhuman animals, but animal ethicists have long claimed that many of our reasons for intentionally causing distress and pain to nonhuman animals (such as our food preferences) are not good reasons. But, this is where the concept of harm becomes tricky. People frequently do not agree when nonhuman animals are experiencing distress or pain. They might not believe that they are intentionally causing distress and pain. Alternatively, they might believe that such pain and distress is justifiable for some larger purpose, and thus, distress and pain do not constitute harm. My response to these objections is that we can know and understand states of distress and pain by observing behavior and physical states. For the purposes of this paper, I hold that causing a nonhuman animal distress and/ or pain for the sake of sport is morally wrong. I also hold that distress and pain are harmful and should be avoided. In addition, I hold that humans have a moral obligation to minimize distress and pain for nonhuman animals that are in our care.

A moral obligation to avoid causing harm to nonhuman animals gives us some tools for condemning many practices. Articulating a moral duty not to harm is important and useful for animal ethics. But, as Giulana Lund writes,

"Victimization should not be the only lens through which we see human relations with other animals. It is not sufficient to say what we *should not do* (inflict pain); it is equally important to say what we *should do* (respect, respond)."[1] Indeed, humans interact with animals in all sorts of ways, and merely not harming animals doesn't make for a very interesting or meaningful human-animal relationship. Lund and others encourage us to ask: what makes for a mutually meaningful human-animal relationship?

The philosophical literature surrounding animals in sport is still sparse, through interest in the subject is growing. Academic research on animals in sport has largely focused on hunting and blood sports. Animal fighting sports have been popular all over the world throughout history. Margo DeMello writes that blood sports include "cricket fighting in China, cockfighting in Southeast Asia to gladiator events in which animals were pitted against animals, people against people, and animals against people."[2] In American sport history, the specter of blood sports is inescapable. Baiting sports, such as bull-baiting or bear-baiting, refer to tying up a large animal and allowing dogs to attack the animal. Spectators take bets on which animal will "win." Colonists in North America largely viewed embracing these "sports" as a rebellion against their English counterparts. As these sports became banned during the Victorian era in Europe, they became more entrenched in the leisure activities of the United States. The South led the way, but Northern cities soon followed and cultivated their own blood sports. Elliott J. Gorn and Warren Goldstein write:

> Rat baiting appeared in New York City around 1830 and achieved sudden favor with gamblers, saloon owners, and the urban underclass. In the "classic," one hundred rats were placed in a pit eight feet long, and a carefully trained fox terrier waded in to kill as many of them as possible in a given period of time. The best dogs could dispose of all one hundred in about twenty minutes. In the "handicap," a timekeeper determined how long a dog took to kill its weight in rats. For variety, men wearing great boots occasionally teamed up with the terriers in timed rat-killing competitions. Like other blood sports, ratting had a certain sophistication—dogs had special trainers and handlers, referees resolved disputes, timekeepers kept watchful eyes on the clock, and old men and boys were hired to catch live rats.[3]

Just as with today's popular sports, the sophistication of the sport appealed to a variety of people and such sophistication enabled greater opportunities for involvement. The rat-catching boys of yesteryear are the ball boys of today's baseball teams.

Though ratbaiting fell out of fashion, dogfighting and cockfighting are blood sports that continue to thrive. Dogfighting involves placing two dogs in an enclosure, usually a square pit, where they "fight either until one is too injured to continue and quits the fight due to extreme pain or severe exhaustion or until one dies."[4] Dogs are trained using brutal techniques and are regularly administered performance-enhancing drugs (sometimes even cocaine).[5] Jim Gorant's devastating book, *The Lost Dogs,* intimately details current practices of dogfighting and the controversy surrounding NFL player, Michael Vick.[6] Dogfighting is currently illegal (a felony charge) in the United States, but this wasn't always the case. Hanna Gibson notes that the United Kennel Club actually sanctioned and sponsored dogfights in the mid-1800s. The sport was so popular that in 1881, railroads in Ohio and Mississippi offered discounted fares to a dogfight in Louisville.[7] Similarly, cockfighting involves fighting two gamecocks in an enclosure until one bird quits from injury, exhaustion, or death. Gamecocks are outfitted with sharp metal gaffs, which look like the business end of an ice pick, that are attached to their legs to inflict injury upon their opponents. Cockfighting is regarded as an ancient sport with roots in many cultures around the world. Andrew Lawler notes, "One of the earliest recorded cockfights took place in China in 517 B.C."[8] The vestiges of these blood sports are on display as many universities in the United States revere bulldogs and gamecocks as their mascots.

Can blood sports be considered sports? The animals clearly suffer harms of stress, injury, isolation, and death. But though they are unethical, do these activities meet the criteria of a definition of sport? These are important questions, and I will return to them shortly.

GAMES, PLAY, AND SPORT

Philosophers of sport have discussed the distinction between games, play, and sport at length.[9] Indeed, defining sport continues to be one of the central problems in philosophy of sport (as evidenced by the existence of this very volume!). In this section, I will briefly outline some of major points of (relative) agreement in the definitional debate surrounding games, play, and sport. My purpose is to understand how these concepts relate to human-animal activities.

Bernard Suits characterizes games as rule-bound, goal-oriented activities, which "involve choice, ends and means."[10] Suits distinguishes between "constitutive rules" and "rules of skill."[11] Constitutive rules prescribe what moves are permissible in attempting to achieve the goal of the game. For example, in basketball, the rule that one must dribble the ball while advancing it up the court is a constitutive rule. In contrast, rules of skill are rules that enable one to play a game well. They are often unwritten conventions of best practices.

For example, today's basketball players shoot free throws like any other shot, one-handed with the shooting hand positioned behind and slightly underneath the ball. According to the constitutive rules, it is still permissible to "granny-shoot" free throws, lobbing the ball underhanded from between one's legs using both hands, but it is considered a less effective method. Thus, shooting free throws one-handed is a rule of skill.

The distinction between constitutive rules, rules of skill, and broader cultural conventions surrounding sport are important. Some conventionalists take the rule of skill concept further, arguing that conventions are powerful not only because they dictate best practices, but also because conventions carry moral weight. The conventions surrounding sport and games are often referred to as "the ethos of the game."[12] The nature of the moral weight of conventions is often a flashpoint for debate. For example, there is often public outcry when one high school team blows out another, especially if the winning team continued to play its starters. These are ultimately disagreements about the moral nature of conventions surrounding games and sports. Other disagreements about training practices and off-field conduct also concern the moral nature of conventions surrounding games and sports. As I will show later, the concepts of constitutive rules, rules of skill, and conventions are important in considering animal sports.

Philosophers of sport agree that play is an important element in defining sport. Johan Huizinga characterizes play in his oft-cited 1950 work, *Homo Ludens,* "First and foremost, then, all play is a voluntary activity. Play to order is no longer play: it could at best be but a forcible imitation of it."[13] For Huizinga, freedom (voluntary engagement) is the first of three main characteristics of play. The second characteristic is a suspension of reality or a separation between play and other realms of life. Play is "stepping out of *real* life into a temporary sphere of activity all of its own."[14] Behaviors and actions that are permitted during play may be impermissible outside the context of play. The third characteristic of play, for Huizinga, is limitedness.[15] Play happens, then it is over. It "contains its own course and meanings" but is "played out within certain limits of time and space."[16] Huizinga and other play theorists argue that though play is often fun, it is also very serious, a necessary and important endeavor. The importance of play oscillates between its instrumental value, in that play can enable players to achieve external goals, and its inherent value, in that play is rewarding in and of itself. Randolph Feezell writes, "At the heart of sport is the ambivalent recognition that sport is both serious and nonserious, real and unreal, authentic and pretend, essential and superfluous."[17]

The characteristic that sets sport apart from play and games is the cultivation of physical skill through physical activity and training. In summarizing Paul' Weiss's view, Randolph Feezell claims, "sport involves the pursuit of excellence in and through the body."[18] Other philosophers of sport echo this view, and phenomenological accounts of embodiment in sport describe athletic experiences of flow, dynamic engagement, and cultivating patterns of movement. Sport, then, frequently involves play, is often conceptualized through games, is rule-bound (both in terms of constitutive rules and rules of skill), time-bound, involves the pursuit of excellence through the body, and is surrounded by culture, conventions, and institutions. The definitional project with regard to sport has never been to find exclusive conditions to be met, as that has proved impossible. Rather, the project is to identify relevant features of sport, and to subsequently strive for an ideal, normative view of how sport ought to be practiced. Not all play is sport, and not all sport involves play. While play is not a necessary condition for sport, some qualities of play contribute to an ideal practice of sport, in which play and sport frequently correlate.

In the context of animal sports, the voluntary nature of play, as embodied by animal players, ought to be conceptualized as a threshold condition for qualifying human-animal activities as sport or not. If play is a voluntary activity, then the question of whether animals are voluntarily offering behaviors that are consistent with playfulness ought to be in the forefront of our minds as we evaluate human-animal activities. An ideal, normative view of animal sport is similar to human-only sports in that some features of play ought to be present in the sport. I hold that voluntariness is the feature of play that is especially important for animal sports, because voluntariness is akin to consent. Because we cannot obtain well-informed consent from animals, and they cannot understand the complexities of sporting activities to grant consent, we have to look elsewhere for indicators that an animal is voluntarily choosing to participate in an activity. Of course, animals' choices are shaped and determined by their human stewards, and the choice to participate in an activity might simply be the best choice between two very bad options. In the following section, I will elaborate upon some features of voluntariness as it applies to animal play.

ANIMAL PLAY, VOLUNTARINESS, AND MOTIVATION

An account of animal play, and animal learning more generally, is necessary for a definition of animal sports for two reasons. First, as I noted earlier, while it is easy to agree that we ought to avoid causing animals harm in an abstract and theoretical sense, human beings have a hard time conceptualizing what constitutes harm in relation to nonhuman animals. Providing this brief account is an attempt to give us a more nuanced account of harm and how it occurs in human-animal relationships. Second, an understanding of animal play and motivation can guide our efforts to evaluate whether animals participating in a sport are doing so voluntarily. This understanding can also help us to identify when practices in animal sports are morally objectionable or permissible.

Nonhuman animals love to play. Play is, simply, a fun and joyful activity. Marc Bekoff writes, "Animals love to play because play is fun, and fun is its own very powerful reward."[19] Bekoff, an evolutionary biologist who studies animal emotions, characterizes animal play in two ways. First, animal play is characterized by "Five S's": spirit, symmetry, synchrony, sacredness, and soulfulness.[20] The spirit of play is evident in the energy with which it is pursued by animals. "The Symmetry and Synchrony of play is reflected in the harmony of the mutual agreements to trust one another—individuals share intentions to cooperate with one another to prevent play from spilling over into fighting. This trust is Sacred."[21] Bekoff claims that play is "soulful" because, like their human counterparts, animals become completely immersed in expressing themselves in play. Second, Bekoff characterizes creativity in animal play through "Six F's": flexibility, freedom, friendship, frolic, fun, and flow. He writes, "As animals play, its not unusual to see known mating behaviors intermixed in highly variable kaleidoscopic sequences along with actions that are used during fighting, looking for prey, and avoiding become someone else's dinner. In no other activity but play do you see all of these attributes and behaviors occurring together."[22] Animals enjoy external benefits through play, learning important skills for survival and successful social interaction. Bekoff emphasizes that animal play, like human play, is dependent upon fairness and cooperation. When the participants cease to be fair or cooperative, the play ceases.

Animals learn through two mechanisms: association and consequences. Learning through association is called classical conditioning. The environment produces a stimulus, which causes an involuntary response in the animal. The animal learns to associate the stimulus with that response, and may act on the environment later to avoid or engage the stimulus in question. For example, let's say Minky the Mongrel Puppy goes for a walk. On her walk, the wind blows a trashcan onto the sidewalk in front of her, making a loud clanging noise. The stimulus in the environment, the leaping clanging trashcan, produces an emotional response of fear in Minky. Minky learns to associate trashcans with fear.

Learning through consequences is called *operant conditioning*. In operant conditioning, an animal acts upon the environment, and the consequences of that action work to increase or decrease the likelihood of that action being chosen in the future by the animal through punishment or reinforcement. B. F. Skinner, a psychologist, conceptualized operant conditioning as four *quadrants*:[23]

	Subtracts something from the situation to achieve behavioral goal	*Adds* something to the situation to achieve behavioral goal
To *increase* the likelihood of a behavior recurring	*Negative Reinforcement*	*Positive Reinforcement*
To *decrease* the likelihood of a behavior recurring	*Negative Punishment*	*Positive Punishment*

Figure 11.1 Operant Conditioning

A *reinforcer* is something an animal is motivated to acquire, while an *aversive* is something an animal is motivated to avoid. Let's say our behavioral goal is to have Minky the Mongrel Dog walk on a leash without pulling. In the case of *negative reinforcement,* let's say that we have outfitted Minky with a prong collar. Minky pulls ahead and her collar pinches her neck and trachea, causing pain and discomfort. The removal of the aversive (pain is the thing Minky is motivated to avoid) will have the consequence of increasing the likelihood that Minky will walk nicely without pulling. In the case of *positive reinforcement,* Minky walks next to us without pulling and she is intermittently fed little bits of her favorite treat, Monterey Jack cheese. The addition of the reinforcer (cheese, the thing Minky is motivated to acquire) increases the likelihood that Minky will walk nicely without pulling. If we want to decrease the likelihood of Minky pulling on the leash, we have two options to help her learn. In the case of *negative punishment,* Minky pulls on the leash and we stop walking and stand still. We are removing the reinforcer (forward movement is the thing Minky is motivated to acquire because forward movement is exciting and fun) to decrease the likelihood of her pulling. In the case of *positive punishment,* Minky pulls on the leash and I kick her in the ribs. We are adding an aversive (pain from being kicked in the ribs) to decrease the likelihood of her pulling on the leash.[24]

This may seem very tedious for a discussion on defining sport. However, the relevance of these concepts to animal sports and a concept of harm cannot be overstated. These principles are present in all animal learning and behavior in animal sports. Animal sports involve learning sequences of behaviors, sometimes intricate and elaborate. How these behaviors are taught and learned is important for formulating guiding practices within animal sporting contexts. I argue that the voluntariness of animal behavior in sporting contexts is compromised when the behaviors are compelled using positive punishment and negative reinforcement, both quadrants that involve the use of aversives.

Nowhere are the justifications for causing animals pain and fear so prevalent and pervasive as in animal training. In dog training, for example, dogs are routinely trained using yelling, kicking, jabbing the neck, toe pinching, ear pinching, choking, scruffing (lifting a dog by the scruff of the neck and shaking her), electric shock, alpha rolling (pinning a dog on her back against the ground until she stops struggling), helicoptering (lifting the dog off the ground by the leash and swinging her around), and strangulation. These methods are often cloaked in language to obscure the fact that humans are willfully using pain and fear to achieve behavioral goals. A "foot tap" is a kick, "gentle pressure" is a pinch, "balanced training" relies on pain and fear, and "stimulation" or "sensation" denotes the use of electric shock. Proponents of these methods often deny that the animal is experiencing pain or fear, claiming that these methods simply inspire the dog to pay attention, or that the method emulates some "natural" behavior. But, in order to work, the aversive or reinforcer has to be something the animal seeks to avoid or is motivated to acquire. If the aversive or reinforcer is a neutral phenomenon, then, logically, it cannot work to either increase or decrease the frequency of a behavior. A movement toward training without the use of pain or fear continues to grow, especially as animal behavior science has demonstrated that the use of punitive methods can lead to learned helplessness, increased aggression, and fearfulness. Governing bodies in veterinary science and canid behavior not only denounce these methods, but also claim they are unethical. In response, proponents of these methods claim that problems only occur when these methods are applied incorrectly. But, to put it simply, there is no correct way to inflict pain or fear.

Certainly, animals are complex organisms who may tolerate pain and fear in a human-animal relationship. A dog might get excited when the choke chain is taken out of the drawer because he associates the appearance of the choke chain with going for a walk, an activity he finds tremendously rewarding. This does not mean that the dog enjoys being choked. A more plausible explanation is that the dog tolerates the pain of being periodically choked because going for a walk is pleasurable. But, this is not a justification for the infliction of pain. The dog would prefer going for a walk without being choked. Also, those of us who do cultivate relationships with nonhuman animals regularly take on responsibilities that interfere with the animal pursuing opportunities to satisfy her own interests. My dog might be interested in roaming the neighborhood, eating out of garbage cans, and chasing the neighbor's horses, but to allow him to satisfy those interests would be irresponsible and dangerous. One might object that my dog suffers a harm of deprivation because he is not permitted to satisfy his interests. However, the potential harm of deprivation that my dog suffers by the restrictions I place upon him is mitigated by my positive obligations to create safe, appropriate outlets for him to explore, chase, and forage. This is all to say that while these issues are complex (we are, after all, dealing with living beings), the negotiation of conflicting interests rarely, if ever, offers us a justification for causing harm through pain and fear.

Training methods that rely upon inflicting pain or fear are not confined to dog training. The history of horse training is remarkably brutal, for example. An examination of punitive methods are important for animal sports because the use of these methods, I argue, compromises an animal's voluntariness and freedom. An animal performing a task to avoid pain or fear is not free. One might object that an animal volunteering behaviors that are likely to result in the acquisition of a reward (positive reinforcement) is also not free. But, the threat of harm is a very different thing from the promise of a reward. The motivation to acquire rewards and further opportunities for satisfying interests represents an opening up of the world for the animal. Denise Fenzi and Deb Jones, dog trainers specializing in dog sports, write, "While force-based techniques exist which may compel an animal to master and perform various behaviors, it is extremely unlikely that the end result will be the picture of teamwork, beauty, and mutual enjoyment that is the 'gold standard' of a successful competition team."[25] Building energy to drive behavior through acquisition of play opportunities, food, or whatever else the animal finds reinforcing, is at the core of a playful, dynamic, meaningful human-animal relationship.

I have described animal learning, play, and harm through the infliction of force and fear at length because the relationship between these elements is, as I will argue in the next section, important for determining whether animal sports meet a threshold condition of voluntary play, and can thus be defined as sport.

ANIMAL SPORTS: GOOD, BAD, AND NOT EVEN

In this section, I distinguish between sports, games, and physical activity in human-animal activities. In doing so, I attempt to map the human-animal relationships that are present when animals and humans engage in sport together. Also, I attempt to evaluate whether current animal sports are not sports, bad examples of sports, or good sports. The view laid out above on animal play, behavior, and motivation provides us with a loose framework for evaluating whether human-animal activities meet the condition of voluntary play for a definition of sport.

Certainly, animals engage in physical activity. However, not all physical activities are sports. Though an animal might be engaged in playing a game, or getting exercise, there is no sport without rules, conventions, and culture. Conversely, some animal games do not involve the cultivation of physical skill or the pursuit of bodily excellence. This distinction is the same distinc-tion philosophers of sport commonly make between human games, sport, and physical activity.

Putative animal sports can be divided according to the human-animal relationship cultivated through the sport. There are two basic relationship configurations:

Animals as opponents: In these sports, animals directly oppose other animals or humans in competition. Sports where animals oppose humans include (but are not limited to) the following: bullfighting, fishing, hunting, alliga-tor wrestling, and many rodeo events such as bull- and bronco-riding, and calf-roping. Sports where animals oppose other animals include (but are not limited to) the following: greyhound racing, cockfighting, dogfight-ing, cricketfighting, and camel wrestling. In sports where animals oppose humans, the primary goal of the activity is for the human to overpower or kill the animal. In sports where animals oppose other animals, the goal may be for one animal to outperform other animals, or, more likely, to overpower or kill other animals.

Animals as teammates: In these sports, animals work together with human teammates during a competition to achieve a common lusory goal. Some examples include (but are certainly not limited to) the following: horserac-ing, polo, dressage, harness racing, rabbit-hopping, dock-diving (dogs), agility (dogs), nosework (dogs), canine freestyle, disc dog, flyball (dogs), and herding (dogs). In these sports, animals work together with a human handler during competition.

This distinction is not a neat one, however, as some sports use multiple species of animals that each play different roles. For example, in the new dog sport of Barn Hunt, bales of hay and straw are arranged to construct an obstacle course. A domesticated rat is enclosed in a PVC tube with some bed-ding, and then the rat is hidden in the obstacle course. A dog is released onto the course and the dog has to alert his human handler when he's located the rat. The team that identifies the location of the rat correctly and with the fastest time wins. The rats are socialized not to be afraid of dogs and are trained to relax in the tube. Dogs must be trained to give up the rat tube willingly, or they are disqualified. The rules for care of the rats and the conduct of rat wranglers (rat handlers) in the sport are extensive. Rats who participate in barn hunt are often adored pet companions. While at a barn hunt, rats are not permitted to work an entire day, and must be given breaks for food and water, and must not incur duress or harm.[26] Similar to barn hunt, competitive herding trials require dogs to move a group of sheep through a course, with direction from a handler. In these cases, it's not clear that the rats and the sheep are players in the game in the same way as the dogs and humans, though they do not incur harm.

Another example of where this distinction between animals as opponents and animals as teammates becomes blurry is in hunting sports. In foxhunting, for example, humans ride horses in a group, following a pack of scenting dogs, to kill foxes. Humans work together with horses and dogs, but they cannot be said to be playing the game because a fox does not volunteer to engage in the activity of being hunted. Whether hunting ought to be considered a sport or not is a complicated problem for animal ethicists and philosophers of sport. S. P. Morris's excellent dissertation on hunting argues that hunting (sport or not) is only morally permissible when all other options to avoid harm are exhausted.[27] I give some broad strokes of a view here to dismiss hunting as a sport. There might be good reasons to argue that hunters engage in a kind of play, cultivate physical skills, and pursue mutual excellence when they compete against other hunters. But, we cannot possibly argue that the animals are engaged in a sport when they are being hunted. In "The Ethics of Interspecies Sports," Morris argues, "We have no moral grounds to justify harming animals for sport because, as experiencing subjects of a life, they have welfare interests that ought not to be infringed upon for the sake of our mere ulterior interests. That is, we have a negative duty that amounts to, roughly, this: Do not harm animals for the sake of sport."[28] There might be good reasons to defend certain types of hunting under certain conditions. It may be that subsistence hunting is preferable to other means of obtaining meat and other animal products for human consumption. But, it is not a sport. Animals who are fleeing from hunters are not playing. If all the sentient beings involved cannot or would not reasonably volunteer or consent to engage in the activity, then that activity fails to meet a basic condition for a definition of sport: voluntariness in play.

However, justifications of animal fighting sports often appeal to the "natural" or "voluntary" quality of the behaviors performed by animals in sporting contexts. Even the most problematic cases in animal sports, such as cockfighting and dogfighting, are defended on the grounds that behaviors such as fighting and chasing prey are natural behaviors performed instinctively by animals. This line of defense ultimately claims that the animals are motivated, by their own volition, to perform the tasks asked of them in sport. For example, along the lines of this argument, roosters will fight each other for territory and access to mates, thus, cockfighting is justified because the fighting behavior between roosters is natural.[29] Fighting is a common behavior across species. Sloths fight. Rabbits fight. Fish fight. It is natural in the sense that it is common and observable outside the context of sport, but that does not make pitting animals against each other to fight morally permissible. Dogfighters regularly claim that their dogs love to fight, a quality referred to as *gameness*, and selectively breed for dog-to-dog aggression.[30] But, even if a dog will readily and quickly aggress in response to encountering another dog (whether that is a trait selectively bred for, a trait that is the result of experience, or just a fluke personality trait) that does not mean a dog enjoys fighting and enters a dogfight voluntarily. Though fighting may be a natural behavior or response to stress, animals cannot be informed about the risks of such activities and cannot volunteer playful behavior under these conditions. An animal cannot give consent to these harms. When the lusory goal of the activity necessarily involves harm to the animal via pain, duress, injury, or death, the activity does not fall within the realm of sport.

Some animal fighting activities have distinct cultural significance and handlers/breeders may identify strongly with their animals. Anthropologist Clifford Geertz's most famous work is "Notes on the Balinese Cockfight," in which he theorizes that cockfights are places where the Balinese enact Jeremy Bentham's notion of *deep play*.[31] The dramatic tension between village, kingroup, and state are not merely a cockfight, but a negotiation of human status and emotion.[32] Like hunting, such activities may be deeply culturally significant, but we ought not fall into the trap of using "sport" as an honorific term. Whatever these activities are, they do not qualify as sport if we are to value our moral obligations to nonhuman animal lives.

The objection that sports are human creations, and only humans participate in sport, regardless of the activity's use of animals is relevant here. One might argue that the humans involved in the Balinese cockfights are certainly engaging in play, and that the activity meets many criteria for a definition of sport. Animals cannot understand the complexities of sport, and while they may be participating in some aspects of the sport, they cannot be said to be fully participating, or so the objection goes. But, I do not think this objection holds weight. If animals have the physical and mental capacity to experience distress, fear, pain, pleasure, and joy, just as humans, then there is no reason to make being a member of *homo sapiens* a requirement for a definition of sport. If a definition of sport relies upon an understanding of the risks, rules, and other complexities of the activity, then small children or other humans who cannot understand said complexities would be barred, also. One might object that some human-only sports necessarily involve injury, pain, and duress, such as boxing, UFC fighting, and American football. But, participants in these sports are presumably able to consent to exposing themselves to the risks involved in these activities. Another relevant objection is that while cockfighting and the like are condemnable and unethical practices, this does not disqualify them from being sports. They are certainly bad examples of sport, but they are sports. My response to this objection is that the lusory goal is central to whether an activity qualifies as a sport. Our ideal practices of sport involve components of play, and nonconsensual harms of injury and death are contrary to play. If lusory goal of an activity necessarily involves harm, and such harms cannot be consented to, then the activity cannot qualify as a sport.

There are sports in which the lusory goal of the activity does *not* necessarily involve harm via pain, duress, injury, or death. However, these sports ought to be rightly condemned for other reasons. The lusory goal of the sport may not itself involve such harms, but the *ethos of the game* may involve profound and systemic harms to nonhuman participants. I maintain that while these activities do qualify as sports, they are bad examples of sport. A culture of harm envelops the activity, such that pain, isolation, duress, and injury are regular occurrences in the lives of these animals. Horse racing is a deeply problematic example of animal sport. Greyhound racing is an outright poor example of animal sport. Though the lusory goal, to have dogs compete against each other in a footrace, is itself devoid of harm, the practices surrounding greyhound racing are bastions of harms. Margo DeMello writes:

> In a world where millions of companion dogs are still euthanized every year for no other reason than there are too many of them, the breeding in the greyhound industry is a cause for concern. . . . More than 1,500 breeding farms produce nearly 30,000 dogs every year for this sport. Breeding greyhounds live stacked in kennels either outdoors or in barns, with no exercise, no toys, no love, and no life outside of the cage. Even racing dogs live in small kennels during their life off the track; sometimes as many as a thousand dogs live at each track . . . In addition to heart attacks, injuries such as broken legs and necks are rampant in the industry. Some dogs are drugged in order to perform, and kennel cough is common due to the close living conditions.[33]

At its peak in 1992, the sport generated $3.5 billion in bets alone.[34] Interest in the sport has been dwindling as criminalization of greyhound racing has increased. There are many reasons to condemn greyhound racing, but the lusory goal itself does not necessarily involve harm to the animals. It is possible to imagine a very different kind of dog racing sport, in which greyhounds live as companion animals who are sufficiently trained and received proper care. They might go race on occasion, in a pleasant environment, taking pleasure in running as fast as possible, pushing their bodies to their limits, tapping into the prey drive that prompts them to chase.

What does a good animal sport look like? In short, it is one where the condition of voluntary play is consistently attended, with the understanding that skills and motivations of animal athletes may change over time and circumstance. Good examples of animal sports resist using force, fear, and pain to compel behavior in the pursuit of a lusory goal, both in competition and training. These sports also avoid practices that compromise the well-being of an animal or its offspring over the life span, and attempt to create a meaningful, reciprocal relationship between human and animal. Some sports, including Barn Hunt, prohibit the use of positive punishment and equipment that facilitates the use of positive punishment or negative reinforcement like prong or choke collars. Still other sports expressly claim that the purpose of the activity is to have fun with your animal.

In "Taking Teamwork Seriously: The Sport of Dog Agility as an Ethical Model of Cross-Species Companionship," Giuliana Lund claims that dog agility is a model animal sport. She argues that rules and ethos surrounding agility encourages the recognition of canine agency and authority. She writes:

> As a demanding cross-species endeavor, agility is constructed in such a way that, felicitously, functional and moral practices tend to coincide. By rewarding teamwork, agility facilitates cooperation amongst significant others. The fact that ever-increasing numbers of people are becoming addicted to the game in spite of its costs in dollars and time indicates that it fulfills a deep-seated desire for closer communication and partnership with our canine companions. To play agility in synch with actual canine teammates, humans must respect their individuality, their divergent perspective and their desires.[35]

Lund's view of dog agility is valuable because it challenges us to think beyond both the avoidance of harm *and* a condition of voluntary play to delineate permissible forms of animal sport. An ideal animal sport ought to not only involve the animal play, but also the cultivation of inter-species communication between human and animal, respect for the animal's unique abilities and perspective, and cooperation. Certainly, there are examples of bad conduct in agility and other ideal animal sports. I once attended a dog agility class where the instructor permitted a student to use a shock collar to shock her dog every time he went off course. For the dog, the choice was to approach the jump (which the dog was afraid of), or experience the pain of being shocked. The choice between fear or pain is not a good one. Eventually, the dog just lied down on the course and stayed there in a state of learned helplessness while his person shocked him for lying down (my dog and I never returned after that). Fortunately, the culture surrounding these sports largely discourages such practices.

One relevant objection to the view I've advanced here is that, regardless of how much fun the animal is having, to use an animal to compete in a sport is to subject the animal to the interests of humans. Winning contests is not an animal desire, after all. My response to this objection is to emphasize the value of a condition of voluntariness in play in these contexts. Though animals may not have an interest in winning or other abstract goods of sport, they do have interests in play, learning new things, and creating partnerships with humans. Sport, under certain conditions, is one way to enable animals to pursue those interests.

I have argued that the voluntary feature of play, as it is defined in both philosophy of sport and ethological accounts of animal play, ought to be of utmost concern in examining animal sports. Voluntariness and motivation are contingent and malleable, but they are important in this context because they are the closest thing we have to consent. I have noted, through the context of American sport history, that animal sports have not only been historically prevalent, but have also followed a similar developmental trajectory as sports without animals. I discussed harm through the lens of operant conditioning, the framework through which all behavior in animal sports is learned. I have argued that blood sports are not sports because they do not meet a basic condition of voluntary play, as animals who are pitted against one another as opponents often necessarily incur serious harms of infliction and deprivation. Further, I have made distinction between ideal animal sports and animal sports where the lusory goal does not involve harm but the pervasive culture and conventions morally requires us to condemn the sport. I hope that these observations will inform future considerations of the role of animals in sport.

NOTES

1. Giuliana Lund, "Taking Teamwork Seriously: The Sport of Dog Agility as an Ethical Model of Cross-Species Companionship," in *Sport, Animals, and Society,* ed. James Gillett and Michelle Gilbert (New York: Routledge, 2014), 104.

2. Margo DeMello, *Animals and Society: An Introduction to Human-Animal Studies* (New York: Columbia University Press, 2012), 118.

3. Elliott J. Gorn and Warren Goldstein, *A Brief History of American Sports* (Chicago: University of Illinois Press, 2004), 56–57.

4. DeMello, *Animals and Society,* 118.

5. Hanna Gibson, "Detailed Discussion of Dog-Fighting," *Michigan State University College of Law Animal Legal and Historical Center,* accessed March 19, 2015. http://www.animallaw.info/article/detailed-discussion-dog-fighting#id-1

6. Jim Gorant, *The Lost Dogs: Michael Vick's Dogs and Their Tale of Rescue and Redemption* (New York: Gotham Books, 2010).

7. Gibson, "Detailed Discussion of Dog-Fighting."

8. Andrew Lawler, "Birdmen." *Salon,* accessed March 20, 2015. http://www.slate.com/articles/health_and_science/science/2014/12/cockfighting_and_chicken_history_the_world_slasher_cup_in_the_philippines.2.html.

9. See Chad Carlson, "A Three-Pointer: Revisiting Three Crucial Issues in the "Tricky Triad" of Play, Games, and Sport" in this volume for a discussion of the issues raised by the intersection of these concepts.

10. Bernard Suits, "The Elements of Sport," in *Philosophic Inquiry in Sport,* ed. William J. Morgan and Klaus V. Meier (Champaign, IL: Human Kinetics, 1995), 8.

11. Suits, 11.

12. Fred D'Agostino, "The Ethos of Games," in *Philosophic Inquiry in Sport,* ed. William J. Morgan and Klaus V. Meier (Champaign, IL: Human Kinetics, 1995), 42–49.

13. Johan Huizinga, *Homo Ludens: A Study of the Play Element in Culture* (Boston: Beacon Press, 1955), 7.

14. Huizinga, 8.

15. Huizinga, 8–9.

16. Ibid.

17. Feezell, Randolph. *Sport, Play & Ethical Reflection* (Chicago: University of Illinois Press, 2006), 31.

18. Feezell, *Sport, Play & Ethical Reflection*, 4.

19. Marc Bekoff, *The Emotional Lives of Animals* (Novato, CA: New World Library, 2007), 94.

20. Ibid.

21. Ibid.

22. Ibid.

23. B.F. Skinner, *The Behavior of Organisms: An Experimental Analysis* (New York: Appleton-Century-Crofts, 1938).

24. The distinction between negative reinforcement and positive punishment can be difficult, since the removal of an aversive necessarily requires the application of an aversive in the first place. The critical literature surrounding operant conditioning is extensive and, in the interests of space, my presentation of these concepts is simplistic.

25. Denise Fenzi, and Deb Jones. *Dog Sports Skills, Book 2: Motivation* (Woodside, CA: Fenzi Dogs Sports Academy Publishing, 2014), 15.

26. "Barn Hunt Association Official Rulebook," *Barn Hunt Association*, accessed April 1, 2015. http://www.barnhunt.com/rules/barnhuntrules_2014_final.pdf.

27. S. P. Morris, "On Hunting: A Philosophical Case Study in Animal Sports," (PhD diss. The Ohio State University, 2010).

28. S. P. Morris, "The Ethics of Interspecies Sports," in *Sport, Animals, and Society*, ed. James Gillett and Michelle Gilbert (New York: Routledge, 2014), 134.

29. "Blood Sports," *Taboo: The Complete First Season*, DVD, (2004; National Geographic Television and Film).

30. *Off the Chain: A Shocking Exposé on America's Forsaken Breed*, DVD, directed by Bobby J. Brown (Woodland Hills, CA: Allumination FilmWorks, 2004).

31. Clifford Geertz, "Notes on the Balinese Cockfight," in *The Interpretation of Cultures* (New York: Basic Books, 1973), 432.

32. Geertz, "Notes on the Balinese Cockfight," 440–441.

33. DeMello, *Animals and Society,* 117.

34. Ibid., 116.

35. Lund, "Taking Teamwork Seriously," 109–110.

Chapter 12

The Mainstreaming of Fantasy Sport

Redefining Sport

Brody J. Ruihley, Andrew Billings, and Coral Rae

When asked whether fantasy sport constitutes the title of sport in its own right, the most apt response is also a hedging one: it depends. Part of that decision depends on the definition of sport one employs. Some definitions are so broadly drawn that fantasy sport participation could qualify, such as David Best's contention that sport "requires the arbitrary selection or creation of difficulties which it is our aim to overcome."[1] Other definitions leave fantasy sport falling short of qualification. For instance, most fantasy sport games are facilitated via some form of new media device, with advanced metrics derived from the computer programs significantly aiding the participant; as such, fantasy sport would not qualify under the definition offered by Hampton Stevens, who claims that "every single sport on earth shares three fundamental characteristics: people compete at it, computers can't do it, and aesthetics don't count. Absent any one of these criteria, and it is no sport."[2] Even one of the more accepted definitions of sport offered by J. Bowyer Bell would disqualify fantasy sport games, since Bell argues that sport is "a repeatable, regulated, physical contest producing a clear winner."[3] The physicality of sport is also stressed by Klaus Meier in his work on the definition of sport, "sport requires the demonstration of physical skill, and, as a consequence, the outcome is dependent, to a certain degree at least, upon the physical prowess exhibited by the participants."[4]

There is little doubt, despite the consensus that fantasy is not sport, of the profound impact on how we consume and understand sport by the rapid ascent of fantasy sport play. Even professional athletes admit to avidly following the statistics as they relate to fantasy sport.[5] Some, such as NFL wide receiver Greg Jennings, admits that an additional level of skepticism to the fan/athlete dynamic is imbued within the fantasy sport experience because an injured player will often immediately receive queries about the fantasy sport impact; Jennings told Jeff Bercovici that "When a player says it doesn't really bother them, they're lying."[6]

Fantasy sport represents a major impact on the sports world, with a gigantic financial imprint on the industry. With 57.4 million North American participants,[7] an overall valuation of $70 billion,[8] and an estimated $6.5 billion in lost worker productivity,[9] the fantasy sport industry is now measured in billions of dollars, not the millions of decades past. As such, it imparts a sizable impact on the consumption of sports media product, with everything from viewership to consumer behavior and purchases positively correlating with the likelihood of playing fantasy sport games. [10] Perhaps the most telling statistic comes from Enoch,[11] who noted that the average fantasy sport participant consumes more than triple the ESPN content of a nonparticipating sports fan. In the perspective of a media industry, in which a half-ratings point is a major shift, fantasy sport constitute a clear "game changer."[12]

The first part of this chapter explores the clear overlapping circles between sports fandom and fantasy sport participation, as well as the clear correlations between the motivations for fantasy sport play and the motivations for sport play. The second part deals with the ways fantasy sport affects sport consumption and thus how we understand sport. In one of the deepest examinations of the relationships between conceptions of fantasy sport and traditional sport, Carlson forges the argument that fantasy sports "constitute a category we might call parasitic games in that they spawn from their real-sport counterparts and in some ways alter how we conceive of these real sports."[13] In sum, it is difficult to discuss and/or comprehend one without inherently discussing the other.

Because, as Dauncey and Hare note, "the trend is towards individualisation of consumption allowed by technological innovations in miniaturization and portability of the new media,"[14] fantasy sport is a response to the desire to have greater control of the sports consumption experience—not just in terms of which players to root for, but also the degree in which a person opts to become a deep fan, as well as their willingness to continually shift loyalties between one's favorite team and one's fantasy sport team. Lee, Ruihley, Brown, and Billings even note that when presented the option of either having one's favorite NFL team win or having a win for one's fantasy sport team, 41 percent of respondents opted for the fantasy sport victory,[15] confirming the connection Carlson finds between participating in fantasy sport and "deep play."[16] Moreover, Carlson believes that "we expend great time and energy participating in fantasy sports but very little time critically exploring their philosophical merits."[17] Because of this lack of critical focus on fantasy sport play, this chapter will (a) explore fantasy sport fandom directly, then relating trends to both (b) motivations and (c) individual consumption before

(d) fusing ties directly to the sports, entertainment, and fantasy sport industries and (e) articulating conclusions about the relationships between sport and increasingly-popular fantasy sport play.

FANTASY SPORT PARTICIPATION

At the time of this writing (October 2016), fantasy sport participation had risen sharply to 57.4 million North American participants—a stark contrast to the 500,000 participants in 1988.[18] Put in perspective, this eighty-two-fold increase over several decades is truly revolutionary: twice as many people play fantasy sport as watch any current serialized drama or sitcom on television; more people play fantasy sport than are actively engaged on Twitter.

The popularity of fantasy sport can be delineated by a variety of reasons. On the surface, many assume reasons for participation revolve around competition, winning a prize, or intense fandom looking for more ways to consume sports. Many agree with Rodney Ruxin, one of the main characters in the FX television series, *The League*, on at least one motivating factor in participation as he claims: "Fantasy football is about proving that you're better than your friends, not equally as good as your friends."[19] Fantasy sport offers, as Ruxin so pointedly asserts, an opportunity for participants to simultaneously flaunt one's prowess and fandom to the friends in which they compete. The average player spends $52 on league fees and an additional $20 on information materials during a season, yet others are high-stakes players, often willing to win at any cost.[20]

Despite such "win-at-all-costs" attitudes adopted by many fantasy sport participants, in order for players to participate in a game, one must engage in the lusory attitude, or "the attitude [. . . that serves as] an explanation of that curious state of affairs wherein one adopts rules which require one to employ worse rather than better means for reaching an end."[21] This lusory attitude is necessary to participate in a game because:

> To play a game is to engage in activity directed towards bringing about a specific state of affairs [a win, a touchdown, etc.], using only means permitted by rules, where the rules prohibit more efficient in favour of less efficient means, and where such rules are accepted just because they make possible such activity.[22]

In the case of fantasy sport, these rules differ among leagues, requiring participants to choose from standard scoring leagues to points per reception leagues based upon their personal view of what "less efficient means" constitute the highest level of entertainment (the highest motivating factor for men to participate in fantasy sport).[23]

While the aforementioned reasons are accurate in painting a representative picture of many participating in the activity, it would be unwise to overlook other explanations for play. Several scholars have assisted in identifying motivations for fantasy sport participation. Utilizing Q-methodology, Farquharand Meeds discovered arousal and surveillance as reasons for participation.[24] Roy and Goss delineated three major areas of influence centered on psychological, social, and market-controlled areas.[25] Psychological areas contain motives of achievement, control, and escape; Social areas house motives of community and socialization; and market-controlled aspects involve marketing concepts of product, price, and promotion. Finally, Spinda and Haridakis identified six motives specific to fantasy football participation: (a) ownership, (b) achievement/self-esteem, (c) escape/pass time, (d) socialization, (e) bragging rights, and (f) amusement.[26]

Taken collectively, these factors often overlap; yet have developed with a great deal of nuance over time. The result has been a comprehensive listing of motivations aiding in not only defining the fantasy sport fan, but also deciphering the inner-workings of the fantasy sport participant psyche. Some of the most examined reasons for consumption involve the following areas rendered by Billings and Ruihley:[27]

* *Arousal*, positive stress and emotion in fantasy sport
* *Camaraderie*, relationship formation and retention through fantasy sport activities
* *Competition*, desire to be better than others through fantasy sport
* *Control and ownership*, managing a fantasy sport roster (i.e., drafting, adding/dropping players, trading, and starting/benching players)
* *Escape*, disengaging from daily concerns and worries while focusing on fantasy sport
* *Pass time*, purposeful allowance of time to pass
* *Self-esteem*, feeling better or worse about oneself as it relates to a fantasy sport outcome
* *Social sport,* socializing about sport or fantasy sport activities
* *Surveillance,* information gathering about a sport, team, or athlete for fantasy sport purposes

Clearly, the aforementioned list features similarities and differences with traditional ways of consuming sport, as the listed motivations can be applicable to both the fantasy and traditional sport realms. While the analyses did not include all the previously cited motives, the work of Billings and Ruihley compared several areas of fantasy sport participation and traditional sport fandom.[28] This work revealed that fantasy sport users indicated significantly higher levels of (a) sport fanship, (b) media consumption, (c) mavenism (sharing of products and news), (d) Schwabism (having a know-it-all mentality), and (e) motives including: self-esteem, surveillance, and passing time. These findings highlighted an amplified fan, a "Sport 2.0."[29] In addition, several studies have found the motivating factor of escape as a lower-tier factor in fantasy sport consumption.[30] As research suggests, this is due to fantasy sport becoming part of the daily routine and not an escape from it. People are competing in fantasy sport with coworkers, friends, and family and incorporating fantasy sport into those circles, making fantasy sport less of an escape from other aspects of ones' life and more of a new layer in which previously forged interactions emerge.

Along with motives for play, another consideration with fantasy sport participation mentioned in the introduction is the idea of deep play. Bentham defines deep play in terms of monetary gain where "equal in regard to pleasure, [the odds . . .] are always unfavourable."[31] Geertz further describes this as "play in which the stakes are so high that it is, from his utilitarian standpoint, irrational for men to engage in it at all."[32] With the time, effort, and—in some cases—money expended on fantasy sport are taken into account, association with deep play is plausible. Interestingly, the average amount of time spent directly consuming fantasy sport content per week is over 8.5 hours, with spending estimated at $111 in league-related costs per season. This means that in a seventeen-week fantasy football season the winning participant of a ten team league stands to make, in a winner take all scenario, $520 ($52 per person in prize fund), or $3.23 per hour at best—while the other participants make nothing.[33] Participants in this range are clearly engaged in deep play by both Bentham's and Geertz' standards as their time, as, from a utilitarian perspective, the time could be better spent elsewhere.[34] Despite this "deep play," fantasy sport users often counter such utilitarian interests, participating in fantasy sport at rapidly increasing rates for reasons other than financial motivations.

Research on participation also helps to create a detailed picture of the fantasy sport user, yet, if participants are sporadically involved in the activity, such trends lack significance. Thankfully for the industry, satisfaction is high. In several examinations, Billings, Hardin, and Ruihley have found fantasy sport participants to be extremely satisfied (6.5 to 6.9 on a 7.0 scales) with the activity and having great intent to return to the play in the subsequent seasons (6.5 to 6.9 on a 7.0 scales).[35] Put simply, there is no known sport-related entity with participants as committed to their activity as fantasy sport, as satisfaction is exceedingly high. As FSTA leader Paul Charchian has noted four out of five participants indicate a commitment to continue participation in fantasy sport for a minimum of the next decade, with two of every five reporting they fully intend to participate in fantasy sport until their death.[36]

Thus, the fantasy sport user is invariably a sports fan, yet with unique qualities. Summarizing participation, fantasy sport players are concurrently represented as a fan that self-identifies as more of a sport fan than others, consumes more sport media, shares information with others, thinks they know more about sports than others, does not consider the activity as a way to escape, engages in deep play, has emotional attachment to the outcome of a plethora of sporting events, is extremely satisfied with the activity, and plans to return. This type of sport fan is invested, interested, amplified, and a sport organization's ideal consumer. Moreover, the fantasy sport participant is simply a more committed sports fan, much more than an anomalous entity; inevitably, breeding larger sports fans appears to beget committed fantasy sport participants in the years that follow. Fantasy sport does not create sports fandom nearly as much as the inverse, with sports fandom becoming an evolution in which fantasy sport participation becomes one of the final stages.

FANTASY IMPACT ON SPORT MEDIA

Fantasy sport impacts traditional sport fandom in many manners. Some are translucent, others more opaque, yet with distinguishing characteristics that make the profile of a participants warranted for comprehensive investigation. From the types of fantasy sport offerings and the industry surrounding the activity, to alterations in media and in-person sport entertainment options, fantasy sport is significantly impacting how sport is consumed, even altering the fundamental reason why people have traditionally watched a sporting contest: to see what team wins.

Sports Encompassing the Fantasy Experience

As described in the aforementioned section on consumption, it can be advantageous for sport organizations to be involved in fantasy sport. It is no surprise, then, that many U.S.-based sports are considered options for the fantasy sport experience. The most popular, fantasy football, is based on the live action of the National Football League (NFL).[37] Other popular sports consist of: baseball (Major League Baseball, MLB), basketball (National Basketball Association, NBA), auto-racing (NASCAR/IndyCar), golf (Professional Golfers' Association of America/ Ladies Professional Golf Association, PGA/LPGA), hockey (National Hockey League, NHL), and soccer (European soccer leagues and Major League Soccer). These sports and sport organizations benefit from the amount of attention fantasy sport can bring, as evident by escalating media consumption rates.[38, 39] Whether this involves consuming additional games, watching the entirety of a match, or tuning in to a sport not normally followed because of fantasy sport interests, the amount and diversity of consumption is part of the added benefit of being associated with fantasy sport.

In addition to sports simply being a part of the season-long fantasy sport equation, the fantasy sport industry has recently increased its frequency of offerings, altering the experience with expansion into daily leagues. On their websites and reading oddly similar to each other, the top two daily offerings, DraftKings and FanDuel, tout "no season-long commitment," a chance to win "real" money, and guaranteed "prizes."[40] In addition, FanDuel highlights the ability to draft in minutes and leagues starting at $1.00 while DraftKings highlights that the company is based in the United States and is "100% legal."[41] Daily leagues offer owners the opportunity to pick a new set of players every day, with the potential to erase the feeling of being trapped with a bad team for a long season. This, in turn, allows for an even more enhanced sport fan, creating increased frequency in interest, research of statistics and player, and game day media consumption. However, without question, such daily league participation more closely correlates with gambling than other forms of season-long leagues, as people invariably spend much more than an average of $52 per season if opting to draft a new team each day or week, altering the previously cited disproportionate utilitarian equation. In contrast to season-long options with free league participation (including ESPN.com and Yahoo), all major daily league platforms operate on direct fee structures, with millions of dollars being exchanged among winners and losers. As such, daily league participants represent a robust area for future definition of not only fantasy sport participation, but also sports fandom in general. Nevertheless, since daily leagues are still relatively new and, in many states legally embattled, this will not be pursed here.

Altering the In-Person Sport Experience

At the time of writing this chapter, two major issues, involving fantasy sport to some degree, are at the forefront of selling tickets to view NFL games in person. The first is adding or increasing the abilities of wireless Internet in stadiums for the more than 60,000 fans in attendance; bandwidth is becoming the major issue for the twenty-first century, first-person fan. Baig discusses the need to appease the die-hard football fans, arguing that the NFL understands and recognizes that people attending a NFL game "typically behave much like their counterparts watching on TV at home . . . they're simultaneously tweeting, posting on Facebook and Instagram, watching video, checking fantasy stats and browsing. At least that's what fans in NFL stadiums want to do."[42] In addition, Casey cites fantasy sport as a reason for technological and spatial improvements in NFL venues.[43] He states that the league is enhancing stadiums from a technical perspective including cameras in locker rooms, video boards, fantasy football lounges, game day audio, team-specific fantasy sport games, and free access to the NFL RedZone.

The second issue, as mentioned by Casey,[44] is the addition of fantasy sport lounges in NFL stadiums. Whether (or not) the construction or renovation of stadium spaces into these lounges will attract new spectators while maintaining long-held fan interests is yet to be determined. Nevertheless, increased phone and tablet accessibility to live games, fantasy sport scores, and fantasy sport rosters, the need for an actual space to change a lineup and view others games, offer some form of value added to the highly-identified fan. Eichelberger quotes Jaguars' Senior Vice President, Hussain Naqi, as concluding regarding such technological innovations that: "Our fans are consuming fantasy sports and stats at a level they never had. . . . We want to remove any obstacles to a fan coming to the stadium. The lounge will provide a comfortable environment where they can check their scores."[45]

In sum, fantasy sport is exhibiting the power to alter not only the in-game experience (with additional screens and bandwidth to accompany fantasy sport user desires), but also the decision on whether to attend a game at all; the 2015 NFL decision to suspend the local market blackout rule seemingly was acknowledging a shift in the economic model of sports consumption, with less revenue coming from general ticketing counteracted by luxury boxes (replete with options catered for the fantasy sport fan) and rising television ratings from the at-home viewer (opting to consume games in a place where fantasy sport information and updates can be more easily accessed).

Sport Information

The manner in which one seeks out fantasy sport information has shifted dramatically in the past two decades. Early on, fantasy sport participants would have to look past simply reading the back of a baseball card or checking a box score and endeavor to find the detailed sports information of today's environment. There has been much effort since then to get fantasy sport participants from simple statistics to comprehensive fantasy sport reporting. Billings and Ruihley's text on the fantasy sport industry provides a prime example of bridging that information gap.[46] In it, *USA Today*'s Steve Gardner discusses *Baseball Weekly*'s launch and how fantasy sport was a part of that, even if others did not know they were consuming fantasy material.

> Fantasy was a dirty word, and if you said *fantasy*, you had already turned off 80% of your potential audience. If you went back and looked at them now, so many of the things that were written, you could see, playing time battles, pitching rotations, injuries and things like that—a lot of those things were written to

where you can get some serious fantasy information from this, but to label it *fantasy* was taboo. It was a big step to actually have a fantasy column.[47]

Another example in the text comes with something that is now taken for granted: the bottom line television scroll "news ticker." Fox Sports' Jim Bernard recounts that as recent as 2004, the information presented was minimal:

> They were just going to put just scores [on the television screen graphics]. [We said], "No, you can't. These guys care. You've got to say who scored that touchdown" . . . We like to keep pushing it forward. You'll see in the halftime shows, they definitely have bullet points that are directed to the fantasy guy.[48]

Within the modern sports media landscape, statistics are everywhere, deconstructed in dozens of ways and patterns, and news is easy to find. With this type of data and information available, two companies have emerged as leaders in the fantasy sport information industry; Rotoworld and Rotowire are major entities in providing fantasy sport information, rising to the forefront of fantasy sport information and news. While on the opposite end of the pay-for information spectrum (Rotoworld is free; Rotowire has a subscription cost), both are providing fantasy sport users with desired stats, information, injury updates, and breaking news, all from a fantasy sport perspective. The result is often a bifurcation of what a sports fan regards as a meaningful statistic, with older fans relying on traditional measures of excellence, non-fantasy sport playing younger fans relying more on sabermetrics, and fantasy sport users opting for measures that more directly impact a fantasy sport game than an enacted game. Players with high value in one league are discounted within another, as formats, statistics, and values shift considerably depending on interests within the sports fan/fantasy sport participant overlapping binary.

How one consumes sport—and through what medium—is also adapting to meet the burgeoning demands of the fantasy sport participant. Satellite radio, a relatively recent technological advancement in and of itself, has committed to and excelled at offering an exclusive radio station devoted to fantasy sports. With its call-in format, expert analysis, constant discussion of fantasy sport, and a myriad of hosts and guests, SiriusXM Fantasy Sport Radio is proudly promoted as *the only 24/7 radio channel dedicated to all things fantasy sports. Hear expert fantasy sports opinion and information.* Radio and television-style programs are also dispersed utilizing the communicative medium of podcasts. Seemingly, any organization with a stake in fantasy sport information has developed an audio or video podcast. Major sport organization like ESPN, CBS Sports, Fox Sports, Yahoo!, *The Sporting News*, the NFL, and MLB are sharing the podcast environment with fantasy-specific organizations like Rotogrinders, Rotowire, Fantasy Pros, and Dynasty League Football. Such podcasts have impact as their regularity (usually ranging from daily to weekly) and length (often 20–30 minutes in duration) equate to several additional hours of sport consumption each week.

Fantasy sport even permeates the avenues of traditional and streaming television. Shows like NBC's *Fantasy Football Live*, ESPN's *Fantasy Football Now*, and the NFL Network's *Fantasy Live* have earned a coveted timeslot on their respected family of cable networks. Discussing the emergence of fantasy sport into television programming, ESPN's Matthew Berry states this about one of the first fantasy-specific television shows, *The Fantasy Show:*

> The show aired Thursday afternoons on ESPN2. Critically, everyone liked the show, but in that time slot, getting huge ratings was a challenge. The internal feeling was that fantasy would work on TV; we just needed to tweak the format and find the right time slot. Next year, we started *Fantasy Insider* on ESPN News and *Fantasy Football Now* on ESPN.com. The success of both those shows proved there was a huge appetite for televised fantasy content on Sunday morning, both on TV and digitally. Currently, we air *Fantasy Football Now,* Sunday mornings, on both ESPN2 and ESPN.com. The show has won an Emmy and the ratings have been terrific.[49]

To address the viewing pleasure of millions of football fans, the NFL and NFL Network "embraced" fantasy sport and premiered the NFL RedZone in September 2009.[50] The basic idea behind the RedZone is to show every scoring play, live and in replay, for every NFL game. For fantasy sport users wanting to see all the action, this is the channel to have and to be watching. The RedZone is a pay-for channel (depending on television provider). Browne suggests "it should cost $3,000 but ends up being around $40 . . . there are no commercials. FOR SEVEN HOURS."[51] With the popularity of the RedZone Channel, DirecTV created a fantasy sport platform called the Fantasy Zone. This channel will also be "broadcasting while games are in progress, but will focus solely on how the live action is affecting the day's fantasy stats, with up to the minute game-to-game analysis, stats and on-screen tickers that offer projections and key player updates."[52] If there is an example of how fantasy sport participants are insatiable, the Fantasy Zone is that exemplar, as the RedZone Channel would seemingly be the ultimate evolution of sport media consumption, and yet fantasy sport players are opting for yet even another layer of committed sport fandom.

A final example of how fantasy sport is changing traditional media consumption is one of the largest undertakings the fantasy sport industry has experienced. For the first time in fantasy sport history, the industry has a television channel. The FNTSY Sports Network, debuting in 2014, can be viewed through online streaming on their website or on a Roku, and has been added to specific cable packages like Optimum's Sports and Entertainment pack.[53]

> FNTSY Sports Network is the first television network to have live studio programming, call-in shows, panels, celebrity and expert drafts, reality programming and on-site commentary from sports venues, all specifically targeted towards the estimated 40 million people who play fantasy sports annually and on a daily basis.[54]

From a sports media standpoint, the primary reason people consume sport is still to see who wins the game, but a subcorrelate of that question is now: which game? Much focus has been placed on the increased role of second screen usage in media consumption,[55] yet little focus has been placed on how second screens facilitate second (and third and fourth) games being played in the sports environment via fantasy sport.

Carlson offers that, "Fantasy sports do a lot of good for their respective real sports. They foster more active participation in particular sporting cultures by building parasitic games on the original sport."[56] The manner in which fantasy sport bolsters their respective sports must be defined beyond just the aggregation of making a sports fan a bigger and better sports fan, but to define the fantasy sport player, one must first decipher the ever-evolving sports fan, one that is increasingly following a multitude of games within an hierarchy of loyalties.

In sum, all of the media offerings now catering to the fantasy sport participant reveal two truths about how sports media regards fantasy sport: (a) fantasy sport participation is, indeed, mainstream and (b) fantasy sport leagues are likely to live beyond the realm of being a fad, instead becoming a primary fixture as part of the modern sport landscape. Fantasy may not be a sport itself, but it is and likely will continue to be an inescapably part of how we consume and understand sport.

NOTES

1. David Best. *Philosophy and Human Movement* (London: George Allen & Unwin, 1978).

2. Hampton Stevens, "Why Cheerleading Isn't a Sport, but Croquet Is," *The Atlantic*, last modified August 5, 2010. http://www.theatlantic.com/entertainment/archive/2010/08/why-cheerleading-isnt-a-sport-but-croquet-is/60949/.

3. Quote in David Rowe, *Sport, Culture and the Media, 2nd Edition* (London: Open University Press, 2004), 12.

4. Klaus Meier, "Triad Trickery: Playing with Sport and Games," *Journal of the Philosophy of Sport* 15, no 1 (1988): 13.

5. Associated Press. "Fantasy Football Isn't Just for Fans—NFL Players are Hooked, Too," *NFL.com*, last modified July 26, 2012. http://www.nfl.com/news/story/09000d5d8145ad3d/article/fantasy-football-isnt-just-for-fans-nfl-players-are-hooked-too.

6. Jeff Bercovici, "Greg Jennings Reveals What NFL Players Really Think of Fantasy Football." *Forbes.com*, last modified March 10, 2012, http://www.forbes.com/sites/jeffbercovici/2012/03/10/greg-jennings-reveals-what-nfl-players-really-think-of-fantasy-football/.

7. "Industry Demographics," Fantasy Sports Trade Association, last modified October 22, 2016, http://fsta.org/research/industry-demographics/.

8. Brain Goff, "The $70 Billion Fantasy Football Market," *Forbes.com*, last modified August 20, 2013, http://www.forbes.com/sites/briangoff/2013/08/20/the-70-billion-fantasy-football-market/.

9. Challenger, Gray and Christmas, Inc. "2012 Fantasy Football Report," @*Work*, last modified September 1, 2012, https://challengeratwork.wordpress.com/2012/09/01/2012-fantasy-football-report/.

10. See Brendan Dwyer, "The Impact of Fantasy Football Involvement on Intentions to Watch National Football League Games on Television," *International Journal of Sport Communication* 4, no. 3 (2011); John A. Fortunato, "The Relationship of Fantasy Football Participation with NFL Television Ratings," *Journal of Sport Administration and Supervision* 3, no. 1 (2011); and Andrew L. Goldsmith and Matthew Walker, "The NASCAR experience: Examining the influence of fantasy sport participation on 'non-fans'," *Sport Management Review* (2014).

11. Glenn Enoch, "Life Stages of the Sports Fan." (Presentation, University of Alabama, Tuscaloosa, AL, October 3, 2011.)

12. Andrew C. Billings and Brody J. Ruihley, *The Fantasy Sport Industry: Games Within Games* (London: Routledge, 2014), 1.

13. Chad Carlson, "The Reality of Fantasy Sports: A Metaphysical and Ethical Analysis," *Journal of the Philosophy of Sport* 40, no. 2 (2013): 188.

14. Hugh Dauncey and Geoff Hare. "Sport and media: representing and Conceptualising Identity and Community." *Movement and Sport Sciences* 86, no. 4 (2014): 9.

15. Jeremy Lee, Brody J. Ruihley, Natalie Brown, and Andrew C. Billings, "The Effects of Fantasy Football Participation on Team Identification, Team Loyalty and NFL Fandom," *Journal of Sports Media* 8, no. 1 (2013).

16. Carlson, "The Reality of Fantasy Sports," 190.

17. Carlson, "The Reality of Fantasy Sports," 188.

18. "Industry Demographics," *Fantasy Sports Trade Association*, last modified July 20, 2015, http://fsta.org/research/industry-demographics/.

19. Dan O'Keefe, Jeff Schaffer, and Jackie Marcus Schaffer, *The League: The Tie*. Television Series, Directed by Jackie Marcus Schaffer (2010; Los Angeles; FX Network, 2010).

20. "FSTA Highlights."

21. Bernard Suits, *The Grasshopper: Games, Life and Utopia, 3rd edition.* (Peterborough, Ontario: Broadview Press, 2014), 52.

22. Suits, *The Grasshopper*, 36.

23. See Ruihley and Billings, *The Fantasy Sport Industry.*

24. Lee K. Farquhar and Robert Meeds, "Types of Fantasy Sports Users and Their Motivations," *Journal of Computer Mediated Communication* 12, no. 4 (2007).

25. Donald P. Roy and Benjamin D. Goss, "A Conceptual Framework of Influences on Fantasy Sports Consumption" *Marketing Management Journal* 17, no. 2 (2007).

26. John S.W. Spinda and Paul M. Haridakis, "Exploring the Motives of Fantasy Sports: A Uses-and-Gratifications Approach," in *Sports Mania: Essays on Fandom and the Media in the 21st Century,* eds. Lawrence W. Hugenberg, Paul M. Haridakis, and Adam C. Earnheardt (Jefferson, NC: McFarland & Company, Inc, 2008).

27. Billings and Ruihley, *The Fantasy Sport Industry.*

28. Andrew C. Billings and Brody J. Ruihley, "The Fantasy Sport Trade Association: An Inside Look into a Billion Dollar Industry," (Presentation, Fifth Summit on Communication and Sport, Peoria, IL, March 2012).

29. Billings & Ruihley, *The Fantasy Sport Industry,* 37.

30. See Billings & Ruihley, "The Fantasy Sport Trade Association;" Billings and Ruihley, *The Fantasy Sport Industry*; and Brody J. Ruihley and Roy L. Hardin, "Beyond Touchdowns, Homeruns, and 3-Pointers: An Examination of Fantasy Sport Participation Motivation," *International Journal of Sport Management and Marketing* 10, no. 3/4.

31. Jeremy Bentham and Etienne Dumont, *Theory of Legislation,* trans. Richard Hilgard (London: Kegan Paul, Trench, Trübner & Company Ltd., 1908), 106.

32. Clifford Geertz, "Deep Play: Notes on the Balinese Cockfight," *Deadalus* 134, no. 4 (2005): 71.

33. "FSTA Highlights."

34. Bentham, *Theory of Legislation*, and Geertz, "Deep Play."

35. Billings & Ruihley, *The Fantasy Sport Industry*; Brody J. Ruihley, Andrew C. Billings, and Coral Rae. "As Time Goes By: Deciphering the Fantasy Sport Playing Teenager," *Sport Marketing Quarterly* 23, no. 4 (2014); and Ruihley and Hardin, "Beyond Touchdowns, Homeruns, and 3-Pointers."

36. Quoted in Billings and Ruihley, *The Fantasy Sport Industry.*

37. "Industry Demographics."

38. Enoch, "Life Stages of the Sports Fan."

39. See Brody J. Ruihley and Andrew C. Billings, "Infiltrating The Boys' Club: Motivations for Women's Fantasy Sport Participation," *International Review for the Sociology of Sport* 48, no. 4 (2013); and Billings and Ruihley, *The Fantasy Sport Industry.*

40. "Home Page," *Draftkings.com,* https://www.draftkings.com and Fanduel.com, "Home Page," *Fanduel.com*, https://www.fanduel.com.

41. "Home Page," *Draftkings.com.*

42. Edward C. Baig, "NFL Goal: Better Wi-Fi in Stadiums." *USA Today*, last modified November 19, 2011. http://www.usatoday.com/story/tech/columnist/baig/2014/11/19/nfl-hopes-to-boost-wifi-in-stadiums-via-extreme-networks/19285451/

43. Matthew Casey, "NFL lagging on stadium Wi-Fi," *Cnn.com*, Last modified September 3, 2013, http://www.cnn.com/2013/09/02/tech/innovation/nfl-wi-fi-stadiums/.

44. Ibid.

45. Curtis Eichelberger, "NFL Stadiums Hope Fantasy Lounges Will Lure Fans," *Sentinel & Enterprise*, Last modified August 23, 2013, http://www.sentinelandenterprise.com/football/ci_23924861/nfl-stadiums-hope-fantasy-lounges-will-lure-fans.

46. Billings and Ruihley, *The Fantasy Sport Industry*.

47. Ibid., 69.

48. Ibid., 79.

49. Ibid., 66.

50. Eichelberger, "NFL Stadiums," and Rembert Browne, "NFL RedZone: The People's Champ," *Grantland.com*, last modified October 23, 2012, http://grantland.com/the-triangle/nfl-redzone-the-peoples-champ/.

51. Browne, "NFL RedZone."

52. Chris Strauss, "DirecTV is Adding a Live Fantasy Football Channel to 'NFL Sunday Ticket'," *USA Today*, last modified July 7, 2014, http://ftw.usatoday.com/2014/07/directv-nfl-sunday-ticket-fantasy-zone-football.

53. "Optimum Sports & Entertainment Pack," *Optimum TV*, accessed 2015. http://www.optimum.com/digital-cable-tv/sports/sports-pak.jsp;   and   Mike Reynolds, "Fight Network, FNTSY Gain First U.S. Berths with Cablevision: Anthem Media Properties Available on MSO's Sports Package," *Multichannel.com*, last modified June 26, 2014, http://www.multichannel.com/news/distribution/fight-network-fntsy-gain-first-us-berths-cablevision/375414.

54. "About Us," *Fantasysportsnetwork.com*, accessed 2015, http://fantasysportsnetwork.com/about_us/.

55. See Mari Ainasoja, Juhani Linna, Päivi Heikkilä, Hanna Lammi, and Virpi Oksman. "A Case Study on Understanding 2nd Screen Usage during a Live Broadcast-A Qualitative Multi-Method Approach," in *UBICOMM 2014, The Eighth International Conference on Mobile Ubiquitous Computing, Systems, Services and Technologies* (2014); and Fabio Giglietto and Donatella Selva, "Second Screen and Participation: A Content Analysis on a Full Season Dataset of Tweets," *Journal of Communication* 64, no. 2 (2014).

56. Carlson, "The Reality of Fantasy Sports," 202.

Chapter 13

E-sport

Video Games as Sport

Joey Gawrysiak

The thrill of a closely contested victory after hours of tension and excitement. The agony of blowing a close competition and coming up just short of winning. The sound of the crowd cheering and hanging on to each moment and move made by professionals competing at the highest level of competition. Sounds like any great sporting event. This is the exciting new world of competitive video game electronic sports, or e-sports. While to some this may not seem like a legitimate concept or notion, competitive video gaming should be considered a sport. E-sports do find themselves, however, in a strange area. Can something be considered a sport when it is a simulation and the actions are relayed to a screen? Can a sport exist in a virtual time and space? This chapter will address these and other concerns about the place of e-sports within the general concept of sport.

It is first important to explore what e-sports are. Competitive gaming comes in many forms and across genres and platforms. Real-time strategy, multiplayer online battle arena (MOBA), and first-person shooters (FPS) make up the majority of e-sports. Tournaments with games such as *DOTA 2, League of Legends,* and *Call of Duty: Black Ops* award millions of dollars to winners.[1] E-sports are gaining popularity and becoming more widespread with their inclusion in the X Games and their coverage by major television networks such as ESPN and TBS. The popularity of e-sport has even resulted in new games being created specifically for play at professional competitions.[2] The e-sport industry is expected to increase its revenue in 2015 by 30 percent and attract more than 113 million fans.[3] These are not just casual activities for kids to play in their free time. Video games have become a legitimate career and professional sport entity. Major League Gaming was even started to act as a governing body for a number of these tournaments.

Competitive tournaments are gaining in popularity and have caught the attention of media and sport brands alike. This is a growing concept that appears to have staying power. The trends in the industry point this way as well. It is already a popular international concept, something that other sports and fans of those sports struggle with at times. Professional tournaments and leagues also exist in South Korea, Europe, North America, Australia, and China. Interestingly, despite its large video game market, Japan remains relatively underdeveloped in terms of e-sport competition and represents a potential area for international growth.[4] And while this suggests that there is opportunity for international growth still, in America the competitions continue to increase. The number and scope of tournaments has increased significantly, going from about ten tournaments in 2000 to about 260 in 2010.[5] So whether or not video game competitions are considered a sport does not seem to be impacting the popularity and drive of the industry.

The viewers and fans of these events are often times the same demographic that tunes in to traditional sports, which may cause a rift in viewership if these two industries do not find a way to cooperate. The breakdown of the audience of e-sports are approximately 85 percent male and 15 percent female, with 60 percent of viewers between the ages of eighteen and thirty-four.[6] Not only are the demographics similar to those that would be watching traditional sports, but the numbers are increasing as well, to the point that they rival the number of viewers of large sporting events. During one day of The International, Twitch recorded 4.5 million unique views, with each view watching for an average of two hours.[7] In 2013, it was estimated that approximately 71,500,000 people watched competitive gaming.[8] These statistics clearly demonstrate the growth of competitive gaming around the world and in the United States, regardless of how sport is defined.

DEFINITION OF SPORT

Sports in American society draws us in and grabs our attention like few other things can. They offer a chance to escape from everyday life and get caught up in something that is simply a form of entertainment and excitement. They matter in the lives of people on an unparalleled scale. But what exactly is a "sport"?

Of course whether or not video games can be considered a sport depend on what definition of "sport" is being employed. While there are many definitions of sport, there are elements that are common to most if not all definitions. These elements are best captured by the following definition: sports are institutionalized competitive activities that involve complex physical and mental skills and that are removed from normal space and time.[9] Obviously even within this broad definition of sport there are terms therein that can be interpreted differently. Nevertheless, the key elements are relatively clear. There must be a governing body with a set of rules to govern the competition. There must also be a winner and a loser. There must be some kind of a ranking system to determine the outcome. The sections below provide clear evidence that e-sports meet these qualifications. The issues come in around the terms of complex physical and mental skills, especially the physical skills. An analysis of the complex physical and mental skills is central to this explanation.

Institutional Structure, Competition, and Mental Skills

E-sports and video game competitions have different governing bodies depending on the type of competition, tournament, and game being played. These governing bodies set rules, requirements and various restrictions to ensure a level playing field. They are a competition in every sense of the word as there is a winner (either individual or team depending on the tournament and game) and a loser(s). Some of these winners receive substantial prizes and rewards. Modern professional e-sports take place more and more often, including large tournaments held at huge, sold-out arenas. Sometimes audiences as large as 40,000 people come to each these events at these specially designated spaces, spaces often times used for traditional sports![10]

In addition, there is an undeniable mental component to e-sports where strategies are employed by teams to create a desired effect. Game intelligence, mental awareness, and strategy are part of the mental skills used during gaming competitions and are needed to be considered sport. Just like in other sports, as games are played there are adjustments made in order to alter strategies within the game. This takes mental awareness of the situation in the game and the ability to plan for the best strategy moving forward.

Physical Skills

Video games do not require the same set of physical skills as other traditional sports, such as football and basketball. Video games do, however, require complex physical skills in order to execute the appropriate movements and combinations in order to be successful, known as "actions per minute," or APM. Professional gamers can execute upward of 400 to 500 APM, or almost 10 per second![11] Certainly this qualifies as complex physical skill, and obviously such movements require substantial amounts of practice time and skill. The physical skills here are fine motor movements that are different from gross motor movements, but are still complex physical skills.

More importantly, the physical skills play an important part in determining the outcome of the competition. This is different from other activities, such as poker or chess, where the physical components do not determine the outcome. Folding differently or holding the cards differently in poker does not determine the outcome of the hand. Similarly, moving a pawn or rook in chess quicker than an opponent does not have bearing on the outcome of the chess match. The skills required for the button combinations and actions of video game controllers, however, do have a direct impact on the outcome. This is an important distinction. The players that execute their desired button combination quicker and more accurately tend to be more successful. For example, in a *Call of Duty* match, the player that can aim at their opponent and fire at them first accurately will eliminate them while the slower or more inaccurate player will not be as successful. While many arguments against video games as sport are grounded in this concept, there *is* physical skill involvement, just not the same as traditional sport, an issue that will be discussed later.

The threshold of physical skills often times separates games from sport.[12] The level of physical skills (fine or gross) becomes important in determining the outcome. Traditional sports have sets of physical skills that must be developed because how adept one is at those skills and movements determines the outcome. Many contemporary sports involve both fine and gross motor movements. Video games obviously focus on fine motor movements, which may seem to separate video gaming from sport because it seems simplistic and isolated where only hands are used and not the whole body. However, as was discussed earlier, expert gamers display an APM of more than 400; a skill set that must be honed over countless hours of practice. These skills need to be practiced just like other movements in traditional sport. The evolution of controllers and complexity of the buttons and joysticks further complicates the training of professional gamers as they must adapt to these changes in not only the controller, but also the games being played. The hand-eye coordination element of watching the screen and translating that into movement and appropriate combinations in the correct order to be successful rivals any other professional athletes' fine motor movement and complexity of physical executions.

While there is certainly a physical element involved in e-sports, the physical aspects of the game do not present much in terms of danger or excitement, something that many other sports do possess. According to Russell, all activities present some form of danger,[13] but the "significant risk" involved in sports such as football or hockey are not present in e-sports. It should be noted that it is not necessary for an activity to be dangerous in order for that activity to be considered a sport, but clearly e-sport is tame in comparison to football or hockey. There is however a mental danger component to video gaming as much of what is done in the competition is in a high stress environment, so there is some sort of danger, just not danger of the physical nature.

There can be significant injuries in most sports that require athletic trainers and medical staff on hand. Video games do not require such resources, but this should not be used in the criteria to determine whether or not something is a sport. The essential core elements discussed earlier are used to define sport, not danger. Most sports seen today have a masculinity aspect and a conceptualization of sport almost like a romantic image of a gladiator type for an athlete, especially contact sports. This masculine-based concept of traditional sports is unnecessarily exclusive and non-essential. This image simply does not need to exist in order for an activity to be a sport.

An interesting area that should be discussed is the concept of motion controlled gaming, such as the Wii, Xbox Kinect, and PlayStation Move. These devices allow the user to physically manipulate themselves using large movements and full body motions to control the action on the screen. As the concept of video games as a sport is discussed, it would be imprudent to ignore the impact of these motion controlled games as the two seem to be interconnected. In actuality, the two areas are not as closely related as it seems. This is a little counterintuitive, but upon examination makes sense.

E-sport and video games as a sport refers to the concept of the whole event, not necessarily to only the game and ways of producing the on-screen movements. Motion controlled games are stripped down versions of actual movements and simulate real world motions, but are often times not used in a competitive atmosphere with a governing body and removed from normal time and space. These types of games are great for what they are made for, commercial and entertainment success. They also provide opportunities for rehabilitation practices and for getting some gamers the chance to be less sedative as they play video games. So while these motion controlled games may appear to be more like sport, they actually are, outside a competitive context, less of a sport than other games that have been discussed.

E-SPORTS USED AND CONSUMED AS SPORT

It is clear that as society continues to provide meaning to video games and redefines sport, e-sports is well positioned. Some examples of e-sports being used as sport are the issuing of sport visas for e-sports participants, the initiation of e-sports as a varsity college sport, the inclusion of e-sports at the X Games and the coverage of e-sports competitions on ESPN.

Competitive video game-players can enter the United States on sport visas just like other athletes from around the world would enter to play in the NFL, NBA, and so on.[14] This essentially says that the United States government recognizes e-sports as a legitimate sport and will allow participants from around the world to come and compete in the United States. This is a huge moment and could be a watershed event as more and more players can come to the United States in hopes of training, competing, and earning significant amounts of money in e-sport competitions." This lends legitimacy to e-sports being a fully recognized professional sport. While providing these sport visas started as a way for only a few players of *League of Legends*, what this does is open the door for more players of more games to come here, helping the sport to grow.

Another significant step toward legitimacy is American universities offering scholarships for e-sport athletes in very much the same way these institutions provide scholarships for football or basketball players. Robert Morris University Illinois started this trend by providing scholarships and practice facilities for their e-sport team.[15] While many other schools have video game clubs that compete in competitions, Robert Morris is the first to recognize competitive video gaming as a varsity sport. Robert Morris could do this more easily than many other schools because they are not part of the NCAA. In order for more widespread acceptance of competitive video gaming as a varsity collegiate sport, the NCAA would have to recognize it and sanction it. This is a big step, however, as colleges are now seeing the importance e-sports may have, with bringing in more students and using this to enrich their lives and help them have more high-achieving graduates.[16]

Competitive video gaming took a major step in being seen as a sport when they were included in the X Games: Austin in 2014, an extreme sports competition that includes skateboarding, BMX biking, and other extreme sports.[17] OpTic Gaming made history by taking home the first ever gold medals awarded to a team in an e-sports event at a major sporting competition.[18] Having video games included in part of this type of mainstream sport competition adds to the validity of competitive video gaming as a sport. Their popularity was also something to take note of as fans packed the stands and had a line wrapped around the venue to get in to watch their favorite gamers compete for the $1 Million prize pool.[19] This popularity may serve as a springboard to get e-sports included in more sport competitions, and may even be a precursor to getting Olympic Committee recognition in the future.

Video games have recently gotten a significant boost in coverage by appearing on ESPN2, the self-proclaimed "Worldwide Leader in Sports." In 2014 and 2015, ESPN2 broadcasted multiple video game competitions as they attempted to capitalize in the growing popularity and acceptance of e-sports.[20] *Heroes of the Dorm* was the latest in this series of televised competitions, as teams competed from various schools to win scholarships. While there has been both positive and negative feedback for such broadcasts, there is no denying that ESPN recognizes the role that e-sports plays and the growing popularity of it. It should be noted that popularity of an activity does not necessarily mean it is a sport and it is not the popularity that is driving the perception or notion that these are sports. It does, however, impact the viability of e-sport as a successful commercial sport.

ESPN broadcasts included announcers and slow-motion replays, mimicking traditional sports, weaving storylines, showing multiple camera angles, exhibiting sponsors, and filling dead time in a manner similar to broadcasts of football games. These methods separate the broadcasts of e-sport from other activities (i.e., spelling bee and poker) that are not generally considered sports.

TRADITIONAL VS. NON-TRADITIONAL SPORT

Modern day competitive video gaming mimics "traditional" sport with competition, strategy, practice, play elements (fun), being unscripted, tournaments, professionalization, wide followings, governing bodies, sponsorships, and even fantasy leagues. These concepts are usually reserved for commercialized professional sport leagues, but competitive gaming has incorporated them to help e-sports grow. Now that e-sports are using these same elements as the "traditional" sports, competitive video gaming can be considered a "nontraditional" sport. An operational definition of "traditional" sport is a sport that has been commercialized by mainstream media for the larger dissemination and consumption by mass audiences and a sport that has been established with decades of history and records being kept by professional governing bodies. In this sense, professional football, baseball, basketball, and so on are all considered "traditional" sport, where e-sports is "nontraditional."

The advancements in technology in our society have created new norms and social constructions to the point that people are re-creating what it means to exist. Everything from online banking to online grocery shopping to online competitions has changed the way that people live. Video game-play fits into this evolution of how we live our lives. The video game evolution has seen video games go from simple in-home activities or arcade hobbies to massive competitions with a technological explosion. Further analysis and categorization may be necessary to answer the criticism of some who are hesitant to consider e-sport as being sport. Breaking sport down into "traditional" and "nontraditional" serves as a way to designate new forms of sport as sport but keeping the sanctity of long-established sports intact.

"Traditional sports" refers to those sports that are played in the natural world (where the action is not a manipulation or simulation), have been around for decades and are widely accepted as "sport." Football, baseball, tennis, hockey, and so on are all considered traditional sports in that they have not fundamentally changed in decades. These sports were established a century ago, if not longer, and have been played in numerous forms. They require gross physical activity and fit other components of the definition of "sport." They also present an element of danger, excitement, and physical contact, which sometimes is a cause of their popularity.

"Nontraditional sports" here refers to those that can be considered sport but may not exhibit the same sense of danger and physical contact that traditional sports may possess. These are sports that are augmented in another sort of reality and use someone manipulating the object performing the visual action. Robot fighting and drone racing can also be considered "nontraditional" sports because of the lack of inherent danger to humans in participating in those sports. The Drone Racing League (DRL) is a startup league where people controlling drones are flying the drones through a course in time trials. The DRL has already said that it wants to be as big as e-sports and be a new form of NASCAR.[21] Competitive gaming certainly fits this model, as it may not be an activity that has the sense of danger of football, but should be considered sport because of what it does have in common.

The idea of "traditional" and "nontraditional" sport extends past the simple notion and categorization; it is important to also look at traditional and non-traditional ways of *consuming* sport. This designation is important because it mirrors further social advancements and alterations to the ways that were previously used to consumer sport products and highlights the acceptance of advanced technology. The very notion of sport consumption has been altered through the use of "nontraditional" sport products, such as fantasy sports and video games.[22] The Internet has created numerous opportunities for consuming sport at an interactive level in contemporary society, thus showing the current general use and acceptance of these methods. Just as these have been accepted, so too will nontraditional sport be accepted.

Generational shifts and an aging demographic that grew up with video games and technology as their norms should phase out steadfast notions of "traditional" sports and sport consumption being the "right" way. The average age of a gamer is thirty-five years old and has been playing for thirteen years.[23] With video games gaining more acceptance in society and increasing in popularity, there is reason to believe that acceptance of video games as a sport will also increase, even if just in the "nontraditional" sense of sport. Keep in mind that all sports were at one point considered new. Many have had to go through periods of growth and acceptance by the public. Skateboarding, for example, did not always have public acceptance as a sport and often times was explicitly banned from public areas.[24] Now skateboarding is a staple of the X Games and seems to be more widely accepted than it ever has been.[25] Modern activities that are turning into sport don't necessarily mirror those sports started decades ago because they were started in different technological eras. This does not mean that modern activities evolving into sport are not sport, they are just different from what the masses are accustomed to, for now.

CRITICISMS TO THE NOTION OF VIDEO GAMES AS SPORT

Criticism to the notion of competitive video games as sport certainly exists. These go beyond the issue of whether or not there is a physical component to e-sports, even though that is the biggest issue for many people in whether or not they consider this a sport. Since this issue has been discussed already, it is appropriate to bring about and address other criticisms to considered competitive video gaming a sport. In addition to the question of whether or not e-sports includes enough of a physical element to be considered sport, there are other criticisms to be addressed.

E-sports Are Too Virtual to Be Sport

A popular criticism is that video games exist in a virtual space and are not "real" like other sports.[26] Technology and virtual worlds exist as part of the new normal in the world. As technology advances its uses become more commonplace and more widespread. This widespread acceptance has led to more work and play being done in virtual spaces. Manipulations of this virtual time and space are different today compared to the past and video games exist today as an extension of the "real world." Definitions of the "real world" are social constructions as signs of the time. With the growing use and acceptance of virtual spaces for work and play, video games should be considered the real world now. In addition to this idea, it is not far-fetched for some traditional sports to do be considered an augmented, or virtual, reality. Sport itself is an artificial human invention as it exists in a separate space and time and imitates various aspects of life and actions. In fact, war metaphors are frequently intermingled into sporting events. Sports are a form of simulation as they create an artificial space to be played on or in, just like video games.

E-sports Are Too Juvenile to Be Sport

Another frequent criticism is that video games are just games for youth.[27] The vast majority of professional gamers are adults, the youth in America and around the world are the generation embracing video games now. This may be true but that does not mean that competitive gaming is not a sport. Sports often times start as games played by children. A staggering 99 percent of boys and 94 percent of girls play a video game before age 13.[28] This shows how engrained and important video games are to youth and how much of a part of our culture they are. It is hard to believe traditional sports get those participation numbers. Some people are ignorant to how widespread gaming has become. The evolution of gaming and growing acceptance from an aging generation has bridged the gaps with Digitals and Millennials. The generational gaps are closing and adults play all kinds of games now, including video games, as the average age of a gamer is thirty-five years old.[29] Video games are not just for kids. Beyond the average age of participants, the games themselves are no longer simplistic and easy to grasp all the time. Video games now are complicated and require more thought and innovation than ever before (just ask someone trying to play a game of *Madden* for the first time!). With this said, even if video games are considered geared toward youth, that should not impact whether or not it is a sport. Youth football is designed just for children, but it is still considered a sport.

Professional Sport as Selective

Professionalized sport in its highest form is something that the average person cannot do, which is why it is so selective and restricted. The same goes for professional competitive video gaming. While it is true that anyone can play video games in a competitive arena, not everyone can compete on the highest level, just like any other traditional sport. Anybody can play football or baseball, but not to the level that Tom Brady or Mike Trout can play their respective sports. Similarly, not everyone can play *Call of Duty* like Matt Haag can. These people that compete on this level are professionals for a reason. The gap between professionals and amateurs is vast and requires time and resources to bridge.

Video Games Are Too Violent to Be Sport

A further criticism of video games as sport is that many of the games involved in competitive video gaming are inherently violent with the goal of "killing" the enemy or destroying a base of some sort. This aspect should not impact the notion of video game as sport since many other traditional sports are also violent, and violent to real people, not to simulations. It should also not be a consideration because the violent aspect of video games is simply a means to an end; a way to achieve a larger goal. The concept is still a sport; it just happens that many of the specifications tend to be violent in some capacity. This also goes a long way in the way of classifying video games as spectator sport, which will be discussed more later.

COMPETITIVE VIDEO GAMING AS A SPECTATOR SPORT?

Spectators are deeply important to any successful commercial sport. Spectators and fans are not essential to define an activity as a sport, but they do provide commercial stability for the growth and acceptance of that activity. Traditional sports as we know are based on commercial success and so cater toward the spectator. In this regard, the capability to garner significant spectator interest is essential is for making a strong case for an activity to be classified as sport.

One stumbling block for wider spectator interest is that video games are constantly changing, even the same game will change form one year's edition to the next. Games like *Street Fighter IV* and *League of Legends* are popular and give people a chance to make money. However, as recent as five or six years before this, this wasn't the case. People were still playing *Third Strike* and *Marvel 2* in the fighting game community, and the MOBA genre wasn't a thing outside of *Warcraft 3* modifications yet. That's just five small years, and the whole face of professional gaming changed. It's even worse in the shooter genre. Games like *Counter-Strike* and *Team Fortress 2* may have staying power, but they don't have near the numbers that *Call of Duty* pulls, and *Call of Duty* puts out a new game every year. Tournament organizers need to figure out whether or not to run the new game or the old one. Everything spectators came to know from last season is invalid the next season. Everything they know is wrong! This can be a big problem. Manufacturers are not going to agree to stop putting out new versions each year. The vast majority of their revenues come from sales to consumers to play, not through television rights or fees for competitive contests. It may be that this becomes a unique characteristic of e-sports; they change every year. That could be marketed as "part of the culture" of the sport. Games like *StarCraft*, *League of Legends*, *DOTA 2,* and *CS:GO* have been around long enough and do not release new versions as frequently than games like *Call of Duty* or *Halo*, so e-sports in America would have to embrace those games or settle on a version of an FPS to play for an extended period of time.

Traditional sporting events tell a story and they are often marketed on that story. The event is much more than just a game between two teams. There are storylines to draw as much interest as possible. Sports weave a narrative that all fans participate in. Super Bowl 50 for instance was billed as the final struggle of an aging veteran (Peyton Manning), against the talented yet much criticized newcomer (Cam Newton). This narrative was related to some extent to the actual playing of the game, but was to a greater extent billed as "the story behind the game." Professional video games, however, largely do not feature such narratives. People who aren't already a part of the community see random names and faces with no meaning when they watch a match. Even when there is no narrative present, fans who don't know who to cheer for in a game just root for their home team out of a sense of pride. Teams in professional e-sports seem random and disorganized with multiple teams from the same city and nearly no teams coming out of the middle of the country. There are no home teams to root for. Even the Olympics, which features athletes almost no one knows, have marketers and broadcasters to weave a narrative. This can be an opportunity for e-sports to capitalize and create a more desirable experience by making their broadcasts mirror other sporting events.

A large potential drawback and barrier to long-term success as a spectator sport is that companies own the games that are being played. For example, Capcom owns *Street Fighter* and if tournament organizer decided that competitors are going to play *Street Fighter IV* from now on so everyone knows how it plays and competitors can come back without learning a new game, Capcom can say "no." All of the actions in regards to tournaments for that game, including what prizes can be, where they can be held, what format they can be held in, and whether or not they can be streamed can be controlled by Capcom, and if they like they can just put a stop to it whenever they like. Networks like ESPN don't want to pick up games for seasons that could stop as soon as a CEO wants to pull the plug.

In order for spectators to really buy into e-sports as a sport they have to see that there is a level playing field. This is the same reason why steroid use in many professional sports has made for such public discussion and fan disgust. When there is an unlevel field and one side has an advantage through some enhancements, fans lose interest. Competitive video game tournaments have a lack of codified equipment. Fighting game tournaments see people using arcade sticks, keyboards, hit boxes, pads, and more. Shooter tournaments see people almost all playing with keyboards and mice (KBAM), or with controllers. It is still to be determined whether or not certain pieces of equipment give an unfair advantage. Most shooter players agree that KBAM players are just faster and more accurate than dual analog stick players. Spectators who see this look at KBAM players as "cheaters" rather than people who became accustomed to playing the game in a certain way. Similarly, many fighting game-players build their own controllers! Spectators have a habit of looking at this as sketchy. Similar to the helmet issue in X Games, the governing body has to have the guts to draw a line in the sand and establish concrete rules. Some will reject this (i.e., those skaters who won't wear helmets) but enough will accept it (i.e., those that will) and play.

CONCLUSION

The growth and popularity of video games and e-sports has made the industry impossible to ignore. Media outlets and business have picked up on this and are jumping on the chance to be involved. E-sport tournaments are rising in popularity with increases in prize pools, followers, and reach. While popularity has nothing to do with defining e-sports as a "sport," the acceptance of gaming in today's society is indicative of the understanding of gaming as a sport. Whether or not individuals consider this a sport all depends on their personal definitions. There will always be those that are opposed to e-sports as a sport, which is part of what makes the discussion interesting. Football is a sport. There are not many that will argue that, but video games have now crept into the discussions being had by people who would never otherwise be talking about them, which is positive for the industry.

So what type of video games should be considered sport? Well, any of them, depending on the circumstances of the games and definitions of sport. Any video game can be turned into a sport if it is a competitions with a governing body, requires physical and mental skills to determine the outcome, and is removed from normal space and time, such as in an arena. Sport games, shooters, strategy games, and even speed runs of platformers can be sport. These all can meet the criteria in the right context, but don't necessarily *always* meet the given criteria. Context matters.

Video games have been a source of escape and a leisure activity for decades now. They are entertaining, socializing, and ubiquitous. Contemporary society is becoming more aware and accepting of how people play video games and people should now recognize e-sports as a sport based on the criteria discussed. There are governing bodies controlling the competitions around the world. There is a physical and mental side to it that have a direct impact on the outcome and success of the event. If what I have argued here is accurate, there is little reason to dispute that e-sports are a sport. Still, there are challenges to the e-sports industry, especially in terms of whether or not it can survive and thrive as a commercial spectator sport. Marketers and sport agencies, however, are starting to catch on to the rise in e-sports. Nothing is ever certain, especially in sports, but competitive video games, as well as video games in general, may just be worth betting on.

NOTES

1. Daniel Tack, "Big Plays, Bigger Payouts," *Gameinformer*, 2014, 16–17.

2. Nick Wingfield, "With Halo 5: Guardians, Microsoft Seeks to Lure E-Sports Players Back," *New York Times*, Last modified August 6, 2015, http://www.nytimes.com/2015/08/05/technology/with-halo-5-microsoft-seeks-to-lure-e-sports-players-back.html.

3. Ibid.

4. Andrew Groen, "Why Gamers in Asia are the World's Best eSport Athletes," last modified May 14, 2013, http://www.pcworld.com/article/2036844/why-gamers-in-asia-are-the-worlds-best-esport-athletes.html.

5. Ben Popper, "Field of Streams: How Twitch made Video Games a Spectator Sport," last modified September 30, 2013, http://www.theverge.com/2013/9/30/4719766/twitch-raises-20-million-esports-market-booming.

6. "Major League Gaming Reports 334 Percent Growth in Live Video," last modified November 14, 2012, http://www.gamespot.com/articles/major-league-gaming-reports-334-percent-growth-in-live-video/1100-6400010/.

7. Popper, "Field of Streams."

8. Phillippa Warr, "Esports in Numbers: Five Mind-Blowing Stats," last modified April 9, 2014, http://www.redbull.com/en/esports/stories/1331644628389/esports-in-numbers-five-mind-blowing-stats.

9. Jay Coakley, *Sports in Society: Issues and Controversies*, 10th edition (New York: McGraw-Hill, 2009).

10. Stephen Evans, "League of Legends Gaming Final Fills Seoul Stadium," last modified October 20, 2014, http://www.bbc.com/news/business-29684635.

11. Yannick Lejacq, "How Fast is Fast? Some Pro Gamers make 10 Moves Per Second," last modified October 24, 2013, http://www.nbcnews.com/technology/how-fast-fast-some-pro-gamers-make-10-moves-second-8C11422946.

12. Dennis Hemphill, "Cybersport," *Journal of the Philosophy of Sport* 32 (2005).

13. J. S. Russell, "The Value of Dangerous Sport," *Journal of the Philosophy of Sport* 32 (2005).

14. Colin Campbell, "Competitive Gaming Recognized in U.S. as a Pro Sport," *Polygon,* last modified July 12, 2013, http://www.polygon.com/2013/7/12/4518936/competitive-gaming-recognized-in-u-s-as-a-pro-sport.

15. Jason Keyser, "Robert Morris University Becomes First to Recognize Video Games as Varsity Sport," *Huffington Post,* last modified October 6, 2014, http://www.huffingtonpost.com/2014/10/06/video-game-scholarship-varsity-sport_n_5940898.html.

16. Campbell, "Competitive Gaming Recognized in U.S. as a Pro Sport."

17. Chris Lin, "Gamers Take Home Gold at X Games," *ESPN,* last modified May 8, 2015, http://xgames.espn.go.com/xgames/events/2014/austin/article/11053677/gamers-break-new-ground-x-games-austin-first-medals.

18. Ibid.

19. Ibid.

20. Jason Schreier, "ESPN Airs Video Games, Twitter Freaks Out," *Kotaku,* last modified April 26, 2015, http://kotaku.com/espn-airs-video-games-twitter-freaks-out-1700333433.

21. Lewis Leong, "VR Drone Racing Makes for a Vomit-Inducing Spectator Sport" *IGN,* last modified January 29, 2016, http://www.ign.com/articles/2016/01/29/vr-drone-racing-makes-for-a-vomit-inducing-spectator-sport.

22. Joey Gawrysiak, Brendon Dwyer, and Richard Burton, "Understanding Baseball Consumption Via in-Home Gaming," *Journal of Applied Sport Management* 6, no. 3 (2014).

23. "2015 Essential Facts about the Computer and Video Game Industry," *Entertainment Software Association*, accessed September 13, 2015. http://www.theesa.com/wp-content/uploads/2015/04/ESA-Essential-Facts-2015.pdf.

24. Sean Mortimer, *Stalefish: Skateboard Culture from the Rejects Who Made It* (San Francisco, CA: Chronicle Books, 2008).

25. For more on skateboarding as a sport, see Chrysostomos Giannoulakis and Lindsay Pursglove, "Evolution of the Action Sports Setting" and Brian Glenney, "Skateboarding, Sport, and Spontaneity: Toward a Subversive Definition of Sport" in this volume.

26. Sean P. Farrell and Alan Feuer, "Are Video Games a Sport?" *New York Times* (video), last modified September 28, 2013, http://www.nytimes.com/video/sports/100000002463420/are-video-games-a-sport.html.

27. For a point of view that children's games might not be sport, see Kevin Schieman, "Hopscotch Dreams: The Cultural Significance of Sport" in this volume.

28. Amanda Lenhart, Joseph Kahne, Ellen Middaugh, Alexandra Rankin Macgill, Chris Evans, and Jessica Vitak, *Teens, Video Games, and Civics* (Washington, DC: Pew Internet and American Life Project, 2008).

29. "2015 Essential Facts about the Computer and Video Game Industry."

References

"2015 Essential Facts about the Computer and Video Game Industry." *Entertainment Software Association.* Accessed September 13, 2015. http://www.theesa.com/wp-content/uploads/2015/04/ESA-Essential-Facts-2015.pdf.

"2015 Reebok Spartan Race World Championship Crowns Champions in Lake Tahoe." *Spartan.com.* Last modified October 5, 2015. http://www.spartan.com/en/race/detail/843/overview.

"About Us." *Fantasysportsnetwork.com.* http://fantasysportsnetwork.com/about_us/.

"The Action Sports Market." *Active Marketing Group.* 2007. http://www.activenetworkrewards.com/Assets/AMG+2009/Action+Sports.pdf

Aggerholm, Kenneth. *Talent Development, Existential Philosophy and Sport: On Becoming an Elite Athlete.* London, Routledge, 2015.

Ainasoja, Mari, Juhani Linna, Päivi Heikkilä, Hanna Lammi, and Virpi Oksman. "A Case Study on Understanding 2nd Screen Usage during a Live Broadcast-A Qualitative Multi-Method Approach." In *UBICOMM 2014, The Eighth International Conference on Mobile Ubiquitous Computing, Systems, Services and Technologies* (2014): 196–203.

Alenda y Mira, Jenaro. *Relaciones de Solemnidades y Fiestas Públicas de España.* Madrid, 1903.

Allen, Kevin. "NHL approves expansion to Las Vegas." *USA Today.* Last modified June 22, 2016. http://www.usatoday.com/story/sports/nhl/2016/06/22/las-vegas-nhl-expansion/86239704/

Álvarez de Miranda, Ángel. *Ritos y Juegos del Toro.* Madrid: Taurus, 1962.

Anglo, Sydney. *The Great Tournament Roll of Westminster.* Oxford: Oxford University Press, 1968.

———. *The Martial Arts of Renaissance Europe.* New Haven, CT, and London: Yale University Press, 2000.

Anshel, Mark H. *Sport Psychology: From Theory to Practice.* San Francisco: Benjamin Cummings, 2003.

Apel, K.O. *Towards a Transformation of Philosophy.* London; Boston: Routledge & Kegan Paul, 1980.

———. "German philosophy." In *The Routledge Companion to Twentieth Century Philosophy*. Edited by D. Moran. New York: Routledge, 2010.

Arcangeli, Alessandro. *Recreation in the Renaissance*. New York: Palgrave Macmillan, 2003.

Aristotle. *Complete Works*. Edited by Jonathan Barnes. 2 vols. Princeton, NJ: Princeton University Press, 1984.

Ashwanden, Christie. "An Insider's Guide to CrossFit." *New York Times* (blog). Last modified August 18, 2014. http://well.blogs.nytimes.com/2014/08/18/crossfit-book-breathe-fire/

Associated Press. "Fantasy Football Isn't Just for Fans--NFL Players are Hooked, Too." *NFL.com*. Last modified July 26, 2012. http://www.nfl.com/news/story/09000d5d8145ad3d/article/fantasy-football-isnt-just-for-fans-nfl-players-are-hooked-too.

———. "Secret Ballot Eliminates Baseball, Softball." *ESPN*, last modified July 8, 2005. http://espn.go.com/olympics/news/story?id=2103234.

Atkinson, Michael, and Wilson, Brian. "Bodies, subcultures and sport." In *Theory, sport and society*, edited by Joseph Maguire and Kevin Young, 375–395. Bingley, UK: Emerald Group, 2002.

Badenhausen, Kurt. "LeBron James Tops World's Most Powerful Athlete 2014." *Forbes*. Last modified June 30, 2014. http://www.forbes.com/sites/kurtbadenhausen/2014/06/30/lebron-james-tops-worlds-most-powerful-athletes-2014/.

Baig, Edward C. "NFL Goal: Better Wi-Fi in Stadiums." *USAToday*. Last modified November 19, 2011. http://www.usatoday.com/story/tech/columnist/baig/2014/11/19/nfl-hopes-to-boost-wifi-in-stadiums-via-extreme-networks/19285451/

Baillie-Grohman, W. A. *Sport in Art*. London: Ballantyne, 1913.

Barber, Richard and Juliet Barker. *Tournaments: Jousts, Chivalry, and Pageants in the Middle Ages*. New York: Weidenfeld and Nicolson, 1989.

"Barn Hunt Association Official Rulebook." *Barn Hunt Association*. Accessed April 1, 2015. http://www.barnhunt.com/rules/barnhuntrules_2014_final.pdf.

Beal, Becky. "Disqualifying the Official: An Exploration of Resistance through the Subculture of Skateboarding." *Sociology of Sport Journal* 12 (1995): 252–267.

Beal, Becky, and Lisa Weidman. "Authenticity in the Skateboarding World." In *To the Extreme: Alternative Sports Inside and Out,* edited by Robert E. Rinehart and Synthia Sydnor, 337–352. Albany: State University of New York Press, 2003.

Beal, Becky, and Charlene Wilson. "'Chicks Dig Scars': Commercialization and the Transformations of Skateboarders' Identities." In *Understanding Lifestyle Sport: Consumption, Identity and Difference,* edited by Belinda Wheaton, 31–54. New York and London: Routledge, 2004.

Beatty, Sally. "ESPN Buys Assets of Bass Fishing Organization." *Wall Street Journal*. April 5, 2001.

Bekoff, Marc. *The Emotional Lives of Animals*. Novato, CA: New World Library, 2007.

Bellamy, Robert V., Jr. "Professional Sports Organizations: Media Strategies." In *Media, Sports, and Society*, edited by Lawrence A. Wenner. Newbury Park, CA: Sage, 1989.

Belmas, Elisabeth. *Jouer Autrefois. Essais sur le jeu dans la France moderne (XVIe-XVIIIe siècle)*. Seyssel: Champ Vallon, 2006.

Bennassar, Bartolomé. *Histoire de la Tauromachie. Une société du spectacle*. Paris: Éditions Desjonquères, 1993.

Bennett, Gregg, Robin K. Henson, and James J. Zhang. "Generation Y's Perception of the Action Sports Industry Segment." *Journal of Sport Management* 17 (2003): 95–115.

Bennett, Gregg, and Tony Lachowetz. "Marketing to Lifestyles: Actions Sports and Generation Y." *Sport Marketing Quarterly* 13 (2004): 239–243.

Bentham, Jeremy, and Etienne Dumont. *Theory of legislation*. Translated by Richard Hilgard. London: Kegan Paul, Trench, Trübner & Company Ltd., 1908.

Bercovici, Jeff. "Greg Jennings Reveals What NFL Players Really Think of Fantasy Football." *Forbes.com*. Last modified March 10, 2012. http://www.forbes.com/sites/jeffbercovici/2012/03/10/greg-jennings-reveals-what-nfl-players-really-think-of-fantasy-football/.

Beresini, Erin. *Off Course: Inside the Mad, Muddy World of Obstacle Course Racing*. New York: Houghton Mifflin Harcourt, 2014.

Berry, Matthew. *Fantasy Life: The Outrageous, Uplifting, and Heartbreaking World of Fantasy Sports from the Guy Who's Lived It*. New York: Penguin Group, 2013.

Best, David. *Philosophy and Human Movement*. London: George Allen & Unwin, 1978.

"Bicycling (BMX) Participation Report 2010." Sports and Fitness Industry Association. Accessed November 10, 2014. http://www.sgma.com/reports/24_Bicycling-%28BMX%29- Participation-Report-2010.

Billings, Andrew C., and Brody J. Ruihley. "The Fantasy Sport Trade Association: An Inside Look into a Billion Dollar Industry." Presentation at the Fifth Summit on Communication and Sport, Peoria, IL, March 2012.

Billings, Andrew C., and Brody J. Ruihley. *The Fantasy Sport Industry: Games Within Games*. London: Routledge, 2014.

Blackstock, Paul W. *The Strategy of Subversion: Manipulating the Politics of Other Nations*. Chicago: Quadrangle Books, 1964.

Boorstin, Daniel. *The Image: A Guide to Pseudo-Events in America*. New York: Atheneum, 1978.

Booth, Douglas. "Surfing 60s: A Case Study in the History of Pleasure and Discipline." *Australian Historical Studies* 26 (1994): 265–279.

———. "Ambiguities in Pleasure and Discipline: The Development of Competitive Surfing." *Journal of Sport History* 22 (1995): 189–206.

———. "Expressions Sessions: Surfing, Style, and Prestige." In *To the Extreme: Alternative Sports Inside and Out,* edited by Robert E. Rinehart and Synthia Sydnor, 315–333. Albany: State University of New York Press, 2003.

———. "Surfing: From One (Cultural) Extreme to the Other." In *Understanding Lifestyle Sport: Consumption, Identity and Difference,* edited by Belinda Wheaton, 94–109. New York and London: Routledge, 2004.

Borden, Iain. *Skateboarding, Space and the City: Architecture and the Body*. Oxford, England: Berg Publishing, 2001.

Browne, Rembert. "NFL RedZone: The People's Champ." *Grantland.com*. Last modified October 23, 2012. http://grantland.com/the-triangle/nfl-redzone-the-peoples-champ/.

Bruegel, Pieter. *Children's Games,* 1560, painting, Kunsthistorischesmuseum, Vienna.

Bryant, Jennings and Andrea M. Holt. "A Historical Overview of Sports and Media in the United States." In *Handbook of Sports Media,* edited by Arthur A Raney & Jennings Bryant. Mahwah, NJ: Lawrence Erlbaum, 2006.

Bullough, Steven J. "A New Look at the Latent Demand for Sport and its Potential to Deliver a Positive Legacy for London 2012." *International Journal of Sport Policy and Politics* 4 (2012): 39–54.

Burke, Monte. "How The National Football League Can Reach $25 Billion In Annual Revenues." *Forbes.* Last modified August 13, 2013. http://www.forbes.com/sites/monteburke/2013/08/17/how-the-national-football-league-can-reach-25-billion-in-annual-revenues/.

Burns, Francis. "Robert Dover's Cotswold Olimpick Games: The Use of the Term 'Olimpick,'" *Olympic Review* 210 (1985): 230–236.

Caillois, Roger. *Les jeux et les hommes. Le masque et le vertige.* "Idées," Paris: NRF-Gallimard, 1st ed. 1958; 1967.

———. *Man, Play and Games.* Translated by Meyer Barash. Chicago: University of Illinois Press, 2001.

Caldwell, John. "The Moneymaker Effect: Five Years Later." Last modified May 23, 2008. http://www.pokernews.com/news/2008/05/moneymaker-effect-five-years-later.htm.

Campbell, Colin. "Competitive Gaming Recognized in U.S. as a Pro Sport." Last modified July 12, 2013. http://www.polygon.com/2013/7/12/4518936/competitive-gaming-recognized-in-u-s-as-a-pro-sport.

Carlson, Chad. "The Reality of Fantasy Sports: A Metaphysical and Ethical Analysis." *Journal of the Philosophy of Sport* 40, no. 2 (2013): 187–204.

Carse, James P. *Finite and Infinite Games: A Vision of Life as Play and Possibility.* New York: Free Press, 1986.

Casey, Matthew. "NFL lagging on stadium Wi-Fi." *Cnn.com.* Last modified September 3, 2013. http://www.cnn.com/2013/09/02/tech/innovation/nfl-wi-fi-stadiums/.

Challenger, Gray and Christmas, Inc. "2012 Fantasy Football Report." @ *Work,* Last modified September 1, 2012. https://challengeratwork.wordpress.com/2012/09/01/2012-fantasy-football-report/.

Chick, Garry and John W. Loy. "Definitions," *The Encyclopedia of World Sport, Ancient Times to the Present.* Edited by David Levinson and Karen Christensen, 1. 247–49. Santa Barbara-Denver-Oxford: ABC-Clio, 1996.

Chopra, Samir. "Crossfit and the Military: A Way Forward." Last modified August 17, 2013, http://samirchopra.com/2013/08/17/crossfit-and-the-military-a-way-forward/

Cianfrone, Beth A., and James J. Zhang. "Differential Effects of Television Commercials, Athlete Endorsements, and Venue Signage during a Televised Action Sports Event." *Journal of Sport Management* 20 (2006): 322–344.

Clarke, Katrina. "Quebec Student Camille Leblanc-Bazinet Crowned 'Fittest Woman on Earth' at 2014 Reebok CrossFit Games." *The National Post.* Last modified July 28, 2014. http://news.nationalpost.com/2014/07/28/quebec-student-camille-leblanc-bazinet-crowned-fittest-woman-on-earth-at-2014-reebok-crossfit-games/

Coakley, Jay. Sports in Society: Issues and Controversies, *10th Edition.* New York, NY: McGraw-Hill, 2009.

"College Sports 101." *The Knight Commission on Intercollegiate Athletics.* 2009. http://www.knightcommission.org/collegesports101/table-of-contents.

Confucius, *Analects.* Translated by E. Slingerland. Indianapolis: Hacket, 2003.

Contamine, Philippe. *War in the Middle Ages.* Translated by Michael Jones. Oxford: Basil Blackwell, 1984.

Cossío, José María de. *Los Toros: Tratado técnico e histórico.* Madrid: Espasa Calpe, 1943.

"CrossFit: Forging Elite Fitness." *Crossfit.com.* Accessed December 16, 2014. http://www.crossfit.com/cf-info/what-is-crossfit.html.

"CrossFit Games Drug Testing Program." *Crossfit.com.* Accessed December 16, 2014. http://media.crossfit.com/games/pdf/2014CrossFitGames_DrugTestingProgram_140104.pdf

Crowther, Nigel. "The Ancient Olympics and Their Ideals." In *Athletika: Studies on the Olympic Games and Greek Athletics,* edited by W. Decker and I. Weiler, 1–11. Hildesheim, Germany: Weidemann, 2004.

D'Agostino, Fred. "The Ethos of Games." *Journal of the Philosophy of Sport* 8 (1981): 7–18.

D'Anjou, René. *Le livre des tournois du roi René,* Edited by F. Avril et E. Pognon. Reproduction of a 1460 manuscript. Paris: Herscher, 1986.

Das deutsches Wörterbuch. http://woerterbuchnetz.de/.

Dauncey, Hugh and Geoff Hare. "Sport and Media: Representing and Conceptualising Identity and Community." *Movement & Sport Sciences* 86, no. 4 (2014): 5–14.

Delaney, Tim and Tim Madigan. *The Sociology of Sports: An Introduction.* Jefferson, North Carolina: McFarland & Company, 2009.

Delattre, Edward J., "Some Reflections on Success and Failure in Competitive Athletics," *Journal of the Philosophy of Sport* 2, no. 1 (1975): 133–139.

DeMello, Margo. *Animals and Society: An Introduction to Human-Animal Studies.* New York: Columbia University Press, 2012.

Dennett, Daniel. *Brainstorms,* Cambridge, Massachusetts: MIT Press, 1978.

Diccionario de la lengua Española. http://www.rae.es/ayuda/diccionario-de-la-lengua-espanola.

Dietschy, Paul. *Histoire du football.* Paris: Perrin, 2010.

Dogtown and Z-Boys. Directed by Stacy Peralta. 2001. Sony Pictures Classics. Documentary.

Donaldson, Laura, and Mark Asbridge, and Michael D. Cusimano. "Bodychecking Rules and Concussion In Elite Hockey." Plos ONE 8.7 (2013): 1–6.

Donnelly, Maureen P. "Studying Extreme Sports; Beyond Core Participants." *Journal of Sport and Social Issues* 30 (2006): 219–224.

Donnelly, Peter. "Sport as a Site for 'Popular' Resistance." In *Popular Cultures and Political Practices,* Edited Richard S. Gruneau, 69–82. Toronto: Garamond Press, 1988.

Dryden, John. *Vergil's* Aeneid … *in the Dryden Translation,* Edited by Howard Clarke. University Park, PA, and London: Pennsylvania State University Press, 1989.

"Home Page." *Draftkings.com.* https://www.draftkings.com.

Duarte, Dom. *Livro da ensinança de bem cavalgar toda sela.* 1435.

Dubin, Jared. "US Defense Department paid 14 NFL teams $5.4M to honor soldiers." *CBSSports.com.* Last modified May 11, 2015. http://www.cbssports.com/nfl/eye-on-football/25181085/nfl-teams-received-54-million-from-defense-department-in-last-4-years.

During, Bertrand. *Des jeux aux sports. Repères et documents en histoire des activités physiques.* Paris: Vigot, 1984.

Dworkin, Ronald. *Justice for Hedgehogs.* Cambridge, MA: Belknap Press of Harvard University Press, 2003.

Dworkin, Ronald. *Law's Empire.* Cambridge, MA: Belknap Press of Harvard University Press, 1986.

Dwyer, Brendan. "The Impact of Fantasy Football Involvement on Intentions to Watch National Football League Games on Television." *International Journal of Sport Communication* 4, no. 3 (2011): 375–396.

Edgar, Andrew. "The Aesthetics of Sport." *Sport, Ethics and Philosophy* 7, no. 1 (2013): 80–99.

Eichelberger, Curtis. "NFL Stadiums Hope Fantasy Lounges Will Lure Fans." *Sentinel & Enterprise.* Last modified August 23, 2013. http://www.sentinelandenterprise.com/football/ci_23924861/nfl-stadiums-hope-fantasy-lounges-will-lure-fans.

Elias, Norbert and Eric Dunning. *Quest for Excitement: Sport and Leisure in the Civilizing Process.* In *Collected Works of Norbert Elias,* vol. 7, Edited by Eric Dunning. Dublin: University College Dublin Press, 2008.

Ellis, Robert. *The Games People Play: Theology, Religion, and Sport.* Cambridge: The Lutterworth Press, 2014.

England, Dan. "Mud, Sweat and a Whole Lot of Tears." *SBnation.com.* Last modified May 20, 2014. http://www.sbnation.com/longform/2014/5/20/5220672/amelia-boone-spartan-world-champion-profile-obstacle-racing.

Enoch, Glenn. "Life Stages of the Sports Fan." Presentation at University of Alabama, Tuscaloosa, AL, October 3, 2011.

Enriquez, Jon. "Coverage of Sports." In *American Journalism: History, Principles, Practices,* edited by W. David Sloan & Lisa Mullikin Parcell. Jefferson, North Carolina: McFarland, 2002.

Evaluation Criteria for Sports and Disciplines. Lausanne: International Olympic Committee, 2012.

Evans, Stephen. "League of Legends Gaming Final Fills Seoul Stadium." *BBC.com.* Last Modified October 20, 2014. http://www.bbc.com/news/business-29684635.

Factsheet on the Programme of the Games of the Olympiad. Lausanne: International Olympic Committee, 2013.

Factsheet on Women in the Olympic Movement. Lausanne: International Olympic Committee, 2016.

Fairfield, P. *Philosophical Hermeneutics in Relation Dialogues with Existentialism, Pragmatism, Critical Theory, and Postmodernism.* London: Continuum, 2011.

"Home Page." *Fanduel.com.* https://www.fanduel.com.

Farquhar, Lee K., and Robert Meeds. "Types of Fantasy Sports Users and Their Motivations." *Journal of Computer Mediated Communication* 12, no. 4 (2007): 1208–1228.

Farrell, Sean P. and Alan Feuer, "Are Video Games a Sport?" *New York Times* (Video). Last modified September 28, 2013. http://www.nytimes.com/video/sports/100000002463420/are-video-games-a-sport.html

Feezell, Randolph. "On the Wrongness of Cheating and Why Cheaters Can't Play the Game." *Journal of the Philosophy of Sport* 15 (1988): 57–68.

———. *Sport, Play & Ethical Reflection.* Chicago: University of Illinois Press, 2006.

———. *Sport, Philosophy, and Good Lives.* Lincoln: University of Nebraska Press, 2013.

Fenzi, Denise and Deb Jones. *Dog Sports Skills, Book 2: Motivation.* Woodside, CA: Fenzi Dog Sports Academy Publishing, 2014.

Fernández de Andrada, Pedro. *Libro de la Gineta de España.* Seville, 1599.

Fernández de Moratín, Nicolás. *Carta histórica sobre el origen y progresos de las fiestas de toros en España.* Madrid: Imprenta de Pantaleón Aznar, 1777.

Finley, M.I., and Plecket, H.W. *The Olympic Games: The First Thousand Years.* New York: Viking, 1976.

Fischer, Wendi. "Educational Value of Chess." *School of Education at Johns Hopkins University.* Accessed April 7, 2015. http://education.jhu.edu/PD/newhorizons/strategies/topics/thinking-skills/chess/.

Flannery, Michael and Richard Leech. *Golf through the Ages: Six Hundred Years of Golfing Art.* Fairfield, IA: Golf Links Press, 2004.

Fortunato, John A. "The NBA Strategy of Broadcast Television Exposure: A Legal Application," *Fordham Intellectual Property, Media and Entertainment Law Journal* 12, no. 1 (2001): 133–155.

———. "The Relationship of Fantasy Football Participation with NFL Television Ratings." *Journal of Sport Administration & Supervision* 3, no. 1 (2011): 74–90.

Fraleigh, Warren. *Right Actions in Sport: Ethics for Contestants.* Champaign, IL: Human Kinetics, 1984.

Friedman, Jon. "Success and the Bull's Eye." *The CrossFit Journal.* March 1, 2014.

Froissart, Jean. Œuvres, ed. Kervyn de Lettenhove, 25 vols. Brussels: Victor Devaux, 1867–1877.

G. de Bedoya, Fernando. *Historia del toreo, y de las principales ganaderías de España.* Madrid, 1850.

Gadamer, H. G. *Truth and method.* New York: Seabury Press, 1975.

Gallagher, Shaun. *Hermeneutics and Education.* Albany: State University of New York Press, 1999,

Gardiner, E. Norman. *Athletics of the Ancient World.* Oxford: Clarendon, 1930.

Gawrysiak, Joey, Brendon Dwyer, and Richard Burton. "Understanding Baseball Consumption Via in-Home Gaming." *Journal of Applied Sport Management* 6, no. 3 (2014): 75–101.

Geertz, Clifford. "Notes on the Balinese Cockfight." In *The Interpretation of Cultures.* New York: Basic Books, 1973.

Geertz, Clifford. "Deep Play: Notes on the Balinese Cockfight." *Deadalus* 134, no. 4 (2005): 56–86.

Gerber, Ellen. "Arguments on the Reality of Sport." In *Sport and the Body: A Philosophical Symposium.* Edited by Ellen Gerber. Philadelphia: Lea and Febiger, 1972.

Giannoulakis, Chrysostomos. In Press. "The 'Authenticitude' Battle in Action Sports: A Case-Based Industry Perspective." *Sport Management Review*.

Gibson, Hanna. "Detailed Discussion of Dog-Fighting." *Michigan State University College of Law Animal Legal and Historical Center*. Accessed March 19, 2015. http://www.animallaw.info/article/detailed-discussion-dog-fighting#id-1.

Giglietto, Fabio, and Donatella Selva. "Second screen and participation: A content analysis on a full season dataset of tweets." *Journal of Communication* 64, no. 2 (2014): 260–277.

Glenney, Brian and Mull, Steve. "Skateboarding and the Re-Wilding of Urban Space," *Journal of Sport and Social Issues* (Forthcoming).

Goff, Brian. "The $70 Billion Fantasy Football Market." *Forbes.com*. Last modified August 20, 2013. http://www.forbes.com/sites/briangoff/2013/08/20/the-70-billion-fantasy-football-market/.

Goldsmith, Andrew L., and Matthew Walker. "The NASCAR experience: Examining the influence of fantasy sport participation on 'non-fans.'" *Sport Management Review* (2014).

Gomez, Brandon. "How did Nike get the Swoosh into Skateboarding? A Study of Authenticity and Nike SB." Master's thesis, Syracuse University, 2012.

Gómez Quintana, Isidoro. *Apuntes históricos acerca de la fiesta de toros en España. Biografía de los más célebres lidiadores*. Cordoba: R. Molina, 1897.

González Aja, Teresa. "La educación heroica y agonal en el mundo homérico y su repercusión en las manifestaciones artísticas." *Historia de la Educación* 14–15 (1995–1996): 31–46.

———. *El deporte a través del arte: El mundo antiguo: Del "agôn" al "ludus."* Madrid: Dirección General de Deportes, Comunidad de Madrid, 2000.

———. "Trionfo e Dominio nell'arena." *Lancilloto e Nausica* 26 (2003): 30–41.

———. "La restauración de los Juegos Olímpicos: Pierre de Coubertin y su época." In *In Corpore Sano. El deporte en la antigüedad y la creación del moderno olimpismo*, Edited by Fernando García Romero and Berta Hernández García. Madrid: Sociedad de Estudios Clásicos, 2005.

Gorant, Jim. *The Lost Dogs: Michael Vick's Dogs and Their Tale of Rescue and Redemption*. New York: Gotham Books, 2010.

Gorn, Elliott J. and Warren Goldstein, *A Brief History of American Sports*. Chicago: University of Illinois Press, 2004.

Freedom's Fury. Directed by Colin Keith Gray. 2006. Documentary.

Greenspan, Bud. *100 Greatest Moments in Olympic History*. Los Angeles: General Publishing Group, 1995.

Greimas, A. J. *Du sens. Essais sémiotiques*. Paris: Le Seuil, 1970.

Groen, Andrew. "Why Gamers in Asia are the World's Best eSport Athletes." Last modified May 14, 2013. http://www.pcworld.com/article/2036844/why-gamers-in-asia-are-the-worlds-best-esport-athletes.html.

Guillaume-Alonso, Araceli. "Tauromaquia para un rey: Fiesta de toros en la inauguración del Buen Retiro." Paper presented at the Fiestas de toros y sociedad, Seville, 2001.

Guttmann, Allen. *From Ritual to Record. The Nature of Modern Sports*. New York: Columbia University Press, 1978.

———. *Sports Spectators*. New York: Columbia University Press, 1986.

————. *Sports: The First Five Millenia.* Amherst: University of Massachusetts Press, 2004.

————. "Rules of the Game." In *The Sport Studies Reader*, edited by Alan Tomlinson. London: Routledge, 2007.

Habermas, Jürgen. *On the Logic of the Social Sciences.* Cambridge, MA: MIT Press, 1988.

————. *Between Facts and Norms: Contributions to a Discourse Theory of Law and Democracy.* Cambridge, MA: MIT Press, 1996.

Hart, H.L.A. *The Concept of Law.* Oxford: Clarendon Press, 1984

Haugeland, John. "Truth and Rule Following." In *Having Thought: Essays in the Metaphysics of Mind.* Cambridge, Mass.: Harvard University Press, 1998.

Havrilesky, Heather. "Why Are Americans So Fascinated With Extreme Fitness?" *New York Times.* Last modified October 14, 2014. http://www.nytimes.com/2014/10/19/magazine/why-are-americans-so-fascinated-with-extreme-fitness.html.

Heidegger, Martin. *Country Path Conversations.* Bloomington: Indiana University Press, 2010.

Hemingway, Ernest. *Death in the Afternoon.* USA: Charles Scribners Sons, 1932.

Hemphill, Dennis. "Cybersport." *Journal of the Philosophy of Sport* 32, no. 2 (2005): 195–207.

Herz, J. C. *Learning to Breathe Fire: The Rise of Crossfit and the Primal Future of Fitness.* New York: Crown Archetype, 2014.

Higgins, Matt. "In Board Sports, Insider Status Makes Gear Sell." *The New York Times.* Last modified November 24, 2006. http://www.nytimes.com/2006/11/24/sports/othersports/24brands.html.

Hillo, Pepe (José Delgado Guerra). *La Tauromaquia o Arte de torear.* Cadiz, 1796.

Hirsch, E. D. *Validity in Interpretation.* New Haven: Yale University Press, 1967.

"History." *National Spelling Bee.* http://spellingbee.com/history.

"The History of BMX Racing." *USA BMX: The American Bicycle Association.* Accessed January 17, 2015. http://usabmx.com/site/sections/7.

"History, The Early Beginnings." *International Ice Hockey Federation.* Accessed April 4, 2015.

"Homenaje a las mujeres toreras En la muestra 'Una mirada femenina del toreo.'" *Republica.* Last modified May 6, 2011. http://www.republica.com/2011/05/06/homenaje-a-las-mujeres-toreras-en-la-muestra-una-mirada-femenina-del-toreo/.

Homer. *Iliada-Odisea.* Translated by Luis Segalá. 1959 ed. Barcelona: Vergara, 1969.

Honea, Joy C. "Youth cultures and Consumerism: Alternative Sport and Possibilities for Resistance." Paper presented at the annual meeting of the American Sociological Association San Francisco, CA, Aug 14, 2004.

————. "Beyond the Alternative vs. Mainstream Dichotomy: Olympic BMX and the Future of Action Sports." *Journal of Popular Culture* 46 (2013): 1253–1275.

Howell, Ocean. "Skateparks as Neoliberal Ground." *Space and Culture* 11 (2008): 475–496.

Huizinga, Johan. *Homo Ludens: A Study of the Play Element in Culture.* Boston: The Beacon Press, 1955.

Humphreys, Duncan. "Shredheads Go Mainstream? Snowboarding and Alternative Youth." *International Review for the Sociology of Sport* 32 (1997): 147–160.

———. "Selling Out Snowboarding: The Alternative Response to Commercial Co-Optation." In *To the Extreme: Alternative Sports Inside and Out,* edited by Robert E. Rinehart and Synthia Sydnor, 407–428. Albany: State University of New York Press, 2003.

Hurka, Thomas. Introduction to *The Grasshopper: Games, Life, and Utopia* by Bernard Suits. Toronto: University of Toronto Press, 1978.

Husserl, Edmund. *Ideas: General Introduction to Pure Phenomenology.* Translated by W.R. Boyce Gibson. New York: Collier Books, 1972.

———. *Ideas Pertaining to a Pure Phenomenology and to a Phenomenological Philosophy.* Translated by F. Kersten. The Hague: Martinus Nijhoff Publishers, 1982.

"Industry Demographics." *Fantasy Sport Trade Association.* http://fsta.org/research/industry-demographics/

"Home." *International Obstacle Racing Federation.* http://www.obstaclesports.org/.

Jaeger, Werner. *Paideia.* Madrid: F.C.E., 1981.

Jakobson, Roman and Morris Halle. *Fundamentals of Language.* The Hague: Mouton, 1956.

James I. *A Declaration Concerning Lawfull Sports to be Used,* in *Minor Prose Works,* Edited by J. Craigie and A. Law, 102–109, 217–41. Edinburgh: Scottish Texts Society, 1982.

Jhingran, Saral *Ethical Relativism and Universalism.* Delhi, Motilal Banarsidass Publishers, 2001.

Jusserand, J.J. *Les sports et jeux d'exercice dans l'ancienne France.* Paris, 1901.

Keener, Steven D. "Sports Teach Kids Valuable Lessons." *New York Times.* Last modified October 10, 2013. http://www.nytimes.com/roomfordebate/2013/10/10/childrens-sportslife-balance/sports-teach-kids-valuable-lessons.

Kellett, Pamm, and Roslyn Russell. "A Comparison between Mainstream and Action Sport Industries in Australia: A Case Study of the Skateboarding Cluster." *Sport Management Review* 12 (2009): 66–78.

Kelly, Stephen. *Bill Shankly: It's Much More Important Than That.* London: Virgin Books, 1997.

Keneally, Scott. "Playing Dirty." *Outside Magazine,* November 2012.

Keyser, Jason. "Robert Morris University Becomes First to Recognize Video Games as Varsity Sport." Last modified October 6, 2014. http://www.huffingtonpost.com/2014/10/06/video-game-scholarship-varsity-sport_n_5940898.html.

Kidd, Bruce. *The Struggle for Canadian Sport.* Toronto-Buffalo-London: University of Toronto Press, 1996.

Klein, Jeff. "Where Hockey Is Growing, State by State." *New York Times.* Last modified February 20, 2011. http://slapshot.blogs.nytimes.com/2011/02/20/where-hockey-is-growing-state-by-state/.

Knight, K. *Aristotelian Philosophy: Ethics and Politics from Aristotle to MacIntyre.* Malden, MA: Polity Press, 2007.

Kretchmar, R. Scott. "Philosophy of Ethics." *Quest* 45 (1993): 3–12.

———. "Why Dichotomies Make it Difficult to See Games as Gifts of God." In *Theology, Ethics, and Transcendence in Sport,* Edited by Jim Parry, Mark Nesti, and Nick Watson, 185–200. London: Routledge, 2011.

Kubatko, Justin. "Keeping Score: The Story Arc of the 3-Point Shot." *Off the Dribble Blog*. Last modified February 10, 2011. http://offthedribble.blogs.nytimes. com/2011/02/10/keeping-score-the-story-arc-of-the-3-point-shot/.

Kuhn, Thomas S. *The Structure of Scientific Revolutions*. Chicago: University Of Chicago Press, 2012.

Kyd, Thomas. *The Works of Thomas Kyd*, ed. F. S. Boas. Oxford: Clarendon Press, 1901.

Kyle, Donald G. "E. Norman Gardiner, Historian of Ancient Sport," *International Journal of the History of Sport* 8, no. 1 (1991): 28–55.

Laclau, Ernesto and Chantal Mouffe. *Hegemony and Socialist Strategy: Towards a Radical Democratic Politics*. London: Verso, 1985.

Laker, Anthony. *Sociology of Sport and Physical Education: An Introductory Reader*. New York: Routledge, 2001.

Law, Alan. "Surfing the Safety Net: Dole Bludging, 'Surfies' and Governmentality in Australia." *International Review for the Sociology of Sport* 36 (2001): 25–40.

Lawler, Andrew. "Birdmen." *Salon*. Accessed March 20, 2015. http://www.slate. com/articles/health_and_science/science/2014/12/cockfighting_and_chicken_history_the_world_slasher_cup_in_the_philippines.2.html.

Le grand Robert. https://www.lerobert.com/espace-numerique/enligne/le-grand-robert-de-la-langue-francaise-en-ligne-12-mois.html.

Lee, Jeremy, Brody J. Ruihley, Natalie Brown, and Andrew C. Billings. "The Effects of Fantasy Football Participation on Team Identification, Team Loyalty and NFL Fandom." *Journal of Sports Media* 8, no. 1 (2013): 207–227.

Lehman, Craig K. "Can Cheaters Play the Game?" *Journal of the Philosophy of Sport*. 8, 1 (1981): 41–46.

Leiris, Michel. *Espejo de la Tauromaquia*. Madrid: Arena Libros, 2014.

Lejacq, Yannick. "How Fast is Fast? some Pro Gamers make 10 Moves Per Second." *NBC News*. Last modified October 24, 2013. http://www.nbcnews.com/ technology/how-fast-fast-some-pro-gamers-make-10-moves-second-8C11422946.

Lemay, Eric. "CrossFit Mirrors American Militarism: The Fitness Craze Reflects the Country's Ongoing Transformation from a Culture of Sports to a Culture of War." *Salon*, September 7, 2013. http://www.salon.com/2013/09/08/ crossfit_nation_partner/.

Lenhart, Amanda, Joseph Kahne, Ellen Middaugh, Alexandra Rankin Macgill, Chris Evans, and Jessica Vitak. *Teens, Video Games, and Civics*. Washington, DC: Pew Internet and American Life Project, 2008.

Leong, Lewis. "VR Drone Racing Makes for a Vomit-Inducing Spectator Sport." *IGN*. Last modified January 29, 2016. http://www.ign.com/articles/2016/01/29/ vr-drone-racing-makes-for-a-vomit-inducing-spectator-sport.

Lin, Chris. "Gamers Take Home Gold at X Games." *ESPN.com*. Last modified May 8, 2015. http://xgames.espn.go.com/xgames/events/2014/austin/article /11053677/gamers-break-new-ground-x-games-austin-first-medals.

Littewin, Mike. "Jordan Hid Allegiance Under Flag, Cover-up Discloses Nike Won Shoe War." *Baltimore Sun*. Last modified August 9, 1992. http://articles.baltimoresun.com/1992–08–09/sports/1992222100_1_reebok-nike-jordan-put.

Loland, Sigmund. *Fair Play in Sport: A Moral Norm System.* New York: Routledge, 2002.

López Frías, Francisco Javier. "William J. Morgan's 'Conventionalist Internalism' Approach. Furthering Internalism? A Critical Hermeneutical Response." *Sport, Ethics and Philosophy 8*, no. 2 (2014): 151–171.

———. *La Filosofía del Deporte Actual. Paradigmas y Corrientes Principales.* Roma, Qua.Pe.G, 2014.

López Pelegrín, S. ("Abenámar"). *Filosofía de los toros.* Madrid, 1842.

López Valdemoro de Quesada Navas, Juan Gualberto, conde de las. *El espectáculo más nacional.* Madrid: Sucesores de Rivadeneyra, 1899.

Loy, John W. "The Nature of Sport: A Definitional Effort." *Quest* 10, no. 1 (1968): 1–15.

Lumer, Christoph. "Rules and Moral Norms in Sports." *International Review for Sociology of Sport* 30 (1995): 263–280.

Lund, Giuliana. "Taking Teamwork Seriously: The Sport of Dog Agility as an Ethical Model of Cross-Species Companionship." In *Sport, Animals, and Society,* Edited by James Gillett and Michelle Gilbert, New York: Routledge, 2014.

Lundry, Wez. "Subvert the Dominant Paradigm," *Thrasher,* October 1, 2002.

MacGregor, Jeff. "Everything Everywhere All at Once." *ESPN.* Last modified May 24, 2003. http://espn.go.com/espn/story/_/id/9308052/ never-easier-follow-niche-sports.

MacIntyre, Alasdair. *After Virtue: A Study in Moral Theory.* Notre Dame, Indiana: University of Notre Dame Press, 1981.

———. "On Not Having the Last Word: Thoughts on Our Debts to Gadamer." In *Gadamer's Century: Essays in Honor of Hans-Georg Gadamer,* edited by H. G. Gadamer, J. Malpas, U. Arnswald, and J. Kertscher. Cambridge: MIT Press, 2002.

"Major League Gaming Reports 334 Percent Growth in Live Video." Last modified November 14, 2012. http://www.gamespot.com/articles/major-league -gaming-reports-334-percent-growth-in-live-video/1100–6400010/.

Malaby, Thomas. "Beyond Play: A New Approach to Games." *Games and Culture* 2, 2 (2007): 95–113.

Manfred, Tony. "People are Making $100,000 a Year Playing a More Intense Version of Fantasy Football." *Business Insider.* Last modified November 8, 2013. http:// www.businessinsider.com/people-making-100000-a-year-on-daily-fantasy-sports -2013-11.

Mangan, J. A. "Militarism, Sport, Europe: War without Weapons," *European Sports History Review* 5 (2003).

Martínková, Irena and Parry, Jim. "Two Ways of Conceiving Time in Sports." *Acta Universitatis Palackianae Olomucensis. Gymnica,* 41, no. 1 (2011): 23–31.

Martzke, Rudy and Reid Cherner. "After 25 Years, ESPN Still Channels How to View Sports." *USA Today.* Last modified August 17, 2004. http://usatoday30.usa-today.com/sports/2004–08–17-espn-25-years_x.htm.

Marx, Karl. *A Contribution to the Critique of Political Economy.* Chicago: Charles H. Kerr and Company: 1904.

Mason, Tony. *El deporte en Gran Bretaña.* Madrid: Civitas, 1994.

McBride, Frank. "Toward a Non-Definition of Sport." *Journal of the Philosophy of Sport* 2, no. 1 (1975): 4–11.

————. "A Critique of Mr. Suits' Definition of Game Playing." *Journal of the Philosophy of Sport* 6 (1979): 49–52.

McChestney, Robert W. "Media Made Sport: A History of Sports Coverage in the United States." In *Media, Sports, and Society*, edited by Lawrence A. Wenner. New York, Sage, 1989.

McClelland, John. "Sport." In *Encyclopedia of Semiotics*, Edited by Paul Bouissac, 593–596. New York-Oxford: Oxford University Press, 1998.

————. "Ball Games, from the Roman Gentleman to the Renaissance Warrior." In *Militarism, Sport, Europe: War without Weapons*, Edited by J.A. Mangan, 46–64. London. Frank Cass, 2003.

————. *Body and Mind. Sport in Europe from the Roman Empire to the Renaissance.* London-New York: Routledge, 2007.

————. "Sports Spectators and (the Lack of) Sports Arenas: From the Middle Ages to the End of the Eighteenth Century," in *Grenzüberschreitung: Sport neu denken*, Edited by S. Scharenberg and Bernd Wedemeyer-Kolwe, 218–232. Hoya: Niedersächsisches Institut für Sportgeschichte, 2009.

————. "The Accidental Sports Tourist: Travelling and Spectating in Medieval and Renaissance Europe," *Journal of Tourism History* 5, no. 2 (2013): 161–171.

————. "Sport and Scientific Thinking in the Sixteenth Century: Ruling Out Playfulness," *Ludica, annali di storia e civiltà del gioco* 19–20 (2013–2014), 134–45.

McClelland, John and Brian Merrilees, eds. *Sport and Culture in Early Modern Europe / Le sport dans la civilisation de l'Europe pré-moderne*, Essays and Studies 20. Toronto: Centre for Reformation and Renaissance Studies, 2009.

McFee, Graham. "Spoiling: An Indirect Reflection of Sport's Moral Imperative." In *Values in Sport: Elitism, Nationalism, Gender Equality and the Scientific Manufacture of Winners*, Edited by Torbjörn Tännsjö and Claudio Tamburrini, 172–188. London: E&FN Spon, 2000.

————. *Sport, Rules and Values: Philosophical Investigations into the Nature of Sport.* London: Routledge, 2004.

————. "Normativity, justification, and (MacIntyrean) Practices: Some Thoughts on Methodology for the Philosophy of Sport." *Journal of the Philosophy of Sport 31*, no. 1 (2004): 15–33.

Mckelvey, Steve. "Industry Insiders: Action Sports Execs." *Sport Marketing Quarterly* 21 (2012): 206–209.

McLaughlin, Thomas. *Give and Go: Basketball as a Cultural Practice.* Albany, NY: SUNY Press, 2008.

McNamee, Michael. *Sports, Virtues and Vices: Morality Plays.* New York: Routledge, 2008.

————. "Ethics and Sport." *British Philosophy of Sport Association Website.* http://philosophyofsport.org.uk/resources/ethics-sport/

Mehl, Jean-Michel. *Les jeux au royaume de France du XIIIe au début du XVIe siècle.* Paris: Fayard, 1990.

Meier, Klaus V. "Restless Sport." *Journal of the Philosophy of Sport* 12 (1985): 64–77.

————. "Triad Trickery: Playing with Sport and Games." *Journal of the Philosophy of Sport* 15, no. 1 (1988): 11–30.

———. "Performance Prestidigitation." *Journal of the Philosophy of Sport* 16, no. 1 (1989): 13–33.

"Member Resources." *USA BMX: The American Bicycle Association.* Accessed January 17, 2015. https://www.usabmx.com/site/sections/77.

Molina, Argote de. *Libro de la Montería.* Seville, 1582.

Montes, Fancisco (Paquiro). *Tauromaquia completa o El arte de torear en plaza, tanto a pie como a caballo.* Madrid: Imprenta de D. José María Repullés, 1836.

Montgomery, Kathleen and Oliver, Amalya. "A Fresh Look on how Professions Take Shape." *Organization Studies* 28 (2007): 661–687.

Morgan, William J. "Some Aristotelian Notes on the Attempt to Define Sport." *Journal of the Philosophy of Sport* 4, no. 1 (1977): 15–35.

———. "The Logical Incompatibility Thesis and Rules: A Reconsideration of Formalism as an Account of Games." *Journal of the Philosophy of Sport*, 14 (1987): 1–19.

———. "On the Path Towards an Ontology of Sport." *Journal of the Philosophy of Sport* 3, no. 1 (1989): 25–34.

———. "Broad Internalism, Deep Conventions, Moral Entrepreneurs, and Sport." *Journal of the Philosophy of Sport* 39, no. 1 (2012): 65–100.

———. "Conventionalism and Sport." In *Routledge Handbook of the Philosophy of Sport,* edited by Mike J. McNamee and William J. Morgan. New York: Routledge, 2015.

Morris, S.P. "On Hunting: A Philosophical Case Study in Animal Sports." PhD diss., The Ohio State University, 2010.

———. "The Ethics of Interspecies Sports," In *Sport, Animals, and Society,* Edited by James Gillett and Michelle Gilbert. New York: Routledge, 2014.

Mortimer, Sean. "Skate TV: Reaching Millions More than Endemic Media, Skateboard TV Shows are Impacting and Dividing the Industry." *Transworld Business,* February 2008.

———. Stalefish: Skateboard Culture from the Rejects Who made it. San Francisco, CA: Chronicle Books, 2008.

Morton, Timothy. *The Ecological Thought.* Cambridge: Harvard University Press, 2010.

Moskowitz, Tobias, and L. Jon Wertheim. *Scorecasting: The Hidden Influences Behind How Sports Are Played and Games Are Won.* New York: Crown Publishing, 2011.

Moyer, Justin. "Why Michael Phelps Can't Be the Man We Want Him to Be." *Washington Post.* Last modified October 1, 2014. http://www.washingtonpost.com/news/morning-mix/wp/2014/10/01/why-michael-phelps-cant-be-the-man-we-want-him-to-be/.

Mueller-Vollmer, K. *The Hermeneutics Reader: Texts of the German Tradition from the Enlightenment to the Present.* New York: Continuum, 1988.

Muñoz, Jacobo and A. M. Faerna. *Caminos de la Hermenéutica.* Madrid: Biblioteca Nueva, 2006.

Nadot, Sébastien. *Le spectacle des joutes. Sport et courtoisie à la fin du Moyen Âge.* Rennes: Presses Universitaires de Rennes, 2012.

"NBA to Alter Traveling Rules." *ESPN.* Last modified October 16, 2009. http://sports.espn.go.com/nba/news/story?id=4563546.

Nelson, Wade. "The Historical Mediatization of BMX Freestyle Cycling." *Sport in Society* 13 (2010): 1152–1169.

Newsweek Staff. "I'm Not a Role Model." *Newsweek*. Last modified June 27, 1993. http://www.newsweek.com/im-not-role-model-193808

Nozick, Robert. *Anarchy, State, and Utopia*. New York: Basic Books, 1974.

"Ode to Fran." *Youtube.com*. Accessed December 16, 2014. https://www.youtube.com/watch?v=KVxzDOYv85k

Off the Chain: A Shocking Exposé on America's Forsaken Breed. Directed by Bobby J. Brown. Woodland Hills, CA: Allumination FilmWorks, 2004. DVD.

O'Keefe, Dan, Schaffer, Jeff, & Marcus Schaffer, Jackie, *The League*, "The Tie." Television Series, Directed by Jackie Marcus Schaffer. Los Angeles; FX Network, 2010. Television.

O'Leary, John. *Drugs and Doping in Sport*. London: Routledge, 2013.

The Olympic Charter. Lausanne: International Olympic Committee, 2014.

"Olympic Day." *USA BMX: The American Bicycle Association*. Accessed January 17, 2015. https://www.usabmx.com/site/bmx_races?series_race_type=Olympic+Dayandsection_id=64andyear=2014.

"Olympics badminton: Eight women disqualified from doubles," *BBC.com*. Last modified August 1, 2012. http://www.bbc.co.uk/sport/0/olympics/19072677.

"Optimum Sports & Entertainment Pack." *Optimum TV*, accessed 2015. http://www.optimum.com/digital-cable-tv/sports/sports-pak.jsp.

Oriard, Michael. *King Football: Sport and Spectacle in the Golden Age of Radio and Newsreels, Movies and Magazines, the Weekly and the Daily Press*. Chapel Hill: University of North Carolina Press, 2001.

Ortega y Gasset, José. "Sobre la caza." In *Veinte años de caza mayor del Conde de Yebes*, Edited by El Viso, 1943. Reprint, 1983.

Orwell, George. "The Sporting Spirit," *Tribune* 468 (December 14, 1945), 10–11.

Osterhoundt, Robert G. "The Term Sport—Some Thoughts on a Proper Name." *International Journal of Physical Education* 14 (1977): 11–16.

Overman, Steven J. *The Youth Sports Crisis: Out-of-Control Adults, Helpless Kids*. Santa Barbara, CA: ABC-CLIO, 2014.

Parry, Jim. "Sport, art and the aesthetic," *Sport Science Review* 12 (1989): 15–20.

———. "Olympism at the Beginning and End of the Twentieth Century." *Proceedings of the International Olympic Academy* (1998): 81–94.

———. "Sport and Olympism: Universals and Multiculturalism." *Journal of the Philosophy of Sport* 33 (2006): 188–204.

Pepys, Samuel. *Diary*. Edited by R. Latham and W. Matthews, 11 vols. Berkeley and Los Angeles: University of California Press., 1983.

Pérez de Guzmán, J. *Origen e historia de las fiestas de toros*. s.d.

Peyron, Jean François. *Nouveau voyage en Espagne, fait en 1777 & 1778*. Londres—París, 1782.

Plato. *Complete Works*. Edited by J. Cooper. Indianapolis, IN: Hackett, 1997.

Popelin, Claude. *Le taureau et son combat*. Paris: Plon, 1952.

Popper, Ben. "Field of Streams: How Twitch made Video Games a Spectator Sport." *The Verge*. Last modified September 30, 2013. http://www.theverge.com/2013/9/30/4719766/twitch-raises-20-million-esports-market-booming.

Poythress, Cullen. "Major Action-Sports Tours and Their Effect on the Core Industry." *Transworld Business,* December 2006.

"Proceedings of the Association, March 27th." *Journal of the British Archaeological Association,* Volume 26 (1870): 240–243. Accessed March 8, 2015. Google Books.

Pursglove, Lindsay K. "Bicycle Motocross (BMX): Transformation from Niche to Mainstream." Master's thesis, Barry University, 2009.

Rabelais, François. *Gargantua,* 1534.

Rawls, John. *Collected Papers.* Cambridge, Mass.: Harvard University Press, 1999.

"Real Decreto 145/1996, de 2 de Febrero, Por el que se modifica y da nueva redacción al reglamento de espectáculos taurinos." In *Ministerio de Justicia e Interior.* Madrid: Official State Gazette, 1996.

Reddiford, Gordon. "Constitutions, Institutions, and Games." *Journal of the Philosophy of Sport* 12, no. 1 (1985): 41–51.

"Reebok CrossFit Games." *Crossfit.com.* Accessed December 16, 2014. http://games. crossfit.com/

Regan, Tom. *The Case for Animal Rights.* Berkeley: University of California Press, 2004.

Reid, Heather. "Olympic Sport and Its Lessons for Peace." *Journal of the Philosophy of Sport* 33 (2006): 205–213. Reprinted with revisions in *Olympic Truce: Sport as a Platform for Peace,* Edited by K. Georgiadis & A. Syrigos, 25–35. Athens: International Olympic Truce Center, 2009.

———. *Athletics and Philosophy in the Ancient World: Contests of Virtue.* Abingdon: Routledge, 2011.

Reynolds, Mike. "Fight Network, FNTSY Gain First U.S. Berths with Cablevision: Anthem Media Properties Available on MSO's Sports Package." *Multichannel.com.* Last modified June 26, 2014. http://www.multichannel.com/news/ distribution/fight-network-fntsy-gain-first-us-berths-cablevision/375414

Rinehart, Robert E. "Inside of the Outside: Pecking Orders Within Alternative Sport at ESPN's 1995 'The eXtreme Games.'" *Journal of Sport & Social Issues* 22, no. 4 (1998): 398–415.

———. "Emerging Arriving Sport: Alternatives to Formal Sport." In *Handbook of Sport Studies,* Edited by Jay Coakley and Eric Dunning, 504–520. London: Sage, 2000.

Rizzi, Alessandra. *Statuta de ludo. Le leggi sul gioco nell'Italia di commune (secoli XIII-XVI).* Treviso/Roma: Fondazione Benetton Studi Ricerche/Viella , 2012.

Rorty, Richard. *Philosophy and the Mirror of Nature.* Princeton: Princeton University Press, 1979.

Ross, W.D. *Aristotle: The Nicomachean Ethics.* Oxford: Oxford University Press, 1998.

Rowe, David. *Sport, Culture and the Media, 2nd Edition.* London: Open University Press, 2004.

Roy, Donald P., and Benjamin D. Goss. "A Conceptual Framework of Influences on Fantasy Sports Consumption." *Marketing Management Journal* 17, no. 2 (2007): 96–108.

Rühl, Joachim K. *Die ,Olympischen Spiele Robert Dovers,* Annales Universitatis Saraviensis 14. Heidelberg: Carl Winter—Universitätsverlag, 1975.

———. 2009. "A Treasure-trove: One of the Four Originals of the Tournament Regulations of Heilbronn 1485." In *Sport and Culture in Early Modern Europe/ Le sport dans la civilisation de l'Europe pré-moderne,* Essays and Studies 20, Edited by John McClelland and Brian Merrilees, 147–84. Toronto, Center for Reformation and Renaissance Studies, 2009.

Ruihley, Brody J., and Andrew C. Billings. "Infiltrating the boys' club: Motivations for women's fantasy sport participation." *International Review for the Sociology of Sport* 48, no. 4 (2013): 435–452.

———. *The Fantasy Sports Industry.* New York: Routledge, 2014.

Ruihley, Brody J., Andrew C. Billings, and Coral Rae. "As Time Goes By: Deciphering the Fantasy Sport Playing Teenager." *Sport Marketing Quarterly* 23, no. 4 (2014): 187–197.

Ruihley, Brody J., and Roy L. Hardin. "Beyond Touchdowns, Homeruns, and 3-Pointers: An Examination of Fantasy Sport Participation Motivation." *International Journal of Sport Management and Marketing* 10, no. 3/4 (2011): 232–256.

Russell, J.S. "Are Rules All an Umpire Has to Work With?" *Journal of the Philosophy of Sport* 26, no. 1 (1999): 27–49.

———. "Moral Realism in Sport." *Journal of the Philosophy of Sport* 31, no. 2 (2004): 142–160.

———. "The Value of Dangerous Sport." *Journal of the Philosophy of Sport* 32, no. 1 (2005): 1–19.

Sailors, Pam R., Sarah Teetzel, and Charlene Weaving. "*Lentius, Inferius, Debilius*: The Ethics of 'Not Trying' on the Olympic Stage." *Sport in Society* 18 (2015): 17–27.

Salome, Lotte and van Bottenburg, Maarten. "Are They All Daredevils? Introducing a Participation Typology for the Consumption of Lifestyle Sports in Different Settings." *European Sport Management Quarterly* 21 (2012): 19–42.

Samtani, Heiten. "A Spelling Champ Whose E-U-O-N-Y-M Should Have Been 'Joy.'" *WNYC.* Last modified March 23, 2015. http://www.wnyc.org/story/302349-a-spelling-champ-whose-e-u-o-n-y-m-should-have-been-joy/.

Saraiya, Sonia. "Mission Impossible: How 'American Ninja Warrior' Masters the Art of Losing," *Salon.* Last modified February 5, 2012. http://www.salon.com/2015/02/05/mission_impossible_how_american_ninja_warrior_masters_the_art_of_losing/.

Sargent, Bill. "ESPN Bets Bass Fishing Is TV Hit." *Florida Today.* October 30, 2005.

Schazki, T.D. *The Practice Turn in Contemporary Theory.* New York: Routledge, 2001.

Schmidt, Sandra. *Kopfübern und Luftspringen. Bewegung als Wissenschaft und Kunst in der Frühen Neuzeit.* Munich: Wilhelm Fink Verlag, 2008.

Schreier, Jason. "ESPN Airs Video Games, Twitter Freaks Out." *Kotaku.com.* Last modified April 26, 2015. http://kotaku.com/espn-airs-video-games-twitter-freaks-out-1700333433.

Schwartz, Nick. "ESPN People Are Freaking Out Because ESPN Televised eSports." *USA Today.* Last modified April 26, 2015. http://ftw.usatoday.com/2015/04/espn-esports-heroes-of-the-dorm-reaction.

Searle, John R. *Speech Acts: An Essay in the Philosophy of Language.* Cambridge: Cambridge University Press, 1969.

Sheridan, Heather. "Conceptualizing 'Fair Play': A Review of the Literature." *European Physical Education Review* 9 (2003): 163–184.

Shenk, David. *The Immortal Game: A History of Chess,* New York: Doubleday, 2006.

Sherowski, Jennifer. "Skatepark Advancement 101." *Transworld Business,* May, 2007.

Shogan, Debra. "Rules, Penalties, and Officials: Sports and the Legality-Morality Distinction." *Canadian Association for Health, Physical Education, Recreation and Dance Journal* 54 (1988): 6–11.

"SI's 50 Most Powerful People in Sports." *Sports Illustrated.* Last modified March 6, 2013. http://www.si.com/more-sports/photos/2013/03/06/50-most-powerful -people-sports.

Sicilia de Arenzana, F. *Las corridas de toros. Su origen, sus progresos y sus vicisi- tudes.* Madrid: Imp. y Lit, de N. González, 1873.

Siculus, Diodorus. *Bibliotheca Historica.*

Simon, Robert L., Cesar R. Torres, and Peter F. Hager. *Fair Play: The Ethics of Sport, 4th Edition.* Boulder, CO: Westview Press, 2015.

Simon, Robert L. "Internalism and Internal Values in Sport." *Journal of the Philoso- phy of Sport 27,* no. 1 (2000): 1–16.

———. "From Ethnocentrism to Realism: Can Discourse Ethics Bridge the Gap?" *Journal of the Philosophy of Sport 31,* no. 2 (2004): 122–141.

———. *Fair Play: The Ethics of Sport, 3rd Edition.* Boulder, CO: Westview Press, 2010.

———. "Theories of Sport." In *The Bloomsbury Companion to the Philosophy of Sport,* 83–98, Edited by Cesar R. Torres. Bloomsbury Publishing: London, 2014.

Skinner, B.F. *The Behavior of Organisms: An Experimental Analysis.* New York: Appleton-Century-Crofts, 1938.

Skinner, Brian. "Scoring Strategies for the Underdog: A General, Quantitative Method for Determining Optimal Sports Strategies." *Journal of Quantitative Analysis in Sports.* 7, 4 (2011): Article 11.

Smith, Chris. "U.S. Athletes Already Owed $240,000 In Olympic Medal Bonuses." *Forbes.* Last modified February 6, 2014. http://www.forbes.com/ sites/chrissmith/2014/02/16/u-s-athletes-already-owed-240000-in-olympic- medal-bonuses.

Smith, Ronald A. *Play-by-Play: Radio, Television, and Big Time College Sport.* Baltimore, MD: Johns Hopkins Press, 2001.

"Spartan Race." *Spartan.*com. Accessed December 16, 201. http://www.spartan.com/#

"Spending on Action and Adventure Sports." *IEG Sponsorship Report.* Accessed September 6, 2013. http:/www.sponsorship.com/iegsr/subonly/topic_article. asp?id=2563.

Spenser, Edmund. *Poetical Works,* Edited by J. C. Smith and E. de Selincourt. Oxford: Oxford University Press, 1970.

Spinda, John S.W., and Paul M. Haridakis. "Exploring the Motives of Fantasy Sports: A Uses-and-Gratifications Approach." In *Sports Mania: Essays on Fandom and the Media in the 21st Century,* edited by Lawrence W. Hugenberg, Paul M. Haridakis, and Adam C. Earnheardt, 187–202. Jefferson: McFarland & Company, Inc, 2008.

"Sport." *The Free Dictionary.* Accessed July 1, 2016. http://www.thefreedictionary.com /sport

"Sporting." *Oxford Dictionaries.* http://www.oxforddictionaries.com/us/definition/ american_english/sporting.

"Sports." *Oxford Dictionaries.* Accessed January 20, 2014. http://www.oxforddictionaries.com/us/definition/american_english/sport.

Staff, Markus. "Sports on YouTube." In *The YouTube Reader*, edited by P. Snickars and P. Vonderau. Stockholm: National Library of Sweden, 2009.

Steen-Johnsen, Kari. "Networks and the Organization of Identity: The Case of Norwegian Snowboarding." *European Sport Management Quarterly* 8 (2008): 337–358.

Stevens, Hampton, "Why Cheerleading Isn't a Sport, but Croquet Is." *The Atlantic*, Last modified August 5, 2010. http://www.theatlantic.com/entertainment/archive/2010/08/why-cheerleading-isnt-a-sport-but-croquet-is/60949/.

Stranger, Mark. "The Aesthetics of Risk: A Study of Surfing." *International Review for the Sociology of Sport* 34 (1999): 265–276.

Strauss, Chris. "DirecTV is Adding a Live Fantasy Football Channel to 'NFL Sunday Ticket.'" *USA Today*. Last modified July 7, 2014. http://ftw.usatoday.com/2014/07/directv-nfl-sunday-ticket-fantasy-zone-football.

Suits, Bernard. "What is A Game?" *Philosophy of Science* 34 (1967): 148–156.

———. "The Elements of Sport." In *The Philosophy of Sport: A Collection of Essays*, Edited by Robert Osterhoundt, 52–60. Springfield, IL: Charles Thomas Publisher, 1973.

———. "Words on Play." *Journal of the Philosophy of Sport* 4, no. 1 (1977): 117–131.

———. *The Grasshopper: Games, Life and Utopia*. Boston: A Non-Pareil Book, 1978.

———. "Tricky Triad: Games, Play, and Sport." *Journal of the Philosophy of Sport* 15, no. 1 (1988): 1–9.

———. "The Trick of the Disappearing Goal." *Journal of the Philosophy of Sport* 16, no. 1 (1989): 1–12.

———. "The Elements of Sport." In *Philosophic Inquiry in Sport, 2nd Edition*, Edited by William J. Morgan and Klaus V. Meier, 8–15. Champaign, IL: Human Kinetics, 1995.

———. "The Elements of Sport." In *Ethics in Sport*. Ed. William J. Morgan. *2nd Edition*. Champaign: Human Kinetics, 2007.

Sullivan, David B. "Broadcast Television and the Game of Packaging Sports." In *Handbook of Sports Media*, edited by Arthur A Raney & Jennings Bryant. Mahwah, NJ: Lawrence Erlbaum, 2006.

Taboo: The Complete First Season. "Blood Sports." DVD, 2004; National Geographic Television and Film.

Tack, Daniel. "Big Plays, Bigger Payouts." *Gameinformer*, 2014. 16–17.

Tamburrini, Claudio M. *The "Hand of God"? Essays in the Philosophy of Sports.* Goteborg: Acta Universitatis Gothoburgensis, 2000.

Tapia y Salcedo, Gregorio. *Exercicios De La Gineta*. Madrid, 1643.

Thomas, Duane L. "Sport: The Conceptual Enigma." *Journal of the Philosophy of Sport* 3, no. 1 (1976): 35–41.

Thorpe, Holly. "Beyond 'Decorative Sociology': Contextualizing Female Surf, Skate, and Snowboarding." *Sociology of Sport Journal* 23 (2006): 205–228.

———. "Understanding 'Alternative' Sport Experiences: A Contextual Approach for Sport Psychology." *International Journal of Sport and Exercise Psychology* 7 (2009): 359–379.

Tierno Galván, Enrique. *Desde el espectáculo a la trivialización.* Madrid: Tecnos, 1987.

Torres, Cesar R. "What Counts As Part of a Game? A Look at Skills." *Journal of the Philosophy of Sport* 27 (2000): 81–92.

———. "Results or Participation? Reconsidering Olympism's Approach to Competition." *Quest* 58 (2006), 242–254.

———. "Furthering Interpretivism's Integrity: Bringing Together Ethics and Aesthetics." *Journal of the Philosophy of Sport* 39, no. 2 (2012): 299–319.

"Tough Mudder." Accessed July 5, 2016. https://toughmudder.com/events/what-is-tough-mudder.

Townsend, Joseph. *A Journey though Spain in the years 1786 and 1787.* London: C. Dilly, 1792.

Turnkey Sports Poll. "Sports Business Journal In-Depth." *Sports Business Journal* 7, 2006.

Ulmann, Jacques. *De la gymnastique aux sports modernes.* Paris: Presses Universitaires de France, 1965.

"United States and World Population Clock." *United States Census Bureau.* Accessed March 8, 2015.

Vamplew, Wray. "Playing with the Rules: Influences on the Development of Regulation in Sport." *International Journal of the History of Sport* 24 (2007): 843–871.

Van Bottenburg, Maarten and Heilbron, Johan. "De-Sportization of Fighting Contests: The Origins and Dynamics of No Holds Barred Events and the Theory of Sportization." *International Review for the Sociology of Sport* 41 (2006): 259–282.

Vande Berg, Leah R. "The Sports Hero Meets Mediated Celebrityhood." In *MediaSport*, edited by Lawrence A. Wenner. New York: Routledge, 1998.

Vargas Machuca, Bernardo de. *Libro de exercicios de la gineta.* Madrid, 1600.

Vertelney, Seth. "TV Viewership Hit Record Highs in U.S. and the District for the World Cup." *Washington Post.* Last modified July 18, 2014. https://www.washingtonpost.com/express/wp/2014/07/18/tv-viewership-hit-record-highs-in-u-s-and-the-district-for-the-world-cup/.

Vigarello, Georges. *Passion Sport. Histoire d'une culture.* Paris: Textuel, 2000.

———. *Histoire du corps I. De la Renaissance aux Lumières.* Paris: Le Seuil, 2005.

Vivoni, Francisco. "Spots of Spatial Desire: Skateparks, Skateplazas, and Urban Politics." *Journal of Sport and Social Issues* 33 (2009): 130–149.

Vossen, Deborah P. "A Grasshopperian Analysis of the Strategic Foul." *Journal of the Philosophy of Sport* 41, no. 3 (2014): 325–346.

Walbancke, Matthewe. *Annalia dubrensia. Upon the yeerley celebration of Mr. Robert Dovers Olimpick Games upon Cotswold Hills.* London: Robert Raworth, 1636, facs. repr. Menston: Scolar Press, 1973.

Wallace, David Foster. "Federer Both Flesh and Not." *Both Flesh and Not.* New York: Little, Brown and Company, 2006/2012.

Warburton, Nigel. "Tom Hurka Interview on Bernard Suits's The Grasshopper." *Virtual Philosopher.* December 13, 2007. http://virtualphilosopher.com/2007/12/tom-hurka-on-be.html.

Warnke, G. "Social Interpretation and Political Theory." In *Festivals of Interpretation: Essays on Hans-Georg Gadamer's Work,* Edited by K. Wright. New York: State University of New York Press, 1990.

Warr, Phillippa. "ESports in Numbers: Five Mind-Blowing Stats." *Redbull.com.* Last modified April 9, 2014. http://www.redbull.com/en/esports/stories/1331644628389/esports-in-numbers-five-mind-blowing-stats.

Weathers, Cliff. "CrossFit is a Cult: Why So Many of its Defenders are So Defensive." *Salon,* Last modified October 22, 2014. http://www.salon.com/2014/10/22/crossfit_is_a_cult_why_so_many_of_its_defenders_are_so_defensive_partner/.

Wein, Sheldon. "A Reply to Morgan." *Journal of the Philosophy of Sport* 7, no. 1 (1980): 46–50.

Wertz, Spencer K. "Is Sport Unique? A Question of Definability." *Journal of the Philosophy of Sport* 22, no. 1 (1995): 83–93.

Wheaton, Belinda. "Mapping the Lifestyle Sport-Scape." In *Understanding Lifestyle Sport: Consumption, Identity and Difference,* Edited by Belinda Wheaton, 1–28. New York and London: Routledge, 2004.

———. "After Sport Culture: Rethinking Sport and Post-Subcultural Theory." *Journal of Sport and Social Issues* 31 (2007): 283–307.

———. "Introducing the consumption and representation of lifestyle sports." *Sport in Society* 13 (2010): 1057–1081.

———. *The Cultural Politics of Lifestyle Sports,* New York and London: Routledge, 2013.

White, Paul. "Why Derek Jeter Remains Admired After So Many Years." *USA Today.* Last modified September 10, 2014. http://www.usatoday.com/story/sports/mlb/2014/09/09/derek-jeter-appreciation/15354565/.

Widdicombe, Lizzie. "In Cold Mud: The Obstacle-Racing Craze Gets Serious," *The New Yorker.* Last modified January 27, 2014. http://www.newyorker.com/magazine/2014/01/27/in-cold-mud.

Williams, Kaylene C., Robert A. Page, Alfred R. Petrosky, and Edward H. Hernandez. "Multi-Generational Marketing: Descriptions, Characteristics, Lifestyles, and Attitudes." *The Journal of Applied Business and Economics* 11 (2010): 21–36.

Wingfield, Nick. "With Halo 5: Guardians, Microsoft Seeks to Lure E-Sports Players Back." *New York Times.* Last modified August 5, 2015. http://www.nytimes.com/2015/08/05/technology/with-halo-5-microsoft-seeks-to-lure-e-sports-players-back.html.

Wittgenstein, Ludwig. *Philosophical Investigations.* New York: Macmillan, 1953.

Wolff, Francis. *Filosofía de las corridas de toros.* Barcelona: Edicions Bellaterra, 2008.

———. ""¡Torero!¡Torero!" La ética del torero y sus diez mandamientos." Paper presented at the Fiestas de toros y sociedad, 2001.

"Word Frequency Data." *Corpus of Contemporary American English.* http://www.wordfrequency.info/free.asp?s=y

Young, Alan. *Tudor and Jacobean Tournaments.* Dobbs Ferry NY: Sheridan House, 1987.

Young, David. *The Olympic Myth of Greek Amateur Athletics.* Chicago: Ares, 1985.

———. *The Modern Olympics: A Struggle for Revival.* Baltimore, MD: John Hopkins University Press, 1996

The Youth Olympic Games—Sports Programme. Lausanne: International Olympic Committee, 2014.

The Youth Olympic Games Vision and Principles. Lausanne: International Olympic Committee, 2014.

Zemper, Eric D. "The Evolution of Track and Field Rules during the Last Century." Presentation at USA Olympic Team Trials for Track and Field, Eugene, Oregon, July 4, 2008.

Zingarelli, Nicola. *Il nuovo Zingarelli, vocabulario della lingua italiana.* Bologna: Zanichelli, 1987.

Index

About the Contributors

Andrew Billings is the Ronald Reagan Chair of Broadcasting and director of the Alabama Program in Sport Communication at the University of Alabama. His research focuses on sport media content and the effects associated with it.

Chad Carlson is an assistant professor of kinesiology and an assistant men's basketball coach at Hope College, his alma mater. He has served in various service capacities among the leadership of the International Association for the Philosophy of Sport and the North American Society for Sport History. Dr. Carlson's research includes metaphysical and ethical issues relating to play, sport, and Christianity, and the history of college athletics—specifically basketball. He enjoys physical activity of almost any sort, especially when it is competitive.

Joan Grassbaugh Forry is an assistant training instructor at the Dog Training Center of Chester County in Pennsylvania. Before leaving academia to study animal behavior, she held academic appointments at Vanderbilt University, Linfield College, and the University of Southern California. Dr. Forry's research interests include animal ethics, sports ethics, and gender issues. She also devotes her time to her ongoing photography project, "Miles on Hydrants."

Joey Gawrysiak is an assistant professor of sport management in the Harry F. Byrd, Jr. School of Business at Shenandoah University in Winchester, Virginia. Dr. Gawrysiak has published and delivered multiple presentations on e-sports across the country and has been featured in numerous television shows, podcasts, and radio shows on the subject. His presentations on e-sports have been delivered around the country at both sport management and video game conferences. He has organized multiple competitive video game tournaments and been featured regionally in media publications. He has competed nationally in *Halo* e-sport events and is beginning to compete in other games such as *Hearthstone* and *Heroes of the Storm.*

Chrysostomos Giannoulakis is an assistant professor of sport administration at Ball State University. His main research interest focuses on branding and marketing aspects of action sports, with an emphasis on board sports (surfing, skateboarding, and snowboarding). He has recently developed a line of research on Action Sports for Development and Peace. Specifically, he examines the contribution of action sports on intergroup togetherness and community development, and their subsequent utilization as a tool for social change and empowerment with underprivileged and at-risk groups. Part of this research includes academic projects with Native American populations, as well as international exchange groups relative to skateboarding interventions through the United States Department of State.

Brian Glenney is an assistant professor of philosophy at Norwich University in Vermont. His research interests include early modern philosophy, philosophy of sensory perception, and the Urban Arts, publishing in an array of journals such as *Journal of Sport and Social Issues*, *Biology and Philosophy*, and *Journal for the Study of the New Testament*. He is also the co-founder of the *Accessible Icon Project*, an effort to raise the visibility of disability by re-imagining its symbols and contexts. If not in class or his study, you may find him skateboarding in the streets of your city.

Teresa González Aja is a professor of history and politics of sport at Polytechnic University of Madrid and the director of the research group Social and Humanistic Studies in Sport and Physical Activity and the educational innovation group "Areté." She is a member and past president of the College of Fellows of the European Committee for Sports History. At Polytechnic University of Madrid, she has been head director of the Department of Social Sciences of Physical Activity, Sport and Leisure, and assistant director at the Faculty of Physical Activity and Sport Sciences in charge of research. Her publications, all related to the history and politics of sport, cover a wide range, from the impact of physical activity and sports in arts to the political use of sports such as football or the Olympic Games. She has also published numerous studies of various personalities such as Coubertin or Mercurial, as well as controversial physical activities like bullfights and the figure of the bullfighter.

Shawn E. Klein is a philosophy lecturer at Arizona State University. He specializes in ethics, popular culture, and the philosophy of sport. He edited *Steve Jobs and Philosophy: For Those Who Think Different* (Open Court,

2015) and *Harry Potter and Philosophy: If Aristotle Ran Hogwarts* (Open Court, 2004). He is the editor of Studies in the Philosophy of Sport, a series from Lexington Books. He has presented at numerous conferences on sports ethics, business ethics, pop culture and philosophy, and other topics. Dr. Klein blogs as "The Sports Ethicist" at SportsEthicist.com. He has appeared in the *New York Times, Los Angeles Times, Washington Post, USA Today,* Bloomberg News, CNN, and other media outlets.

Francisco Javier López Frías is an assistant professor at Penn State University with a joint appointment in the Rock Ethics Institute and the Department of Kinesiology. He holds a PhD in philosophy from the Faculty of Philosophy of the University of Valencia, where he completed a master's program in Ethics and Democracy at the Department of Moral Philosophy. His doctoral dissertation entitled "Human Enhancement and Doping in the Recent Philosophy of Sport" addresses current debates surrounding the introduction of biotechnologies in sport. Dr. López Frías has published numerous papers in international journals, as well as book chapters, book reviews, and books in the philosophy of sport.

John McClelland is professor emeritus of French literature and a retired associate professor of sport history at the University of Toronto. His main focus has been the culture of the European Renaissance, especially in France and Italy, but his publications have reached back to ancient Rome and forward to the early twentieth century. In addition to books and articles on literary studies, he has written extensively on music and rhetoric, but since 1980 has largely concentrated on the history of early modern sport. He is the author/ coeditor of *Die Anfänge des modernen Sports in der Renaissance* (1984), *Body and Mind: Sport in Europe from the Roman Empire to the Renaissance* (2007), and *Sport and Culture in Early Modern Europe/Le sport dans la civilisation de l'Europe prémoderne* (2009). He sits on the editorial boards of *European Studies in Sport History* and *Ludica, annali e civiltà del gioco.*

Lindsay Krol Pursglove is an assistant professor of sport administration at Ball State University (Muncie, Indiana). She earned her PhD from Texas Woman's University, and her scholarly research evolves around marketing and branding elements of BMX racing. Prior to her academic studies, Dr. Pursglove was exposed to BMX racing as a track volunteer, and subsequently became an official with the National Bicycle League. She has also worked at the Homestead Miami Speedway hosting NASCAR Championship events.

Coral Rae is the manager of partnerships and adjunct lecturer in the Graduate Program in Sports Management at Columbia University. Her research focuses on sports and deviance, as well as on-and off-field analytics.

Heather L. Reid is a professor of philosophy at Morningside College in Sioux City, Iowa, a fellow of the American Academy in Rome, the director of Morningside's Semester in Italy program, and the founder of the Fonte Aretusa organization. She has published numerous books and articles in ancient philosophy, philosophy of sport, and Olympic studies. She has also been invited to lecture on these topics in Beijing, London, Rome, Seoul, and at the International Olympic Academy in Olympia, Greece. She is past president (2005–2007) and recipient of the distinguished service (2009) and distinguished scholar (2015) awards of the International Association for the Philosophy of Sport. Her monographs include *Introduction to the Philosophy of Sport* (2012), *Athletics and Philosophy in the Ancient World: Contests of Virtue* (2011), and *The Philosophical Athlete* (2002). She is also coauthor of *The Olympics and Philosophy* (2012), *Aretism: An Ancient Sports Philosophy for the Modern Sports World* (2011), and *Filosofía dello Sport* (2011).

Brody J. Ruihley is an assistant professor of sport management at Miami University in Oxford, Ohio. His research interests lie in the areas of fantasy sport motivation and participation and public relations activities in sport.

Pam R. Sailors is the associate dean for the College of Humanities and Public Affairs and a professor of philosophy at Missouri State University in Springfield, Missouri. Recent publications include work on sex segregation in sport and an ethical evaluation of American football. The common thread in her research is focus on and concern for equity and fairness, often particularly as applied to gender.

Kevin Schieman is a Strategic Plans and Policy Officer in the United States Army. His military background includes two combat deployments as a UH-60 Black Hawk pilot, but he is currently assigned to the Joint Staff, where he doesn't fly much of anything. Previously, he served as an assistant professor in the Department of English and Philosophy at the United States Military Academy. While at West Point, he taught courses on normative ethics, the ethics of war, and advanced composition. His areas of interest include the ethics of war, specifically lethal autonomous systems, and roughly any topic germane to the philosophy of sport.

Keith Strudler is the director of the Marist College Center for Sports Communication, which he founded in 2011. He is also an associate professor of communication at Marist, teaching a variety of sports communication courses. Dr. Strudler created Marist's degree concentration in sports communication in 2002. He also served six years as chair of the communication department at Marist. As director of the center, Dr. Strudler has built a partnership with the Marist Poll to release co-branded sports-issue polls and extended this partnership to HBO Real Sports. Dr. Strudler has published on the topic of televised sports heroes and the portrayal of race in sports television. He airs a weekly radio commentary on sport and society for WAMC, a public radio station in Albany, New York, and serves as the executive producer and co-host of "The Classroom," a weekly sports program through the Center for Sports Communication that airs on ESPN Radio of the New York Hudson Valley. Dr. Strudler has also written sports commentary for the *Poughkeepsie Journal* and has been an expert source for many national and international media outlets, including the *Washington Post*, CBS Radio, and the *Christian Science Monitor*.

Sarah Teetzel is the associate dean for undergraduate education and an associate professor in the faculty of kinesiology and recreation management at University of Manitoba in Winnipeg, Canada. Her research focuses on applied ethical issues in sport, and has been funded recently by SSHRC-Sport Canada, the International Olympic Committee's Olympic Studies Centre, and the World Anti-Doping Agency. Dr. Teetzel's main areas of expertise include the Olympics, doping and drug testing in sport, and gender issues in sport.

Charlene Weaving is an associate professor in human kinetics at St. Francis Xavier University in Antigonish, Nova Scotia, Canada. She publishes in the sport philosophy field from feminist perspectives. In 2010, she coedited *Philosophical Perspectives on Gender in Sport and Physical Activity* (Routledge). Recent research involves analysis of Ultimate Fighting Championship (UFC), and the *Sports Illustrated* Swimsuit Issue. Dr. Weaving is the current president of the International Association for the Philosophy of Sport.